KNOTS LANDING™

ALSO BY LAURA VAN WORMER

DALLAS: The Complete Ewing Family Saga

KNOTS LANDING™
LANDING™
The Saga of Seaview Circle

Laura Van Wormer

INTRODUCTION BY

David Jacobs
CREATOR OF THE TELEVISION SERIES

A DOLPHIN BOOK
Doubleday & Company, Inc.
GARDEN CITY NEW YORK
1986

In Loving Memory of

William Sidney Fairgate, Jr.
1936–1981

DESIGN BY M FRANKLIN-PLYMPTON

Knots Landing is derived from the television series of the same name.
Executive Producers: Michael Filerman and David Jacobs.

Library of Congress Cataloging-in-Publication Data
Van Wormer, Laura, 1955–
    Knots Landing.
    "A Dolphin book."
    1. Knots Landing (Television program) I. Title.
PN1992.77.K583V36   1986   791.45'72   86-6395
ISBN 0-385-23636-0

CONTENTS

THE OUTSIDER

INTRODUCTION

A couple of years ago, when the "Dallas" and "Dynasty" rivalry was raging hot and heavy, a magazine writer asked me, as the creator of "Dallas," to define the difference between the shows. Because my wife and I had just returned from our first visit to Paris, an incident that had occurred there was fresh in my mind, and I told the writer about it.

We had gone into a fabulous toy store to choose something to take home for the kids. While we were looking, two other American couples came in. One couple, stylishly dressed and speaking flawless French to the clerks, bought an exquisite porcelain doll; their local address was not a hotel but an apartment, which they kept in Paris for their frequent visits. The other couple arrived in a chauffeur-driven Rolls-Royce; their wardrobe was much more casual (but still tasteful and obviously expensive) than that of the first couple; they spoke no French and bought the largest and most expensive item in the store—a rideable, motorized, lavishly decorated Indian elephant with one of those roofed chairs on its back—which they ordered shipped home to Texas; when they gave their Paris address it was that of the grandest hotel in town. We all chatted a little, and I remembered thinking: Well, nobody can say Americans abroad are one thing or another: these two are poles apart.

And, I told the interviewer, the two couples could be considered representative of the people on "Dallas" and "Dynasty." Send the "Dynasty" folk to Paris and they're right at home; send the "Dallas" folk there and they remain Texans.

But what about *you?* the writer asked when I drew the analogy; Where did you and your wife fit on this little sociological curve?

Although I hadn't thought of that, the answer popped straight out.

Oh, Diana and I were just tourists, I said; we were from "Knots Landing."

Thus, spontaneously and without much thought, I had, I think, put my finger on the quality that makes "Knots Landing" unique. While "Dallas" and "Dynasty" (and "Falcon Crest" and "Flamingo Road" and "Berrenger's" and most of the other serials that have come along in the 1980s) are situated in the world of the rich and powerful, "Knots Landing" remains middle-class.

While the other serials are about Them, "Knots Landing" is about Us.

Actually, and contrary to the usual perceptions, "Knots Landing"—the most mid-

dle-class of the prime-time serials, the one regarded as most *different*—was the one conceived first.

When, in 1977, Mike Filerman and I developed the idea of "Knots Landing," there were no nighttime serials on television. When we presented the notion to Richard Berger and Kim LeMasters at CBS, they were intrigued, but hesitated precisely because "Knots" was so middle-class. Inasmuch as we would be breaking new ground, they said, could we come up with something on the same order, only glossier, more sensational, easier to promote—more saga than serial?

The answer was Yes, we could, and the result was "Dallas."

"Dallas" was of course a hit, and because hits breed spinoffs, Bob Silberling of CBS retrieved my old "Knots Landing" presentation from a bottom drawer and asked if there were some way to make it a "Dallas" spinoff. Oh, no, I said, "Dallas" is rich and "Knots" is middle-class; I don't see how . . . Pain stopped me from finishing the thought as Filerman kicked my shin. I mean, *Yes,* I said, a spinoff? Sure, no problem, leave it to us.

So one of the four couples in the "Knots Landing" cul-de-sac became Gary and Val Ewing, whom I'd already created on "Dallas." The rest of the ensemble remained pretty much as it had been in my original presentation.

But if the truth be told, "Knots Landing" was never comfortable as a "Dallas" spinoff. Its aggressive middle-classedness always got in the way. There's no better actor on television than Larry Hagman, yet when he'd come to visit Knots Landing every once in a while, we'd invariably find ourselves with an episode that didn't work. The scale was all wrong. J.R. is bigger-than-life, as is Dallas (the show and the city); he's a Them who too easily overpowers the Us gang on "Knots Landing."

"Knots Landing" had trouble making ends meet for a while. Though never a failure, it wasn't a success, either; it just hung in, with no identity of its own, either ignored in the press or seen as "Dallas's" tagalong little brother who could never live up. Still, it did what it had to do to get along; it was a survivor.

And to survive we had to tell some pretty un-middle-class stories—especially when we went head-to-head against "Hill Street Blues," the most celebrated television show of its time. To deal with that competition we pulled out all the stops. We started making our characters richer. We took them out of the cul-de-sac and put them in the corridors of power. People got threatened, blackmailed, murdered. Karen took pills and Val's babies were stolen. Sumner built a secret station from which he could almost rule the world . . . and Gary Ewing blew it up.

It worked. It took us a season and a half, but we finally overcame the "Hill Street Blues" lead and won our time slot and never gave it up.

But the funny thing was, though we changed "Knots Landing," we didn't really make it different. Its heart and substance remained middle-class, its base familiar. "People like us don't get involved in murder," Mack said once, and the statement reflects the way we do things. We keep people ordinary. Ordinary people in extraordinary circumstances.

I think—one never can be too sure, or one would have nothing but hits, and one doesn't—that this aggressive middle-classedness is what makes "Knots Landing" so easy to identify with and, ultimately, so successful.

It's certainly what makes it fun to do week after week. Fun, at least, for someone who, when he goes to Paris, wears his camera around his neck and buys his kids not Indian elephants or exquisite dolls, but a little toy grocery store so they can play not oilman or banker but checkout cashier and bagger.

David Jacobs

Los Angeles, 1986

 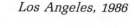 

Who Is Related to Whom in Knots Landing

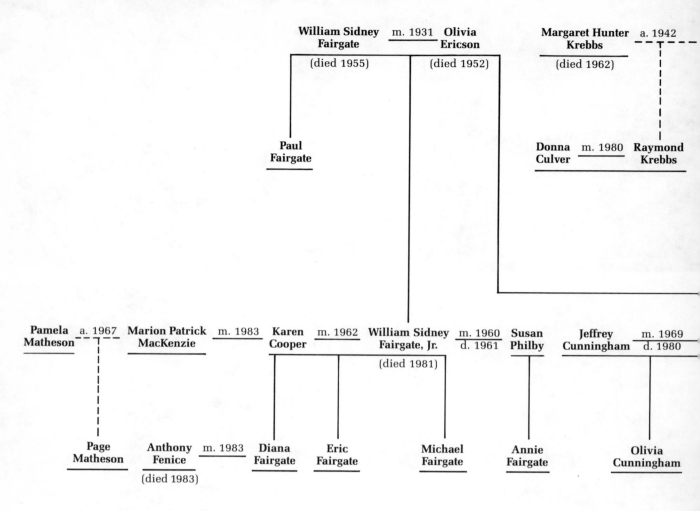

William Sidney Fairgate m. 1931 **Olivia Ericson**

(died 1955) (died 1952)

Margaret Hunter Krebbs a. 1942

(died 1962)

Paul Fairgate

Donna Culver m. 1980 **Raymond Krebbs**

Pamela Matheson a. 1967 **Marion Patrick MacKenzie** m. 1983 **Karen Cooper** m. 1962 **William Sidney Fairgate, Jr.** m. 1960 **Susan Philby** **Jeffrey Cunningham** m. 1969

d. 1961

d. 1980

(died 1981)

Page Matheson **Anthony Fenice** m. 1983 **Diana Fairgate** **Eric Fairgate** **Michael Fairgate** **Annie Fairgate** **Olivia Cunningham**

(died 1983)

KEY

a. = **affair**

m. = **married**

rm. = **remarried**

d. = **divorced**

| = **child sanctioned by marriage**

¦ = **child born out of wedlock**

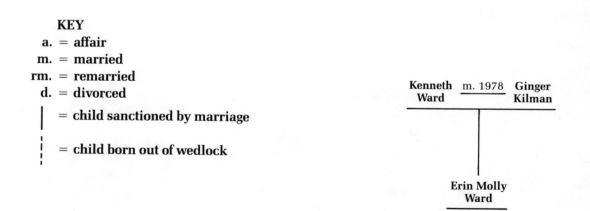

Kenneth Ward m. 1978 **Ginger Kilman**

Erin Molly Ward

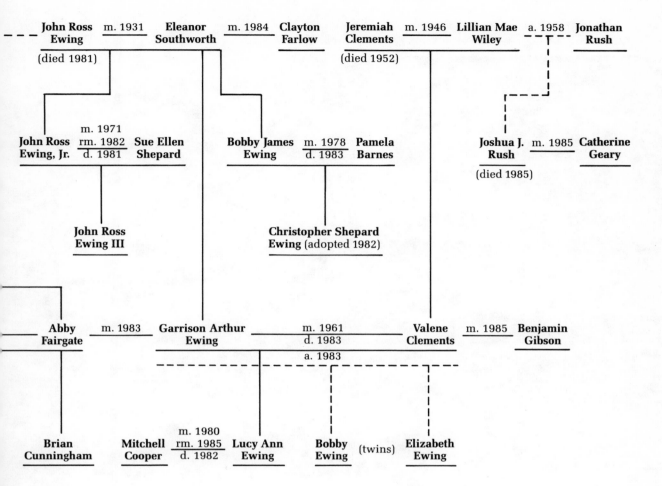

John Ross Ewing — m. 1931 — **Eleanor Southworth** — m. 1984 — **Clayton Farlow**   **Jeremiah Clements** — m. 1946 — **Lillian Mae Wiley** — a. 1958 — **Jonathan Rush**
(died 1981)   (died 1952)

John Ross Ewing, Jr. — m. 1971 / rm. 1982 / d. 1981 — **Sue Ellen Shepard**   **Bobby James Ewing** — m. 1978 / d. 1983 — **Pamela Barnes**   **Joshua J. Rush** — m. 1985 — **Catherine Geary**
                                                                                                                                                      (died 1985)

John Ross Ewing III   **Christopher Shepard Ewing** (adopted 1982)

Abby Fairgate — m. 1983 — **Garrison Arthur Ewing** — m. 1961 / d. 1983 / a. 1983 — **Valene Clements** — m. 1985 — **Benjamin Gibson**

Brian Cunningham   **Mitchell Cooper** — m. 1980 / rm. 1985 / d. 1982 — **Lucy Ann Ewing**   **Bobby Ewing** (twins) **Elizabeth Ewing**

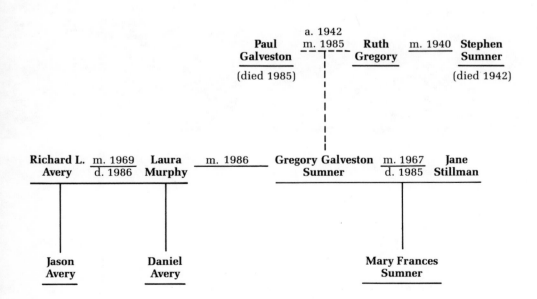

Paul Galveston — a. 1942 / m. 1985 — **Ruth Gregory** — m. 1940 — **Stephen Sumner**
(died 1985)   (died 1942)

Richard L. Avery — m. 1969 / d. 1986 — **Laura Murphy** — m. 1986 — **Gregory Galveston Sumner** — m. 1967 / d. 1985 — **Jane Stillman**

Jason Avery   **Daniel Avery**   **Mary Frances Sumner**

THE
TOWN

"By and by, Lord, by and by,
There's better land a-waiting."
—From the song by
    Lilimae Clements,
    "Will the Circle Be Broken?"

Valene, Lucy, and Gary Ewing running through the surf at the Knots Landing Public Beach.

Knots Landing

There it is. . . .

Just a small pocket of humanity lodged in the hills of the Southern California coastline. The residents here, however, are not in the least self-conscious; for this place, this closely drawn community, is nourished on the strength of the American Ideal. It is a town united in a collective dream—of security, lasting love, and the regeneration of all things lifting the heart and spirit.

The town is called Knots Landing.

Standing at a scenic outlook on the Pacific Coast Highway—with the Palo Verdes Estates to the south behind you, and Redondo Beach to the north—one draws an involuntary breath at the outward vision of the townspeople's dream. To the left, the startling blue of the Pacific, her slow undulations rolling in toward shore, passing over the sandbar, changing to fierce white crests, ending in lashes against the cliffs. Farther north on the horizon, there is a sudden drop-off, the cliffs giving way to a flat white expanse of beach.

Above the cliffs, to the right, we see the first string of houses. The eye traveling back, there are more houses lined in systematic rows. And then as the rows reach back into the hill, they begin to curve and wind and then twist, climbing, until there are swirling patterns covering the hillside, not unlike the swells of the ocean. With each house is the splash of a burnt orange roof, awash in the green of lawn and trees. The sky is empty of all but the most vivid blue. And, oh—but the sun! That valiant, brilliant, loving caretaker of Southern California, its rays diffusing into a golden glow over the land, flashing into sheet radiance on the beach, scattering into fragments of silver across the water.

And the air—this mixture of cool sea breezes and warm fertile earth—carries something else in it, something intangible but heady that sets the heart racing. It carries the air of hope, the hope that this new place offers a better life than the place left behind.

Texas, Tennessee, New York, Washington D.C., Pennsylvania. . . . The list of places left behind is endless, but the place of hopeful arrival is the same. Knots Landing. Home.

In the beginning of its human history, the land was called "The Place of Great Fish." Native Americans had settled on the east side of the hill in a permanent village. Fruit and vegetables were abundant; the temperatures were beautifully mild year round. Its name boasted of the place's most appreciated feature. Between middle and low tide, deepsea fish were often caught in the current and were pulled in between the sandbar and the beach; trapped at low tide, they made for easy spearing.

Village life was, in modern terms, quite sophisticated. The Native Americans maintained an autonomous community whose population was kept in strict

1

The neighbors of Seaview Circle, September 1979. From left to right: Ginger Ward, Kenny Ward, Diana Fairgate, Karen Fairgate, Sid Fairgate, Eric Fairgate, Jason Avery, Michael Fairgate (sitting), Richard Avery, Laura Avery, Valene Ewing, and Gary Ewing.

Although the descendants of Captain Alexander Knot did not find oil in Knots Landing in the 1930s, J. R. Ewing located offshore deposits and tried to drill there in 1979. Karen Fairgate (foreground) was instrumental in stopping him.

Mack MacKenzie barbecues chicken in the backyard, with friend and neighbor Ben Gibson looking on.

balance with the carrying capacity of the land through the use of birth control. In fact, they had developed effective oral contraceptives from local herbs. Their life was peaceful, bountiful, close-knit, closed off, and presumably, fairly happy.

Spanish missionaries arrived by boat in the late 1780s and the villagers' young people were lured to a nearby mission, impressed by the magic the newcomers had brought from a faraway land. Tragically, along with their culture and technology, the missionaries also brought smallpox and venereal disease with them. The Native Americans had no resistance against these imported diseases and their village was nearly wiped out. What people did survive, under the care of the mission, were merged with Native Americans from other villages into one large rancheria. "The Place of Great Fish" had lost its people.

The missions, on behalf of the Spanish Crown, ruled the land until the 1820s, when their brothers in Mexico (having represented Spanish rule for some three hundred years) revolted against the Crown. The missionaries could hardly support the Crown with Mexican armed forces at their back door, and so, in 1823, when the Mexican Republic was formed, California was part of its domain.

Also included in the new republic was Texas—at least according to Mexico. American traders and settlers begged to disagree. Trouble kicked up throughout the Southwest region, and the California missions nervously watched the developments. Texas revolted against Mexico and established its own republic in 1836; Mexico refused to recognize it, but couldn't maintain enforcement there any longer. Traders and settlers, made bold by dreams fostered in the robust American East and the "victory" in Texas, were straggling in over the Rockies to California. Their numbers grew and so did the missions' alarm. By 1846, American troops had moved into Southern California, declaring war with Mexico. The war lasted for two years, ending when Mexico ceded all their lands north of the Rio Grande. The missions, once a ruling arm of Spain, then Mexico, were now voluntary religious parishes. Their land, the huge rancherias, were assumed by the United States for public sale.

The United States had been given an additional incentive to ending the war as quickly as possible; on January 24 of that final year of battle, 1848, gold was discovered in California. Forget the fertile ground, beautiful skies, plentiful forests, plains and oceans—gold was *gold*. Word swept across the land like wildfire, bringing a deluge of eighty thousand prospectors into California in 1849.

What became readily apparent about the Gold Rush was that few were actually going to strike it rich and most, in fact, were more likely to die from hunger in search of it. Unless prospectors had brought their own tools, there were virtually none to be had, and certainly none for the cultivation of food. With the sudden population explosion, the land was being stripped and the demand for food and tools clamored up and down the California coast.

At this time, in Galveston, Texas, Captain Alexander S. Knot, proprietor of the S.S. *Seaview,* was in search of a cargo. Knot had been lured to the Southwest by his friend John Neely Bryant, founder of Dallas, and his scheme to start a shipping line on the Trinity River from Dallas to the Gulf of Mexico, a plan which proved unfeasible. When the news of the prices to be had in California came his way, Knot loaded his ship with tools (and whiskey) and set sail around Cape Hope for California.

He meant to land in San Francisco, but a storm forced him in toward shore about four hundred miles to the south, where he anchored in a small inlet protected by cliffs. When the storm blew over, he rowed into shore to see what there was to see and met a couple of traders. By afternoon, all along shore were what must have been two hundred men and women—all there because of the cargo they heard he was carrying! Knot didn't have to reach San Francisco to make his fortune; he sold

Friends and neighbors wait for the bridal bouquet to be thrown after the marriage of Joshua Rush and Cathy Geary in 1985. From left to right in the first row: Gary Ewing, Abby Cunningham-Ewing, Lilimae Clements, Valene Ewing, Eric Fairgate's girlfriend Whitney, Laura Avery, and Gregory Sumner.

his cargo there on the beach for prices he had never imagined. Pleased at his good luck and attracted to the blossoming nearby Los Angeles, Knot purchased a hundred acres of land surrounding the inlet, visualizing a burgeoning mercantile port. And so, in 1850, "The Place of Great Fish" had a new name: Knots Landing.

Knot sailed back to pick up his family and another cargo, but came down with scarlet fever and died in Galveston, leaving all his worldy goods to his wife. Emily Knot moved to Dallas, where, under the kindly protection of the Bryant family, she raised her son and daughter. The son, Alexander S. Knot, Jr., inherited the bulk of his mother's estate, but daughter Amy was given twenty acres of the California land as part of her dowry.

In 1912 there was a gigantic oil strike at Spindletop in Beaumont, Texas, signaling an oil-rich new era for the Southwest. Jealous Californians took note of the geological composition of the oil sites and began scouting in their own backyard—with phenomenal success. Between 1917 and 1929 fifteen major oil fields were opened in California, some of which were located in the Los Angeles Basin. The grandson of Captain Knot, who had inherited the eighty acres from his father, drilled for oil there in 1932, with no success, and he let the land lay idle for almost thirty years. Meanwhile, back in Dallas, Amy Knot's son lost his estate in a mortgage foreclosure, and his twenty-acre deed in Knots Landing was acquired by the Cattleman's Bank of Dallas.

Also in Dallas, a man named Jock Ewing had founded the independent oil company called Ewing Oil in 1930. Ewing, a wildcatter, had made his fortune by discov-

ering new wells, and with no one knowing yet just how much oil was in Texas, he ensured his company's future by buying up any parcel of land he could get his hands on. In one of the deals he made through the Cattleman's Bank in 1936, Ewing made a bulk purchase of over 600,000 acres of odd lots. They were duly inventoried into Ewing Oil and over the years were explored for oil, natural gas, and minerals, or leased out for growing cotton.

Years later, Ewing would say that he didn't even know that Ewing Oil owned twenty acres outside of Los Angeles and, if he had, would have sold it since, "if it's not a part of the Great State of Texas, then it must be something Texas didn't want."

The 1940s and 1950s brought wild expansion to the city of Los Angeles. Los Angeles wasn't shaping *up* like other cities; it was, quite literally, shaping *out* in every direction. The booming prosperity and expansion were wonderful, materialistically speaking, but the sudden diffusion and mobility created a sense of personal isolation for many of its citizens. Who had a sense of community in a city where the East Side and the West Side were over forty miles apart? Yes, there were neighborhoods in places like exclusive Bel Air and Beverly Hills where the millionaires lived, and yes, there were tract developments and apartment complexes and urban sprawl, but where were the good old-fashioned middle-class neighborhoods? It was precisely that question which prompted developers to buy the available eighty acres of the original Knot property, and oceanfront land on either side of it, with the intent to build. And in early 1960, the ground was broken for the first house of the planned community of Knots Landing—reenvisioned, reborn.

The concept of Knots Landing was to offer each new resident a sense of ownership and belonging. Their lot was to be their own special place, where they could plant a tree and it was theirs; let their children run around in the backyard; cook outdoors on weekends; snooze in the hammock; plant gardens; put a guest in the spare bedroom and a playroom in the basement; and wake each morning to hear birds singing on their land. Knots Landing was to be the kind of town where the back door could be left unlocked, where the neighbors could be hailed by their first names and be known for years, with their children almost as familiar to you as your own. It was to be a town with annual picnics at the beach, and parades and fireworks on holidays. And to a great extent, Knots Landing became that town.

Thanksgiving at the cul-de-sac, 1984. Holidays are no exception for the resident organizer for the neighborhood, Karen Fairgate-MacKenzie, who was hostess for the day. Here she gives last-minute instructions to sons Michael and Eric before a sit-down dinner for sixteen.

The Thanksgiving feast. From left to right: Abby Cunningham–Ewing, Cathy Geary, Joshua Rush, Olivia Cunningham, Eric Fairgate, Mack MacKenzie. On the right, that's Laura Avery.

In 1978, Jock Ewing's youngest son, Bobby, spun off a subsidiary from Ewing Oil to create Ewing Construction. His first endeavor with family housing was sparked by the discovery of the Knots Landing deed of twenty acres. Bobby flew out to see the land and was excited by what he found. A confirmed idealist, he applauded the vision that had been behind the town and was eager to experiment with a contribution of his own, which, if it succeeded, would be used as a model for construction elsewhere.

The existing Knots Landing houses were largely on half-acre lots on the open hillside facing the ocean, and along a strip on the oceanfront. The Ewing land, in contrast, ran across the grassy ridge that overlooked the town and water. Bobby built exactly what he envisioned on his first visit: an offshoot from Seaview Drive (a major artery that ran up the hill) to be called Seaview Circle. The road ended in a cul-de-sac and here is where Bobby created his idea of a neighborhood. He built five houses right up on the road, with each home's 1½-acre lot extending back into a lovely, private refuge. While the five houses were warmly nestled into a little community of its own, each family could enjoy their own beautiful land, trees, grasses, and views from the ridge. The houses were finished in early 1979, waiting only for their new owners to bring the neighborhood to life.

This book is about the five neighboring families who bought these houses. It is about from where they came, how they earned their way here, in what they came in search of, and what has happened to them since they arrived.

The Ewings, the Fairgates, the Averys, the Wards, the Cunninghams. Their lives have changed mightily since 1979. Like the Native Americans who lived here over two hundred years ago, the families have placed their faith in communal intimacy as the best defense between them and the dangers of the world at large. For the Native Americans, their way of life could not withstand the pressures from the outside; for the neighbors of Seaview Circle, theirs is undergoing the test of time.

THE

NEIGHBORHOOD

The First Families of Seaview Circle

"You never know what goes on
behind people's doors."
—Karen Fairgate, 1979

The Ewings

GARY Is Knots Landing as far as you want to go?

VALENE What's wrong with that? We were a couple of very
sad cases, Gary. Me waiting on tables and you, drinking
and getting into fights. Now we have a beautiful home and
nice friends.

GARY Val, when you get like this, I want to kick a hole in the
wall and bust out of here!

—Gary and Valene Ewing, 1981

Garrison Arthur Ewing
Gary

"Five years from now, Gary Ewing's going to make J.R. seem middle-class."

—Paul Galveston, 1985

Yes, *that* Ewing.

The Ewings of Dallas, Texas,* the family who controls the most powerful independent oil company in the United States. The *billionaire* Ewings, who call "home" a 100,000-acre cattle empire. All over the world people fantasize about being a Ewing, about what they would do if they had that money, that power, that *name*. But for all the excitement that comes in connection with the family, just having been born a Ewing has been enough to nearly kill its middle son, and on a number of occasions.

Gary Ewing has spent his life fighting his heritage, while desperately trying to live up to it at the same time. He is a man of startling contrasts and maybe, just maybe, one day he'll find some middle ground upon which to live. Something less dangerous than living on the edge.

Garrison Arthur Ewing was born in 1945 in Braddock, Texas, a suburb of Dallas. His father, John Ross "Jock" Ewing, made his fortune by wildcatting for oil in the late 1920s, and Jock's marriage to Eleanor "Miss Ellie" Southworth united what would become one of the country's largest oil kingdoms with the premiere cattle empire of Southfork Ranch. Gary has an older brother, John Ross "J. R." Ewing, Jr., born in 1939; a younger brother, Bobby James Ewing, born in 1949; and one half-brother, Raymond Krebbs, born in 1943. Gary was named after his mother's only brother.

Gary's mama was, and still is, one of the most gracious creatures to ever walk the earth. Like her father, Aaron Southworth, Miss Ellie thrived on the regenerative forces of Southfork Ranch, in its cattle, horses, wildlife, trees, and grasses, and in the people who cared for them. She adored her husband, cherished her children, was warm, affectionate, playful, and generous, and she helped the community of Dallas as much as she did her own family.

Gary's father, on the other hand, in those days absolutely abhorred ranching and most anything else that wasn't related to the oil business (except Miss Ellie). He didn't understand the word "competitive," because he only did things to win. His idea of a song of nature was the rhythmic thump-thump-thump of the oil pump.

Jock did not like his son Gary. While Jock was of booming voice, heavy stride,

---

* For a history of the Ewing family, see *Dallas: The Complete Ewing Family Saga*, published by Doubleday & Company, Inc.

Gary with his brother, J. R. Ewing, visiting from Dallas. When Knots Landing residents asked Gary to help them stop J.R. from drilling offshore in 1979, Gary explained, "All my life, every time I've tangled with my older brother, I've lost." He did, however, stand up to him on this occasion and *won*.

At Knots Landing Motors, Frank Kolbert and Roy Lance inform Gary he is now in business with them in a stolen car parts ring.

While still working at KLM, Gary and Abby Cunningham went into a side partnership in methanol-powered cars. Gary found himself increasingly attracted to her; as Abby said, "Val tries so hard, and she's really quite charming, but Gary's growing by leaps and bounds. He knows what he's doing, what he's after. Every day he outgrows the little country girl more."

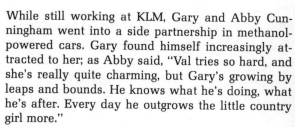

heavy hand, and cocky assurance with more than a tinge of arrogance, Gary was quiet, dreamy-eyed, and moody; his greatest wish in life was to be left alone with animals, music, painting, and his mother. Ewing Oil meant everything to Jock; to Gary, it was another cog of a monstrous industry that threatened the Great Ranches of the Lone Star State. Jock wasn't a team player; he was always a captain, bellowing out orders and demanding they be carried out to the letter. Gary wondered what his father's problem was, why he couldn't leave people alone—including him. But Gary did have two traits which Jock shared: die-hard stubbornness and an infrequent but violent temper.

And what made matters infinitely worse was that J.R. was just like Jock—except a *mean* version. He was the loudest, toughest, most aggressive kid around, and as if that were not enough, the most *jealous* kid around when it came to the attention of his parents. Satisfied that his father despised Gary, J.R. was incensed over his mother's clear preference for Gary. Like his mother, Gary was a gifted painter and would ride out to parts of the ranch with Miss Ellie to do still lifes. J.R. would literally cut them to shreds and make it look as if Gary had done it in a tantrum (not that Miss Ellie ever believed that, but still, the paintings would be gone). Gary and Miss Ellie shared a love of music; J.R. would leave Gary's records out in the sun and set fire to his piano music. By the age of twelve, Gary had abandoned his artistic talents. Since Miss Ellie didn't seem to understand why she shouldn't punish J.R., that it only made his attacks worse, Gary stopped trying to explain to his mother. He just said he didn't like painting or music anymore.

By the age of fourteen, Gary was showing overt signs of inner turmoil. He could and would be silent for days, had no friends at school or on the ranch, and began having inexplicable rages. Since he was shooting up in height, J.R. started backing off, but even when J.R. went off to college, Gary did not, as Miss Ellie would say, "come back." Something had broken inside Gary, something not easily fixed.

One night Gary slipped into the mainhouse through the kitchen door, and Miss Ellie, downstairs getting some hot chocolate, stopped dead in her tracks. Her Gary, her fourteen-year-old Gary, was dead drunk. She demanded to know where he had gotten the liquor, but all Gary would do is laugh and say, "Mama, be happy. I feel happy!" She was horrified; things had gotten out of hand and now she had to do something about it.

For the next four months, she curtailed other activities to spend time with Gary before school—not in her usual dress, but in her blue jeans and boots. Together they milked cows, fed horses, and pitched hay. After school, Gary was assigned to the ranch foreman, learning to round up cattle, cool down horses, brand, and rope. Miss Ellie was doing with Gary what her father had done with her: taking the energy used to get in trouble and rechanneling it into the working rhythm of Southfork Ranch.

Gary loved it. He began to loosen up, even talk a little, gain some self-confidence. Some of the hands liked him, and since Gary respected them, he believed them when they said he was good. And he *was* good, once he put his mind to it. When the annual Ewing rodeo approached in the spring, one of the hands suggested to Gary that he practice his bronco riding and enter the rodeo. At first Gary refused, but then thought, Why not? The idea of the nomadic rodeo life appealed to him. And there was another reason, too. Surely Jock would approve of him in such an event. An event that J.R. wouldn't be caught dead in! (J.R., to this day, can barely sit on a horse.) And so Gary began practicing on the meanest Southfork horse in the corrals.

The big day arrived, but "somehow" (J.R.) Jock caught wind of Gary's entry and had his name withdrawn. Gary demanded to know why and Jock said that Miss

Gary confides in his brother Bobby Ewing, in the nursery at Southfork Ranch in Braddock, Texas. Gary was there for the reading of his father's will; he was the only son to have special provisions on his inheritance because Jock was sure he'd blow it all.

With Abby in their love nest in Playa Del Rey Apartments. Gary was still living with Val at the time. "When I went home the first evening and got into bed beside Val, I thought, 'Oh, boy, here it comes.' I thought sure I'd be overwhelmed by guilt, but it never came. . . . For a while it was like waiting for the other shoe to drop. But when it didn't, all I was left with was a happy feeling."

Trouble in paradise. Now partners in business as well as in life, Abby vehemently protests the ways Gary has started investing his inheritance.

Ellie would kill him if Gary got killed, and since Gary was such a screw-up, surely that'd be the outcome. Furious, Gary stormed off.

That night, Gary returned to Southfork, drunk. With the help of some cowboys from the bar in town, he broke into the pens, found the horse whom no one had successfully ridden that day, and put him in the chute. On his back he went and fling went the gate and Gary went bucking out, staying on the horse for *two* minutes. The screaming and yahooing that went on woke the Ewings, and Jock and J.R. hurried outside just in time to see Gary ride him again. He stayed on for about a minute and a half before the horse, with a buck and a twist, slammed Gary into the corral boards. Gary slid to the ground and lay there, motionless.

He had broken his back.

In the five months he was in Dallas Memorial Hospital, Gary was in heaven. His father, *his* father, told him he was proud of him and stopped by to say hello once a week. And, of course, Miss Ellie came every day, little Bobby with her, and perhaps the nicest thing of all—a lot of the hands came by to joke and kid and swap stories, just as if Gary was one of them.

Gary spent the rest of his long recovery immersed in learning about motorcycles. By the time he was fully mobile again, he was begging, pleading with Jock to buy him one, which Jock refused to do. Finally, however, he gave in to a compromise— Gary could *earn* one. For ninety straight days over his sixteenth summer, Gary was up at 4 A.M., shoveling out the barns and pitching fresh hay. In the afternoon, he'd catch a ride out to Ewing fields and slave in the blazing sun on the oil rigs. Come September, Jock dropped him off at the motorcycle dealer with a slap on the back and a blank check in hand. Gary knew exactly what he wanted, paid for it, started her up, revved her up, and proceeded to drive it right through the showroom window. Respect from his father was thereby withdrawn . . . almost forever. Life went back to "normal" at the ranch, with Gary the outstanding failure.

Gary continued working on the ranch, but made no secret of his drinking. It wasn't as if he was falling down drunk; he just always faintly smelled of liquor. He refused to listen to his mother on the subject, saying that if she wanted him around at all, this was the way it had to be. It was the only thing that made him feel good. He

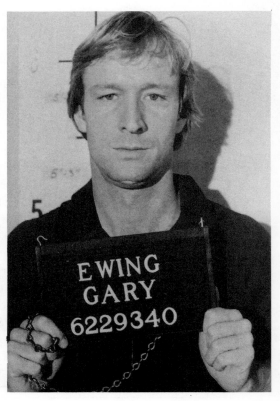

Gary's drinking spree in 1983 was very similar to his one in 1979.

SID He just had a couple too many. He'll be home as soon as he gets it out of his system.

VAL No. He won't.

SID Sure, he probably went to an all-night movie or something. I've done it myself. I doubt there's a married man who hasn't.

VAL But that's the thing, Sid. It's not like it is for other people. Gary isn't like other people. Gary's an alcoholic.

Gary in jail for the murder of Ciji Dunne. Every visitor brought him a painful reminder of wrongs done in the past. As Kenny Ward said to him, "Don't get me wrong—I think you're a weak, selfish son of a gun who'd sell his best friend down the river—but I don't think you're a killer. I wouldn't go into business with you if you paid me, but I still think you're getting a raw deal." Gary said, "Thanks."

started staying out all night, occasionally appearing at the breakfast table with the traces of a fight on his face, but volunteered nothing.

And then, in 1960, Gary met a girl and fell in love. Fourteen-year-old Valene Clements was a waitress in Forth Worth, and Gary quickly made that the destination of his free time. Valene stirred in him all the things that Miss Ellie could get to in years before—his confidence, his sense of self-worth, well-being, and a sense of life being worth it. Valene was beautiful and she was *his.* His drinking stopped and Miss Ellie, while relieved, hadn't a clue as to what had brought the change about.

In early 1961 Valene found out she was pregnant, and not hesitating a moment, Gary insisted she marry him. And then, drawing a deep breath and putting on a brave smile for the benefit of a scared Valene, Gary brought his bride home to Southfork.

Gary worked his tail off at the ranch as a hand, determined to support his wife and coming child. At the end of 1961 Valene gave birth to Lucy Ann Ewing, just the blondest, *loudest,* most beautiful little girl you ever laid eyes on. Gary was mad about her, sweeping her up in his arms at night, waltzing her around, making her laugh, all while crooning "Rock-a-Bye Baby" to her. Even Jock had a soft spot for Lucy right away.

Whatever happiness Valene and Lucy had brought to Southfork, J.R. more than countered with ugliness. He harassed Valene endlessly (saying, for example, that Lucy was the spitting image of her old boss at the diner), complained about Lucy, and engineered run-in after run-in between Gary and his father. Valene pleaded with Gary to move out of the house, but Gary sided with his mother, who insisted Lucy deserved the care she could receive at Southfork.

Gary started drinking again. But now his drinking had taken on a different light. Instead of drinking out of spite, or for good times, it was "just to get the hell away for a while." He started experiencing blackouts, not remembering what he did or said, and the more he promised Valene he would stop, the worse his drinking seemed to become. At the end of 1962, Gary got horrendously drunk one night after a fight with J.R. In the morning he found Valene with a black eye, holding Lucy protectively, cowering from him. Gary broke down and sobbed, feeling his heart break over the apparent evil he had inside. Hating himself, feeling unable to cope, incapable of handling the responsibility and pressure, he started drinking again that day. When Jock threatened to lock him up in a psychiatric hospital, Gary ran away, counting on his mother to look after Valene and Lucy. He felt he just had to get himself together, get his willpower under control, and then he would be back.

For the next fifteen years Gary drank and drifted his way across the country. Sometimes he held a job, controlling his drinking, but then he invariably was pulled into a bender, spending all of his money, losing his job. Moving on, he started gambling as well, rarely hitting it big, mostly losing his shirt and skipping out of town one step ahead of the racketeers. He started picking up women; heck, why not? He had failed Valene in every other way. He worked at a racetrack, pumped gas, and every once in a while, landed in the slums. He'd stop drinking for a few weeks, clean himself up, get himself a girl and a job, throw both away on a bottle, and move on.

He was sick and confused, a heavy cloak of guilt always weighing on his shoulders; his good intentions never materialized. The bottle always won.

In 1977 he landed in Las Vegas, where a friend offered him a casino job on the provision he stop drinking. For a time, he did. And then "a time" became months, which in turn built into a year. He had started as a waiter and worked his way up to a blackjack dealer, making good money and winning friends and respect. In 1978, when Bobby checked into his hotel with his new wife, Pamela, Gary was eager to see them. They had a wonderful reunion and at Bobby's urging, Gary returned to Southfork to see Lucy and his mother.

Gary and Lucy made peace with each other, and Lucy, proud of her dad for not drinking anymore, begged him to stay on in Dallas. She also gave him another big reason why—Valene. His first instinct when he saw her was to run, but the look in her eyes told him he didn't have to.

With renewed hope and energy, Gary stood up to his father and asked to be given a job at Ewing Oil. Gary wanted to start over and show his family what he could do. With Miss Ellie, Lucy, *and* Valene at his side, how could he fail? Easily, he found out. J.R. put incredible pressure on him, and Gary quickly realized that he could not stay sober and be near J.R. at the same time. Sadly, but still not drinking, Gary bade farewell to his family.

But not to Valene. He secretly moved in with her in Fort Worth, where they both worked, kept a low profile, and tried to put their marriage back together. It wasn't as hard as Gary had feared, basically because he had never stopped loving Valene and was grateful, down to his marrow, to her for giving him a second chance. How could he ever not love Val? With her strength, support, love, courage, *belief* in him. And how beautiful she was!

Although technically they were still married, Gary formally asked Valene to remarry him and move to California to start a new life. She accepted and Gary, still dazed at his good fortune, was happier than he had ever been. *Ever.*

They remarried in September of 1979, and as a wedding present, Miss Ellie bought them one of the houses Bobby had built in Knots Landing, California. Gary wouldn't be a millionaire Ewing; Gary wouldn't be a skid row bum; Gary was going to be middle-class! It made him wildly happy.

Gary had never had neighbors before. Sure, there had been Jenna Wade and her daddy on their ranch, some nine miles "next door" to Southfork, and on skid row he had slept in the same alley with a couple of guys, but this cul-de-sac of such friendly, diverse personalities amazed him. He wasn't there for ten minutes before they were into his business; however, it had only been five minutes before all kinds of help had been extended to him and Val. He was amused, pleased, and grateful.

The neighbor he liked best, and vice versa, was Sid Fairgate, who offered Gary a job as a salesman at Knots Landing Motors. Gary accepted the job and vowed to

work hard. He did and excelled, rapidly earning more responsibilities and learning to handle them adeptly. Val was so proud of him and Gary, too, was proud of himself. Sid sponsored him into the Jaycees and the Chamber of Commerce, where he was respected and well liked. Just after Christmas, Sid promoted him to vice president.

When the announcement came during a neighborhood party at the Fairgates', Richard Avery pressed a glass of champagne into Gary's hand. Gary had no intention of drinking it, but then, out of nowhere, the thought came—heck, why not? It's a celebration! The champagne tasted wonderful and Gary could feel the old warmth spreading down through his body, the wave of well-being coming up in his head. He sipped another drink and felt like dancing. More sips followed and by the time they left the party, Gary was high and Valene was scared to death. They argued and Gary, feeling resentful, went out to a bar. And as always in the past, once he started drinking, Gary couldn't stop. Any sense of well-being was long gone by the end of the first night.

The on-and-off drinking of a couple of days was enough to make Gary tell Sid Fairgate to take his job and shove it, make him try (unsuccessfully) to have sex with a prostitute, take on a half-dozen fist fights, spend all of his money, and terrorize every neighbor in the cul-de-sac. As the days went on, his drinking stretched to round the clock and at the Averys' one night he blacked out. The next thing he knew he was under guard at a hospital. In the process of getting himself a drink at the Averys', he had punched his fist through the liquor cabinet glass to get it. He was apprehended after Laura Avery told the police his foray was a suicide attempt so they'd lock him up. They moved him into alcoholic rehabilitation, and after resisting therapy, Gary escaped and returned home, with the intention of getting some money and continuing to drink. He'd show 'em! But Valene finally got through to him. If he continued to drink, he no longer continued to live there. Furious, Gary stormed off, but deep down from somewhere, a little voice of sanity told him he had to try and stop. After much deliberation, Gary sought help from Alcoholics Anonymous.

The minute Gary resolved to attend AA meetings regularly was the minute the damage stopped and the smoke started to clear. Sid took him back at KLM, Valene was relieved to have the Gary she loved back, and with time, Gary forgave himself for what he had no control over—the disease of alcoholism. All his life he had thought drinking was a question of willpower and morality. It wasn't until AA that he understood it was a disease that could be kept in remission. He found strength and an enormous sense of hope from the meetings, and gradually started to feel his lifelong shame fall away. Most importantly, he lost the desire to drink for long periods of time. Valene joined Al Anon, which was an additional help.

In October of 1980, Gary agreed to sponsor a newcomer to AA, Earl Trent. Earl was very, very sick and angry, and had a very, very frightened and miserable pretty wife, Judy. Earl wouldn't take any AA suggestions and Gary spent an inordinate amount of time chasing after him, with a hysterical Judy urging him on. Gary lost a lot of sleep at a time when the pressure at work was escalating.

KLM was, in Gary's view, running the risk of going under, and Gary was determined to drum up profits. A couple of admittedly sketchy characters, Roy Lance and Frank Kolbert, came to him, wanting to buy a fleet of taxis from Gary. It looked like easy money and Gary, with a lot of other things on his mind, ignored his instincts and closed the deal.

Meanwhile, Judy Trent had become more and more dependent on Gary to "fix" Earl and their marriage. In fact, the dependency was turning to love, something which Gary tried to ignore. He only wanted to help, really, but admittedly, the

Mr. and Mrs. Gary Ewing, 1983, with Abby's children Olivia and Brian. The first night of their honeymoon, Abby said to Gary, "From the first time I laid eyes on you, I wanted you. I've moved heaven and earth to get you. And now I've got you. I'm the happiest woman on earth. . . . I *love* getting what I want!"

Gary flew to Tennessee in 1984 to bring Valene home. He was stunned at what he found; from the shock of losing her babies, Valene had regressed into a fantasy world, with absolutely no memory of her real life. As Verna Ellers, she said, "Well listen, Gary, I'd love to jaw, but this isn't making the baby a coat, as my mother used to say. What can I get you?"

drama of the whole thing was a lure. After one particularly horrendous night of fighting and chasing a drunk Earl around, Gary consoled Judy at her home and *it* just happened. He slept with her. Gary felt so guilty about innocent Valene, he could barely look at her. Vowing to be a better husband, he trudged on with a facade and work.

Gary was then faced with the outcome of his taxi fleet deal. The money KLM had made up front on the car sales was more than lost by the repair guarantees Gary had written into the contract to make the deal. Lance and Kolbert, claiming to feel bad about it, offered Gary a deal in cut-rate auto parts to make up for the loss. Gary, realizing the auto parts had to have been stolen, backed out of the deal. Or he *thought* he had. Sid's sister, Abby Cunningham, who had just come to KLM, was there when the two gangsters told Gary that he *had* accepted the deal, whether he liked it or not. And if Gary didn't come up with the $50,000 to purchase the parts, he wouldn't have to worry about his future because he wouldn't be having one.

In the subsequent days of indecision, Gary found himself getting in deeper and deeper confidence with Abby, who pushed him into borrowing the money from, of all people, J.R.! It was the most peculiar thing, actually. Talking with J.R., seeing in his eyes a flicker of respect (for this deal, no matter how it smelled, would make a fortune), unlocked something in Gary, a thought, a fantasy. What if he *did* make his own fortune? The idea kindled and took hold, Abby fanning it into even brighter visions.

The parts were purchased and resold to Sid's regular jobber, who then could undersell every other jobber in the area while guaranteeing KLM unlimited parts at half of his already discounted price. Abby played magician with the KLM books, making the profits appearing from elsewhere. J.R. was paid back, the jobber made a bundle, and Sid was guaranteed first-rate parts at dirt-cheap prices. Sid was ecstatic with KLM's rosy balance sheet, and Gary and Abby smiled, keeping a tight lip.

And then FBI agents arrived at KLM to investigate a stolen car parts ring. Terrified, Gary initially denied any knowledge of it, but then after Sid's wife, Karen, pointed out discrepancies in Abby's bookkeeping, he came clean with the whole story. Gary and Sid went to the FBI together, and Gary was promised a pardon if he would cooperate in catching the crooks.

It turned out to be the single most terrible experience of his life. No, not setting the crooks up to be caught, but the fact that Gary's best friend, Sid Fairgate, was murdered instead of himself. Sid's death seemed a confirmation of what Gary had always believed—that he was no darn good to anybody and, in fact, hurt everyone he cared about. Wrapped in guilt and despair, it was a miracle he stayed sober and that Karen (who did not blame Gary) could talk him out of leaving Knots Landing for good.

Karen came to KLM as the new boss and owner, and Gary did everything he could to teach her about the business and increase her profits. She learned quickly and the two worked well together. In December of 1981, under Gary's guidance, KLM conducted tests on Pete Dorado's conversion method for turning regular gasoline engines into ones using methanol. The tests proved the method to result in cleaner, better cars, running on significantly cheaper fuel. Abby joined in the excitement and the three eagerly presented the opportunity to Karen. As impressed as she was, Karen reluctantly declined on investing because of a short cash flow. Pete didn't mind since he had another company, Petrolux, lined up to invest, but Gary and Abby couldn't let the opportunity to make a fortune slip by. Without Val's knowledge, Gary mortgaged the Ewing house for $150,000 and Abby came up with $50,000 of her own and the two were in business.

When Val found out, she hit the roof. She demanded to know how Gary could dare do such a thing. Gary, frustrated at what he saw as a lack of confidence in him, demanded to know why she couldn't believe in him. It was the first time that Gary saw Valene in a different light; he thought she was holding him back. And too, for the first time, he saw that Abby not only shared his vision, but believed that he could carry it out.

For weeks Gary and Abby met outside of KLM to work on their business. Their hours were long, working terribly hard, side by side. Gary got more and more attracted to Abby as Val's jealousy and complaints increased. Val was just so—*undaring*.

And then came what felt like treason. Valene showed Gary the first draft of her novel, which a New York publisher wanted to buy. Gary was proud of her, but when he sat down to read it, his pride turned to incredulous anger. The whole novel was not a novel at all—it was one long kiss-and-tell story about his family! They argued and eventually arrived at an agreement: Gary wouldn't spend time with Abby outside of office hours, and in return, Val wouldn't publish the book. Gary, however, violated his own agreement when Abby claimed an emergency, so Val went ahead and signed the publisher's contract. Their marriage did not recover.

When Gary and Abby closed a tricky deal that ensured the success of their venture, their night of celebration turned into lovemaking. Gary felt guilty, but sex with Abby was unlike anything he had ever experienced. She was, simply, *thrilling*. For about five minutes he considered never sleeping with her again, and instead started seeing her whenever, wherever he could. Gary was actively addicted again, not to alcohol, but to Abby.

He was living with Val and brooding over Abby. The neighbors began to catch on, but Gary was beyond reason now. It all came to a head in March, when Karen led Val to an apartment where Gary and Abby were in a state of incriminating undress. Val disappeared and Gary stayed home with his scowling mother-in-law, sneaking over to Abby's and then back to his own bed before daybreak.

Val's departure prompted Abby to take Gary out to look for a new house, a presumption that annoyed him. He was beginning to have his doubts. As long as he had

21

had Val, Abby had seemed thrilling. Now, without Val to fall back on, Abby seemed a bit scary. Karen did not approve of Abby *or* Gary, and she canned him at KLM. When Val returned to the neighborhood, every stick of his mother's furniture, all his belongings, were moved out of the house on Val's order. Maybe Gary hadn't come to a decision about what to do, but Valene had—Gary was out! Gary turned to Abby, who set him up in an apartment by Knots Landing Marina and joined him there at every opportunity.

In the fall, Gary was notified that Jock Ewing had been killed in a helicopter crash in South America. He was deeply grieved, angry, too, at all the memories, and at a loss at how to put his relationship with his father to rest. So much had happened recently—he had lost his friends and his career, and with all the guilt surrounding his betrayal to Valene, he couldn't face his friends in AA and hence stopped going to meetings.

Jock's will was read in October; he left Gary 10 percent of the Ewing Oil stock and $10,000,000 in cash, with the stipulation that Gary could receive only the interest and dividends on that money, since he had been convinced that Gary would find a way to blow it all. It depressed Gary enormously, the fact that his father, though dead, could still humiliate him. But Abby, who came down to join him in Dallas, helped him put his anger to rest and be grateful for the new life he had been given. Gary, who had never seen this side of Abby—her understanding, nurturing side—began to fall in love with her for real.

The first thing Gary wanted to do was buy a horse ranch outside of Santa Barbara, but Abby freaked out at the prospect of living "way out in the middle of nowhere." Gary backed down, but came up with other spontaneous ideas: to go into business with Kenny Ward and produce an album by Ciji Dunne, a young beauty of his own discovery, and to loan money to Richard Avery for his new restaurant, Daniel. Gary would do as he liked with his money, but he had to admit, Abby had a head for numbers and an ability to undercut risk which he himself did not possess, and he grudgingly (but secretly willingly) made her a partner in all of his business affairs.

Also as a concession to Abby, Gary bought a gorgeous beach house, into which they moved with Abby's two children, Olivia and Brian. Gary got along extremely well with her children; he had missed all the joys of parenting with Lucy and, in particular with Olivia, happily threw himself into the role of loving parent and co-guardian.

Gary became good friends with Ciji Dunne and had enormous faith in her talent. Problems with his partnership with Kenny arose almost immediately and it wasn't clear whose interference was doing the most damage—Abby's or a cocky pipsqueak named Chip Roberts. Disagreement after disagreement broke out between Gary and Kenny about how Ciji should be handled, and whether G&K Records should be sold out to a bigtime producer. The matter was settled by Abby's financial wheeling and dealing and then somehow the deal was done and Kenny was blaming Gary, claiming he had sold him out behind his back. When Gary pleaded innocence, Kenny said, right, sure, just like the way he had fixed Sid and betrayed Val. That hit Gary very hard. It had the ring of truth.

Depressed, confused as to why his new life was not turning out well, he received another blow. On the front page of a scandal sheet, there was a long excerpt from Valene's unpublished new book that was all about how Gary's drinking and womanizing had ruined her life. Gary was stunned. How could Val write all this stuff? Abby was ready to sue, but Gary pointed out everything she wrote was true. Val told Gary that someone had stolen the material, that she had no intention of ever letting anyone see those pages, but the damage had been done.

In secret, Gary started to drink again. Pretty soon, however, it was no secret. He was on a roaring drunk all over again, its days of destruction touching everyone near and dear to him. The drunk ended with his coming to on a Knots Landing beach. Farther down, lying in the middle of a crowd, was the dead body of Ciji Dunne. A day later, Gary was arrested for murdering her during a blackout.

Gary was consumed with such guilt that even when it appeared that Valene was more likely the murderer, he insisted that he had done it. Whether he had killed her or not, Gary felt duty bound to be punished, if not for this, then for his whole life, for leaving Val, for Lucy, for Sid, for Kenny, and on and on. Valene, after she was cleared, finally convinced him to defend himself. Gary's case was dismissed on insufficient evidence in October and he returned home to Abby. A few days later, however, he had a reconciliation with Valene that lasted for one long loving night in bed.

After that special night, when Gary was thinking about getting more involved with Valene and *less* involved with Abby, Laura Avery reminded him that Val couldn't be "just friends" with him, that he was an obsession with her. He argued he wanted to make amends to her, to which Laura responded, "If you really love her, the best amends you can make to Val is leave her alone." Knowing what Laura said was true, that all he ever did for Valene was mess up her life, Gary veered back to Abby and married her.

Gary started life anew with the purchase of a multimillion-dollar ranch and a career raising quarterhorses. The ranch was christened Westfork. He also got back into AA, and if he didn't get himself regularly to a meeting, Abby or Olivia or Brian did. Feeling better than he had in years and years, content to ride the ranch and work hard every day with his hands, Gary left Abby in control of Gary Ewing Enterprises. As a precaution he hired Laura to keep him informed of Abby's business endeavors.

In the meantime, Gary had been trying to get to know a young woman who was the spitting image of Ciji Dunne. Cathy Geary, leery of him, knew a lot about horses and she finally agreed to come and live and work at Westfork as a hand. Gary and Cathy worked closely together, sharing other interests as well: bodybuilding and

With Paul Galveston, 1985. Gary was thrilled to be his partner in the colossal Empire Valley project, but Karen Fairgate, whom Paul refused to work with, kept getting on his back about Galveston. Gary wrote it off to "sour grapes. People used to talk like that about my dad all the time. Galveston *is* using me, all right? He's building some kind of empire, and I'm his architect. Great. Terrific. I'm using *him*. How many chances does a guy have to build pyramids?" Karen replied, "Egyptian architects got buried in their pyramids, Gary."

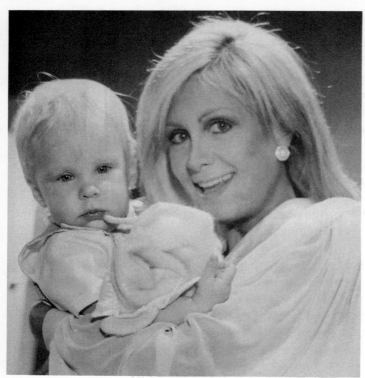

After studying photographs like this one of Valene holding her daughter, Elizabeth, Gary knew the twins must be his.

music. She protested against Gary's initial effort to make her more like Ciji, but once he let her be herself, he came to cherish Cathy's special qualities. She was a beautiful, exciting young friend to have around.

In January of 1984, Gary was alarmed to hear that Abby was somehow mixed up in an environmentally unsound resort project called Lotus Point, which in addition appeared to be connected somehow with organized crime. Getting no information from Abby or Laura, Gary blew his top at their denials and ordered an audit of Ewing Enterprises to find out what was going on. The audit didn't turn up anything on that front, but it did turn up the fact that Cathy was receiving weekly checks from Abby for $1,000. Upon further investigation, contrary to Abby's account that Cathy was from the Midwest, Gary discovered that her last residence had been a prison in Arkansas. As a convicted murderess!

Everything started to fall down around Gary. He learned that Valene was pregnant by Ben Gibson, which, while being happy for her, also made him feel very lonely for her. Cathy confessed why Abby had hired her—to distract him from getting involved in Ewing Enterprises. And then, to top it all off, Abby turned out to be the *mastermind* of Lotus Point, using Ewing Enterprises to do it!

Feeling betrayed on the deepest level, Gary threw Abby off the ranch and, as far as he was concerned, out of his life. He froze all the assets of Ewing Enterprises, slapped Abby with a lawsuit for fraud and embezzlement, sued her for divorce, and replaced her in the bedroom with Cathy. When the scandal around Lotus Point ballooned and he found that Laura Avery, too, was deceiving him, he was quite happy to bid them all good-bye and focus on ranching and Cathy.

Cathy's ex-husband showed up on the ranch, and on Thursday, March 8, he was prowling around the stable when he was shot dead. Mack MacKenzie had just arrived on the scene and, before anyone saw Gary, yanked him aside and explained quickly. A hit man had mistaken Ray for Gary; the Wolfbridge mob group wanted him dead so that his widow, Abby, could unfreeze his assets, including Lotus Point. Would Gary be willing to play dead so Mack could nail the Wolfbridge Group? Gary agreed.

The police hid him away in a cell, and while everyone else grieved his death, Cathy was allowed to see him. He was very upset over Abby and, as he said to Cathy, "Whatever else Abby may have done while we were together, I never doubted that she loved me. But I know now." But in the end, in October, it was Abby who willingly risked her life in order to save Gary's. At that moment, Gary realized that he had been wrong. Whatever Abby had done, she did indeed love him.

Gary and Abby went home to Westfork together, Cathy departed, and Gary and Karen joined Abby full-time at Lotus Point, converting it into what Gary thought it should be. First he built gorgeous offices that, like everything on Lotus Point, fit into the land to the point of building over and around existing streams. They built tennis courts and swimming pools indoors and outdoors, saunas, hot tubs, a golf course. All buildings were powered by solar energy; the garbage and sewer systems were environmentally sound. They built cabins—their designs based on the work of Frank Lloyd Wright—that fit into the landscape.

In November of 1984, in a quest for obtaining an adequate water supply for Lotus Point, Gary met with the mighty Paul Galveston of Galveston Industries. Galveston reminded him a lot of Jock, but with a big difference—Galveston thought Gary was the greatest thing since V-day and was eager to have him as a protégé. He sealed his commitment to Gary with a prize horse and a partnership in building Empire Valley, a planned community on a massive scale. Galveston would provide the land and drum up federal funds, and Gary would be the architect and builder.

Gary threw himself full force into Empire Valley, thriving under the mentorship of Galveston, but in March of 1985, Galveston disappeared and then turned out to be dead. To further confuse matters, Gregory Sumner announced to the world that Galveston had been his father and that he was stepping down from the U.S. Senate to run Galveston Industries, and by virtue of that, become partners with Gary in Empire Valley. To further murk the waters, Galveston left all the land under Empire Valley to Gary, and not to his own son.

In April, Sumner took Gary aside, introduced him to some international business-man, and Gary learned the real story of Empire Valley; at least part of it. Empire Valley was going to be a major economic center all right—as Gary had known, with the installation of light industry in the form of computers, satellites, telephone net-works, and central data banks—but Greg hinted it was secretly going to be a com-munications center vital to America's prominence as a world power as well. He would tell Gary no more unless he agreed to join his group. And then John Coblenz, Galveston's top advisor, took him aside and said that *he* was working with the government and that Sumner was *not*. He wanted Gary to report to him what Sum-ner and his gang were up to, in the interest of national security. In short, would Gary be a spy? After debating, Gary agreed to cooperate with Coblenz and joined Sum-ner's group. Sumner then filled him in. Empire Valley was going to be capable of intercepting and decoding any and every electronic transmission, anywhere in the world. With it, the United States could get into any computer, intercept any military directive, listen in on any phone, radio, or satellite.

Gary acted as a spy until Coblenz proved rather unreliable. Gary was being fol-lowed, someone was watching his house, and Mack and Ben—whom he could not confide in—told him that something very ugly had been brewing in Galveston Indus-tries, something directly connected with Coblenz, something now linked to Empire Valley. Gary told Coblenz the deal was off, that he was on to him and was swinging his lot in with Sumner's group.

At the end of May, Gary received the heartbreaking news of his brother Bobby's death. He flew down to Dallas for the funeral and, deeply depressed over the loss, called Abby and told her he would drive back, taking time to think, and requested she take his place overseeing Empire Valley for a while. His depression lingered into the fall, killing his enthusiasm for Empire Valley. In October, he handed the whole project over to Abby, maintaining authorization for any major decision.

In November, Gary attended the christening of Valene's twins. While looking at pictures of the babies and seeing them up close, Gary could hardly believe his eyes. One child, Betsy, looked just like his mother! There was no mistaking it, that mouth, those eyes. . . . And the little boy, Bobby, who favored Val, also clearly had some of Gary's features. Counting months backward in his head to the night of their lovemaking, Gary's mind went ablaze with the notion that the children might be his. They had to be! At first elated, Gary was then confused about what to do about it, and so for a while, did nothing. When he questioned Karen, she struck down his assertion with a vehement denial—too vehement, Gary thought. And finally, when he came face to face with Val about it, she wouldn't admit it, but she also would not deny it. He knew, without a doubt, those children were his. Only trouble was, Valene was now married to Ben Gibson, who wanted to formally adopt the children.

That same month, Gary got reinvolved with Empire Valley on a limited basis, still heavily relying on Abby. Sumner was causing trouble, trying to move the placement of Abby's television station to an environmentally unfavorable location. When Gary's trusted engineer, Frank Elliot, and Abby showed him geological reports that, in fact, made Sumner's desired location more sound than Gary's, Gary okayed the new placement. Elliot was electrocuted on the site a few weeks later, and Gary, convinced it was no accident, started investigating with Mack.

Gary learned that Abby had somehow blackmailed Elliot into falsifying his geological report, but before he could properly confront her about it, she came to him, frantic and clearly terrified, begging him to sell out Empire Valley to Sumner. When Gary tried to question her, she was nearly hysterical, saying that Coblenz had a contract out on him *and* Abby, one that would surely be fulfilled if Gary didn't sell.

Gary went out to the television site, where Elliot had been killed, and after snooping around in its basement, realized he had stumbled on the global spy center. So that was why everyone—including Abby—had been lying and fighting over the placement and layout of this building.

Gary, reasoning that Coblenz would want them both dead whether he sold or not, since they knew so much about the project, quickly raced through the possibilities of what to do. *Now.* How to stop Coblenz? Answer: Get rid of what he's willing to kill for—Empire Valley. Gary blew the whole complex up sky high, an explosion seen for some twenty miles and costing hundreds of millions of dollars. Fortunately, he had guessed right. Now that there was nothing left to fight over, now that the press was investigating what had been going on at Empire Valley, Coblenz slithered away.

But back at home, that was a different story. Gary knew Abby had been mixed up with Sumner, who in turn had been mixed up with Coblenz, and her involvement and deception were disgusting to him. Out of regard for the children, they continued to live together, but Gary swung into an affair with the governor's special assistant, lovely young Jill Bennett. The Ewings fought constantly at home and Gary came to loathe Abby, and tried to cheer himself up by giving the twins half (some 25,000 acres) of Empire Valley for their birthday.

His affair with Jill escalated toward love and after a near-fatal accident in his race car in March of 1986, Gary moved off the ranch and filed for divorce from Abby.

With Jill Bennett, 1986. After Abby's deceit on the Empire Valley project, Gary sought a personal life elsewhere. His affair with Jill was thrilling, alternating between racing high-speed cars and raising the roof of her hotel room. After he fell in love with her, he filed for divorce from Abby.

Things did not work out the way he hoped, however. Willing to give Abby one half of everything they owned, he was unprepared for her attempt at reconciliation and, when he spurned her, her rage that in turn promised the messiest divorce in history. When his relationship with Jill fell apart in May (she had been using him as a means to get Empire Valley), Gary found himself—for the first time in his life—without a woman to lean on.

He didn't have time to panic over it, however. A toxic waste dump buried under Empire Valley began leaking deadly arsenic, and after several Lotus Point guests and employees were hospitalized (one died), the resort complex was shut down. Gary desperately sought financial help to clean up the Empire Valley site but was forced to sell it back to Galveston Industries on the strength of Sumner's promise to clean it up. Putting the land and the cleanup in the hands of Sumner, however, also put in his hands the future of Lotus Point. And, heaven knew, Sumner was no friend of Gary Ewing's.

Gary has never pretended to be a saint. Problem is, in his determination to overcome his past by gaining respect in the present, he strives to be one, and thus establishes standards of behavior that are impossible for him to maintain. And when he fails to hit the mark, he does it with great gusto, swinging with all his might in the other direction.

Some say one extreme is his Ewing blood at work; the other the Southworth blood he carries from his mother. Valene will quickly point out that it is the Ewing side that sets off his alcoholic attitudes; the Southworth is the only ground receptive to sobriety. Whatever, Gary is always appearing as the saint or the sinner, and his feelings of extreme willfulness and guilt alternate accordingly. Admidst this constant movement, back and forth, the inevitable question arises: Which is the real Gary Ewing, the saint or the sinner?

Exactly. Really a bit of both.

Valene Clements Ewing Gibson

"You ought to eat when you're sitting at a full table, Valene.
Never can tell how long your good luck's going to last."
—J. R. Ewing, 1980

To look into her eyes is to know how far awry the rest of humanity has gone. In them you can see what has been discounted in the whirlwind 1980s—compassion, gentleness, warmth, and perhaps most precious of all, faith. For you are looking into the eyes of the rarest of all creatures—the one who, in the face of darkness, continues to move forward in the light of her own heart.

Valene Clements was born in 1947 in Husky Corners, Tennessee, the only child of Lillian Mae and Jeremiah Clements. They lived in a ramshackle farmhouse that had no electricity or running water. Valene's earliest memories were of lullabies sung by her mother, and laughter and bear hugs from her doting father. She distinctly remembers the day, however, when she was five, that her mama and papa had a terrible fight. Mama was holding a suitcase and Papa was trying to wrest it away from her, but another man came and Mama ran out of the house and drove away with him in a big fancy car. Her papa had cried and sobbed and rocked little Valene, and she tried to comfort him as best she could.

The two struggled along for a year until Jeremiah took sick and died. Valene was six and didn't quite understand where her papa had gone, but when her mama reappeared, she was happy. But not for long. Mama explained that she had to earn a living singing, and after the funeral, she left Valene with Jeremiah's mother. Granny was nice and loved Valene a great deal, but she was getting on in years and couldn't get around very well. She taught Valene how to cook and sew, and not even two years later, when Valene was just turning eight, Granny suffered a heart attack and died. Lilimae reappeared briefly, this time leaving Valene with her sister Rosalie, and took off again.

Valene became withdrawn. She was frightened and very lonely. Aunt Rosalie was loving, but by now Valene feared that to love her would mean she would disappear. She was a good little girl; she did her chores without being reminded, got A's in school, but otherwise kept very much to herself. What saved her in those years were books. Reading, Valene discovered, was a reliable comfort. In books she could go anywhere, do anything, be with anybody. She could read about love, about families, about mothers and fathers and their children and their pets.

That Christmas of 1954, Aunt Rosalie promised Valene that she could spend the holiday with her mother. Valene was terribly excited and worked for weeks on a present for her. And the time finally came! Aunt Rosalie put Valene on a bus for the

Gary and Valene in 1980. He swore to her, "There's no me without you. I know that every minute of every day. I could never betray you. You know it, don't you?" Unfortunately, Valene believed him; he was having an affair with Judy Trent at the time.

hundred-mile trip to her Aunt Jane's, where she would be met by her mother. Lilimae wasn't there. In fact, she never showed up, never sent any word.

Something came to Valene then—an awful feeling, a knowledge that was devastating. She could never *(would* never) rely on her mother again. Apparently the whispers of her relatives were true: Mama didn't care about anybody else, not even Valene, and the sooner she knew it, the better. It did not, however, make Valene love her mother any less.

The next few years were kind enough—despite a serious bout with whooping cough—and Valene spent, as usual, an enormous amount of time reading. Just before Christmas of 1957, her mother arrived and stayed for a few days. After Valene got over her initial anger at Lilimae, they had a close, warm visit. They made fruitcake together, strung popcorn, all interwoven with songs and hugs from Lilimae, and also a frequent "Darling thing, how I love you!" On Christmas Eve they stayed up all night talking. Lilimae coaxed Valene into sharing her dreams and Lilimae confided hers—to be the biggest country and western singing star in the world! Valene fell asleep near dawn with a smile on her lips. When she awakened, Lilimae was gone. No note, no good-bye. Valene wouldn't see her again for two years.

In 1959, Aunt Rosalie put Val on a bus to Nashville, where Lilimae had written she would pick her up. She wasn't there. Valene walked clear across the city to the theater where her mother was appearing; her mother the singing star. But Valene got scared. The theater was old and dirty, her mother was in a scanty little costume, just standing there on stage smiling while Alfonso the Great did magic tricks. Men in the audience were whistling, making cat calls, and yelling obscene remarks—all directed to her mama!

Backstage, Lilimae told Valene she was late for an audition and she was sorry she couldn't stay and talk. Valene walked back to the bus depot and went home. She lied and told Aunt Rosalie about the wonderful day she had spent with her mother, her mother the singing star, appearing in a fine Nashville theater.

When Valene was fourteen, Aunt Rosalie sadly informed her that she could no longer afford to keep her and shipped her off to Fort Worth, Texas, to where Rosalie's other sister, Jane, had just moved. Jane couldn't afford her either and got Valene a job waitressing every day after school and on weekends at Jake's Place, a diner.

Her boss, Ernie, was kind, and Valene, who was terrific with the customers, liked her job a lot. At her new school she was befriended by an English teacher, who encouraged her to write stories, many of which were published in the high school literary magazine.

On one Saturday morning in 1960, the diner was packed, and with one waitress out sick, the place was a madhouse. Valene was working faster and faster, truck drivers and cowboys yelling at her from every direction, and just when Valene was about to throw a tray in the air and give up, "This blond god got up from the counter and started helping me out. He didn't say a word to me. He just smiled. And . . . right then and there I knew everything was going to be all right." The god's name was Gary Ewing.

Their almost immediate mutual love, over the next weeks, turned to passion and shortly thereafter Valene found out she was expecting a baby. Gary insisted on marrying, and she, grateful that Gary really wanted to, smiled all the way down to Mexico and back. And then they arrived at Southfork Ranch.

Fifteen-year-old Valene had never set foot in anything larger than a three-bedroom house her entire life, so the mainhouse came as an inconceivable shock. And so did the Ewing family in it. Miss Ellie was an angel of mercy; Jock was an arrogant bully to Gary (and no one else); Bobby was a sweet little fellow; and J.R. was a complete monster; and the family had more money than God. Not for one moment did Valene feel as though she belonged there. J.R. was constantly spewing off about white trash and knowing it wasn't Gary's baby, and his ongoing veiled threats made Valene grow to fear him.

Lucy's birth in late 1961 made everything seem possible. This blond little princess was a beauty. Valene never left her, not for one minute, so wrapped up she was in the wonderment and joy of this tiny creature. Her daughter. Her *family,* Gary and Lucy. The Ewings.

Gary, however, did not stay happy. Over the next couple of months Valene watched him change. He had always been moody; Valene was used to that, either brimming over with excitement or feeling despondent and hopeless. But now, there was real trouble with J.R., and Val was acutely aware that Gary came to bed with liquor on his breath more often than not. It got worse; Gary'd get into a skirmish

Brother-in-law Bobby Ewing comforts Valene just before her exploratory operation for cancer of the colon. Valene bravely faced the possible colostomy. While reading *You and Your Colostomy:*
VALENE   This really is something.
GARY   What?
VALENE   It says here I'll be able to scuba dive. I never could scuba dive before.
They found her body clean of cancer.

Walking in to discover the truth about Gary and Abby Cunningham, 1982.

with J.R. at the dinner table and then bolt out of the house, returning much later, drunk. And then one night Gary came home and hit Val. That didn't scare her; it was baby Lucy in her crib in the corner that had Val terrified. She threw him out of the bedroom with a great ruckus, which all the family awakened to witness. The next day, Gary took off, as he always did, but this time . . .

Valene waited a month before she knew for sure he wasn't coming back. With Gary out of the way, J.R. resumed his torture of Valene, and after a particular threat —that he would "prove" Valene was an unfit mother and would have Lucy taken away from her—Valene packed up and fled. She and Lucy flew back to Tennessee and drove to Henderson County, where her mother was currently living. Lilimae was the only chance she had left; heaven knew, if there was a way to outfox J.R., Lilimae would know it.

Valene left the car at the side of the road and ran along the path through the woods to Lilimae's house. Something in the air told her to hurry; she had this feeling of being watched. She reached the house, tried the door, and found it locked. Knocking and calling out to her mother, Valene didn't believe her ears when her mother, from the other side of the door, yelled at her to go away. Valene pleaded, tried to explain the pending danger, but Lilimae just kept yelling, "I don't know who you are! Go away!" There was male laughter inside. Frantic, Valene kept pounding on the door. She heard something behind her and whipped around to see two burly men standing there. Valene tried to fight them off with her free arm—Lucy started crying —but the men grabbed hold of Lucy and shoved Valene down to the ground, giving her the parting message of, "You don't want us to hurt your daughter."

Valene was wild with grief. She flew back to Dallas and didn't even get out of the airport arrival gate before J.R. had strong-armed her. It was simple, he explained. The Ewings would raise Lucy, and if Val should so much as show her face, she would be arrested for prostitution. The chief of the Braddock Police was standing behind him, reading off her alleged multiple crimes, and Valene knew J.R. was not kidding.

What to do? Where to go? They said if she didn't leave Texas. . . . J.R. put her on the next plane out, but Valene came back to Fort Worth by bus. She got a waitressing job and hid out from J.R.'s people. Ernie, her old boss and friend, promised to relay word if Gary should try to make contact. He never did.

In quiet despair, deeply lonely, Valene started keeping a journal and immersed herself in reading. In 1970, after eight years without companionship, she dated a rodeo cowboy, Rusty Daniels. He reminded her a little of Gary (namely, his drinking and fighting and disappearing), but she was not in love with him. One of Val's waitressing friends asked her once what it was with her that she cared only for guys who couldn't be there for her. Val was taken aback and a little hurt by the question, but after thinking about it for a while, had to confess that her friend was right. Maybe that was what she was used to. . . .

Well, she had more important things to worry about, namely, Lucy and how to stay near her without being detected. Every morning Valene eagerly scanned the Dallas, Braddock, and Fort Worth papers for mention of Lucy, or the Ewings in general. She was able to keep amazingly close track of her daughter, since anything the Ewings did or said was news. Valene cut out every article and every picture of Lucy and pasted them in a big scrapbook. Lucy was growing into a legendary beauty, favoring Valene (but with Miss Ellie's eyes and height), and apparently, from what the newspapers said, inheriting a lot of Gary's high-flying temperament. Every year Valene gave packages to truck driver friends, who sent them to the ranch from out of state; packages containing gifts and cards for Lucy's birthday, for Christmas, for any holiday appropriate. Val never knew if she got them, but it made her feel better at least to try.

There were times when Valene considered trying to see Lucy, but then she would change her mind. Watching the lifestyle of her daughter, the rich and powerful people who were her friends, she began to think that Lucy would be ashamed of her, her background, her job. In fact, the more she thought about it, the more convinced she was that Lucy was best left alone in the care of a great lady like Miss Ellie.

The years passed slowly, with still no word of Gary. Valene was at work one day in October of 1978, busy setting up for breakfast, when a young woman caught her

A publicity photo for *Capricorn Crude.* Her new life as a bestselling author frightened her, and her beau Jeff Munson urged her, "Reach for it, Val. You're a fabulous, beautiful woman. Loving and intelligent. So stop being so unimpressed with yourself and soak up the limelight. It's no longer a dream."

Autographing books in Los Angeles. Valene appeared on "The Mike Douglas Show" the day *Capricorn Crude* was published.

DOUGLAS Some people are saying that the whole book's a roman à clef.

VALENE Roman à clef? I didn't write the book in French so I wouldn't know.

DOUGLAS Touché.

VALENE Yes, I have a little of that in the book too. . . .

DOUGLAS No, I meant that your book seems to be a thinly disguised story of the real life Ewing family.

VALENE Nothing the Ewings do is ever thinly disguised.

attention. Looking up, Valene felt her whole body go electric with shock. It was Lucy; Lucy was standing there, looking directly into her eyes, saying, "It's taken me a long time to find you, Mama. Why didn't you ever come to see me?" Valene's heart nearly burst and she took Lucy into her arms, rocking her, the years of pain flowing freely from her eyes in tears.

They had a lot to catch up on. That first day was halting, careful, tender, but that soon gave way to a torrent from both sides. Stories were compared, J.R.'s lies untangled and resolved, and the bond between mother and daughter reformed, strong with love. Lucy came every other day to see Valene, and then one day showed up with company.

Gary.

It was all such a jolt, such a wonderful crazy jolt. He was sober—for almost a year now—and had lost none of his feeling for Val. For Valene, it was a dream come true. She had always believed that he would come back to her if he stopped drinking. The question in her mind had always been if he could. Valene remarried Gary in September of 1979 and, with a joyous heart (the only sadness, leaving Lucy in Dallas), set out with him for a new life in Knots Landing.

Valene was overwhelmed by their good fortune. She never dreamed she would ever live in such a fine house: four bedrooms, with little terraces off of each in the back; a huge living room; dining room; big eat-in kitchen; and a tremendous backyard with lovely trees and view over the town and ocean. *Their* house.

Valene initially felt awkward around their neighbors. Almost all of them had been married awhile, had "better" backgrounds, had gone to college. She felt nervous and shy, but she was immediately befriended by her next-door neighbor, Karen Fairgate, whose boundless energy and wit and warmth and support did much to assuage Val's self-consciousness. With Gary as her husband, a house in which to live, Karen as a friend, and all of Knots Landing to get to know, Valene was thrilled anew each day. Almost each day.

In October, Lilimae showed up. Valene was resentful at how casually she dropped in, now that Lilimae had nowhere else to go. They had long talks, however, and by the time Lilimae left, Valene felt more kindly toward her.

In November, Valene secretly applied to take a high school equivalency test. She was terrified she'd fail and more terrified to risk finding out that she was as dumb as

she felt sometimes around her neighbors. She studied hard and aced it. Then she enrolled as a part-time student at the community college, majoring in English. Her professors brought her wonderful new adventures in literature and she thrived under their guidance. She also started to write again.

However wonderful Valene's own life was shaping up, the life she shared with Gary was not trouble-free. His drinking spree in December of 1979 landed him in Alcoholics Anonymous, thank God, and Valene in Al-Anon. She and Gary were unsuccessful in conceiving another child, but after a while Valene thought perhaps it was for the best. Their marriage just wasn't as strong as she had hoped. Gary had his affair with Judy Trent and it really hit Valene hard—an affair while he was sober! And while Gary's job at KLM was going well, the business was changing Gary; a part of him was evolving that Valene did not feel comfortable with. The *Ewing* side. He started to talk of making his own fortune, and Valene also cast more than a nervous eye at the new neighbor on the cul-de-sac and KLM employee, Abby Cunningham. She recognized the look in Abby's eyes when she was watching Gary.

In October of 1981, Lilimae turned up in Knots Landing again. After a difficult time trying to get everything out in the open about their relationship, Valene was finally able to put the past to rest in the belief Lilimae had changed. Her mother was older, homeless, and starving for love. Valene invited her to live with them.

On the writing front, Valene was rather pleased with her efforts. Maybe she was kidding herself, but she thought her teachers over the years might have been right— there *was* something appealing about the way she wrote a story. And the writing class she was taking now seemed to agree. Meanwhile, on the marriage front, Gary was giving her cause for worry. His methanol business with Abby meant spending endless hours with her outside of KLM—*alone.* It was obvious to Valene that Abby was making a play for her husband, but Gary continually denied it.

After having warned Lilimae to keep her hands off her manuscript for class, Val was flabbergasted when Karen's brother, Joe Cooper, announced that he had read it and loved it! And more unbelievable to Valene, he wanted to send it to a friend of his who was an editor. Glowing in his praises, Valene consented, and could hardly be angry with Lilimae for pussyfooting around behind her back.

Neal Henning at Kismet Press in New York liked the book and made a formal offer, zipping a contract off to Valene. She wouldn't accept the offer until Gary read the manuscript. When he finally got around to doing so, he said it was well written, but then surprised Val by adamantly forbidding her to publish it.

> GARY   It's all the skeletons in my family's closet, laid out on paper. Every character in the book is a member of my family. My brothers, my mother, my father, our daughter, you, me—how could you do it?
>
> VALENE   I made up half of what's in the book.
>
> GARY   Nobody's going to know that. They're going to think it's the real people.
>
> VALENE   Why should they think that?
>
> GARY   *A Family in Texas* by Valene Ewing. Come on, Val.

Valene struck a deal with Gary. She would not publish the book if he would stop seeing Abby outside office hours. He violated their agreement, and in anger (and because she wanted to), Valene signed the contract and sent it off.

In March of 1982, Valene was startled when Lilimae asked her how long she was going to close her eyes to what was happening between Gary and Abby. Val didn't know what she was talking about, specifically, but she found out. On the night of a party for regional booksellers given by Kismet Press, Gary didn't show up. Val at

"Thank you, Val honey, this is going to go in my special collection. Next to the knitting needles of Madame DeFarge."

The first "morning after" at Ben's house on the ocean. He was the only man besides Gary that Valene felt capable of loving.

Ben and Lilimae rush Valene into the house after she doubled over in pain. It was a sign of a delicate pregnancy, and Valene had to cancel her plans to accompany Ben to El Salvador.

first was too busy being upset with her publisher to notice—they were changing the title to *Capricorn Crude* and had a jacket mock-up Val thought was "lurid, cheap, vulgar. I can't tell you how disgusting it is"—but later on followed Karen out when she went in search of Gary. They found him—making love to Abby.

Valene, as rationally as she could, packed up her manuscript and typewriter and checked into a motel. She was betrayed, angry, hurt beyond words. She needed to think—or rather, *not* to think, and so threw herself into manuscript revisions. Let *Gary* think it through. Abby Cunningham! Of all the selfish, arrogant, underhanded floozies . . . And yet, Valene knew what Abby had over Gary—she was attracted by the *Ewing* side of Gary, the side Valene cared least for. Well, if that was the direction Gary was going, then Abby could have him.

Lilimae arranged for her to spend a lovely, platonic week at her old beau Rusty Daniel's ranch, where she completed her revisions, further disguising her characters to the satisfaction of her publisher's lawyers (J.R. became C.R. and then E.R.; Sue Ellen became Mary Sue and then Lili Sue). Then with renewed strength, she went home, changed the locks, packed Gary's clothes, and called a mover in to take every stick of Miss Ellie's—and thereby Gary's—furniture out of the house and back to Southfork Ranch. If Miss Ellie wondered what was going on, she'd have to ask Gary.

Kismet Press was taken over by Needham Enterprises and that company was eager to put a lot of money into the promotion and advertising of *Capricorn Crude*. Valene redecorated and refurnished her house with the advance money, and began doing some early interviews to help launch her novel. She was scared to death about it, but with her marriage evidently out the window, Valene needed to focus on her own life, and that meant supporting herself and her mother.

Her first interview was with nationally syndicated columnist Hilda Grant, known in the industry as the "Bouncy Barracuda." Her questions were more like accusations: "I hear your sister-in-law [Pamela Ewing] begged you not to publish the book for fear it would block the adoption of her baby. Is this true?" "Is it true your husband, Gary, was so upset when he read the book that it led to the breakup of your marriage?" Valene muddled through the interview, hating it.

In October, Valene's publicist, Beth Riker, sent over a young man named Chip Roberts, who was apparently some kind of assistant publicist. He was a somewhat suspicious character, but he knew more than Val did and so she was grateful for his advice and support; however, there was something that didn't seem right about him.

Gary's father died that fall and he came over to discuss the will with Valene. She assured him she wanted the house and that was it. Gary, surprised, agreed. It was painful to see him; Valene was still so much in love with him.

Valene went on a publicity tour, and by the time she returned in November, *Capricorn Crude* was number one on the fiction bestseller lists across the country, the New York *Times* hailing it as "Dynamic reading!" She also had a new resident in her home, Chip Roberts, whom Lilimae had invited to stay temporarily. Val didn't like it, but she didn't have it in her to take her mother to task.

By January, Valene was adjusting better to her new status as a single woman, and Jeff Munson—a powerful record producer and supernice guy—was an eager escort. It helped enormously to have him at her side when she invariably ran into Gary and Abby around town. But still, when she had the divorce papers drawn up, Valene was hesitant about signing them. Somehow it was inconceivable to her that her marriage to Gary, whom she loved so much, was over. She went to New York with Jeff for a change of scene and, while there, went to bed with him (which was marvelous). Afterward, she signed the divorce papers.

With Gary allegedly dead, and Ben missing in El Salvador, Lilimae was a rock of support in those agonizing weeks.

Her new manuscript-in-progress wasn't for anyone else to read for a long while. The first draft was a kind of exercise in grief therapy over Gary, what had happened to them since moving to Knots Landing. She wrote about his drinking, about Judy Trent, about Abby, about everything. Shortly after returning from New York, Valene found two chapters missing from it, and the next thing she knew, the *Global Gossip* was on the newsstands with the screaming headline: BOOZE AND WOMEN MADE MY LIFE HELL—EWING EX TELLS ALL IN NEW BOOK. There, for all the world to read, was her angry rehashing of the horrors of her marriage. Gary was incensed when he saw it and Val was hard-pressed to convince him she had no idea how it had happened. And when, a few days later, Valene heard that Gary had started drinking again, she blamed herself.

Her guilt had her chasing around all over town after him, trying to get him to stop. When Gary called her, dead drunk, from Ciji Dunne's apartment, Valene raced over there. He was gone. Valene got into an argument with Ciji, and losing her temper, Val slapped her. Ciji fell backward and hit her head, but got back up while Val stormed out. The next day Ciji was found dead and the authorities arrested Gary. When Val learned that Ciji had been pregnant, she assumed that that was what Gary had been calling her about that night, that he was in a bind. And when she found out that Ciji had died from a blow on the head in her apartment and died there, that someone had dumped the body in the ocean, Val assumed that it was *her* blow that had killed Ciji, and that Gary, trying to protect her, had moved the body and taken the rap.

Valene turned herself into the police, but was released when it was proven that her slap had nothing to do with Ciji's death. Meanwhile, Gary, still in jail, refused to defend himself. Val eventually convinced him to clear himself and the days of contact with him brought up all their old feelings for each other. Val knew he still loved her.

At Gary's hearing, Valene was befriended by Ben Gibson. After Gary was re-

leased and he went straight back to Abby, Valene began seeing Ben as more than a friend. His gentle nature, striking good looks, and bright personality were very appealing.

In November of 1983, during Lilimae's unstable period after trying to kill Chip Roberts, Gary had to bring Lilimae back to the house late one night. After Valene put Lilimae to bed, Gary stayed to comfort her. The comfort turned to a night of lovemaking. The next day, Gary left with the agreement that they'd meet later to discuss the Lilimae problem. He never showed. When Valene called Westfork Ranch to find out what had happened to him, she was sick with pain when Olivia Cunningham told her that Gary and Abby had suddenly gotten married.

Meanwhile, she had no recourse but to commit Lilimae to a psychiatric hospital. It broke Valene's heart to do it. Ben was the sole source of comfort and support in those horrible, agonizing days. By December, her affection for him turned to a tentative love and they began a romantic involvement in the fullest sense.

Valene finished a new manuscript, *Nashville Junction*, which was based on the stories Lilimae told about herself. Her publisher loved it, claiming, "It has the best heroine in it since Scarlet O'Hara." More good news came—Valene, after all this time of trying, was pregnant! She was ecstatic, filled with fantasies of a little boy like Ben. And then the bad news—she was *three* months pregnant. This was February, she had started sleeping with Ben in December . . . oh no—it had to be Gary's.

Valene never considered anything but carrying the child, but what went with it did not go easily. She tried to tell Gary, but couldn't. She wanted to correct everyone's assumption that the child was Ben's, but couldn't. She did, however, tell Ben who the father was. Although he broke off with her for a while until he sorted his feelings out, Ben did not divulge Val's secret. When they reconciled later, Val agreed to accompany him on a three-month overseas assignment, but Val suffered the symptoms of a delicate pregnancy and her doctor forbid her to go. Ben left a marriage proposal with her before his departure.

March brought extraordinary news—Valene was carrying twins! Her joy was cur-

As Verna Ellers, waitress extraordinaire at the Waldorf Luncheonette in Shula, Tennessee. Abby was the first to locate her, and didn't believe that Valene had no memory of who she really was.

ABBY You're making me crazy.

VALENE I'm sort of swamped, you know? You're not my only customer.

ABBY I just need to know one thing, are you coming home or not?

VALENE Miss, you've got a real problem.

Gary finally starts to break through to "Verna," when he shows her the author photograph on the back of Valene's second novel, *Nashville Junction*. With all the publicity surrounding her disappearance, the novel hit the bestseller lists, while its author was preparing to marry Parker Winslow. The reception was to have featured a jug band called Snake-Eyes Billy McCloud and the South Fork Rattlers, and the couple was to honeymoon in Parker's Winnebago.

tailed by the news that Ben had disappeared in El Salvador and was presumed dead, although the state department was unable to find his body. Valene tried every means to find out more, and Gary offered his help and support. Driving out to his ranch one afternoon, feeling alone and terrified, Valene arrived just in time to hear a gunshot. Mack MacKenzie dragged her away, telling her that Gary had been murdered.

No one but Valene knows what those days were like for her. One thing was for sure—the twins were the only thing that made her feel like living. At Gary's funeral, Laura Avery told her that Gary had loved her; in fact, she said he had not met her that day after they made love because he had known how he would mess up her life all over again. Val found it consoling. And then Ben reappeared, alive and recovering from his injuries.

While terribly relieved and happy at having Ben back, Valene was still determined to find out who had killed Gary. Ben, who was openly jealous, was upset, which Valene understood. But what she didn't understand was that when Ben found out that Gary was alive, he didn't tell her. Livid, Valene broke off their engagement, feeling unhappy, happy, enraged, heartbroken—a number of things.

In October of 1984, Valene's half-brother (whom she never knew she had), Joshua Rush, moved in with her and Lilimae. It cheered her enormously to have more family around her, and her vision of the future, of the babies, looked brighter.

In November, Valene's obstetrician was called out of town and she was referred to Dr. Mitchell Ackerman, who put her on a new medication. When she started experiencing pains, Ackerman told her to increase her dosage of pills. At 7½ months pregnant, Valene went into early labor and was rushed to the hospital by the Fairgate boys. Her labor was not very long or difficult, but Ackerman insisted on giving her some kind of anesthesia regardless. Both babies were born, she heard them cry, and then she was out. When she reawakened, eager to see her children, Ackerman told her, with great sorrow, that the babies had been stillborn. Gone. Dead. Valene was frantic—they had made a mistake! No, they told her. Valene got hysterical, screaming for her children, and her friends and neighbors were enlisted to help her through the aftermath of grief. Val knew the babies were alive; it was as if the whole world had gone crazy. Or was *she* going crazy? She *heard* her children! Her grief and despair and shock pushed Val into a deep, vacuous depression. One that, in time, pushed her over the edge of reality.

She thought she was Verna Ellers, the lead character of *Nashville Junction,* and went to Shula, Tennessee, to begin a new life, with no recollection of her old one. She worked as a waitress in the Waldorf Luncheonette and almost married a guy named Parker Winslow before Gary got through to her and brought her back to Knots Landing. It was all so confusing; she remembered Gary, her mother, but no one else. Gradually her memory came back and so did the grief over the twins. She cried and cried and admitted to Karen that she still believed them to be alive. Ben, understanding and patient, stood by her side as long as she would let him.

When things began to settle a bit, Valene noticed how strange and selfish Joshua had become. Val didn't want to interfere, and to a large extent didn't, but she and Joshua were no longer close, nor trusting of one another. Trying to pull herself together, she toyed with a new novel, one about the perfect childhood. Her relationship with Ben was moving smoothly again and by the end of April 1985, they entertained the notion of something more permanent. Val put off an official engagement until she could feel more at rest about the twins.

Then, one day in May, Abby came rushing to find her with the news that someone had called her—thinking she was Mrs. Ewing as in Valene—and told her where the babies were. Val got into the car and Abby drove her to a house, all the while Val not feeling surprised. She had this odd sensation of having known all this before, that her children were alive, only somewhere out of her reach. She saw the children —a boy and a girl—in the care of illegally adoptive parents. Not since the birth of Lucy had Valene felt like this; no greater light has been seen than what was shining in her eyes at that moment of recognition.

There were endless legal complications involved in proving that the twins were her children. Valene didn't understand why she just couldn't have them, but the court placed a restraining order on her, barring her from the Fishers' property. Valene, miserable, longing for her babies, would stake herself across the street, hoping for a glimpse of them. And then one evening in October, the doorbell rang and Val came downstairs. Karen had succeeded in getting the children. They were hers now, really hers. Her babies.

With her half-brother, Joshua Rush, Gary, and Abby at Lotus Point. Valene was very nervous about Joshua's going to work for Abby at Pacific World Cable—and for good reason.

It is an emotional moment for all as Karen brings Bobby and Elizabeth home to their mother. Home to stay.

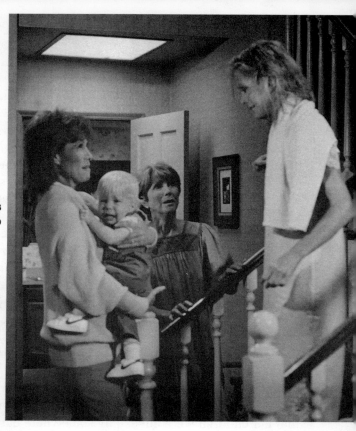

Ben teaching Valene how to use a word processor in his office at Pacific World Cable. Everything was going fine until a file labeled "Ackerman" came up. Valene wanted to know if that was the same Ackerman as the doctor who had delivered her children. Ben denied it, not wanting to get her hopes up if his investigation didn't pan out.

Valene was in euphoria, carrying Elizabeth "Betsy" in one arm and Bobby in the other. And Ben, wanting to raise the children as his own, proposed marriage. Valene accepted. They married in November and went on a short but heavenly honeymoon, after which Ben moved into the Seaview Circle house.

Joshua, at this point, was in Valene's opinion psychotic and she barred him from the house in fear for the children. Lilimae fought her tooth and nail over it, but Valene was firm. She wasn't without compassion, however; she pleaded with Joshua to let her take him for psychiatric help, but he refused.

After Joshua died in December, Valene prayed that things would settle down. They didn't. The biggest problem was, as always, Gary. He started showing up at the house to visit the twins, dropping off presents, conspiring with Lilimae to see them in the park. Valene knew he had somehow found out the children were his, *biologically,* but she refused to confirm it. On one hand, she wished she could share the children with him, but on the other, the realistic hand, Ben Gibson was her husband and, for all intents and purposes, their father.

On the twins' first birthday, Gary gave them the multimillion-dollar present of 25,000 acres of Empire Valley. Valene quickly moved to return the gift but was pained by *Gary's* pain in wanting to give his children something. Ben, in the meantime, was in agony, incensed over what seemed like a public announcement of paternity. Val tried to reassure Ben and assuage his insecurities by staying away from Gary (and keeping him away), but Gary's behavior had her worried. His racing cars, his flaunting an affair in front of Abby, the money he was throwing around, all signaled one thing to Val—that Gary was on a "dry drunk." As hard as she tried, she couldn't detach from Gary's situation, and her badly handled attempts at hiding

After finding her walking on the beach, Abby drops Valene off across the street from the Fishers', the couple who illegally adopted the twins.

it from Ben caused a breach in their marriage. But she was so caught up in the children, and in Gary, that it was only when Ben walked out the front door with a suitcase that it dawned on Valene that she was losing him to Cathy Geary.

The moment of truth had at long last arrived.

Martyr /mart-er/n 3: VICTIM: *esp.:* a great or constant sufferer.

Given the circumstances of her childhood, Valene was hardly equipped for any role other than as described above. But up until recent years, her life could accommodate her addiction to people who cause her pain (namely, Gary), and no one else had to endure the ramifications. But now with Ben Gibson in her life, she has not only continued to be a victim, but has become a victimizer as well. For whatever pain she feels in connection to Gary, it is now Ben's pain too—perhaps even more so.

All's fair in love and war as an *adult,* but now Valene has two small children to think of as well. As a loving parent, one teaches one's children everything one knows about how to live. So one can only hope that Valene will come to realize that unless she learns a new way of living, she may well be condemning her children to follow in her footsteps, to making the same mistakes, to feeling the same pain, over and over again.

Benjamin Gibson

"If there's a story, there's Ben Gibson."
—Charles Coker, 1983

There is a timeless quality to his talents. Sir Arthur would have considered him a windfall for the Round Table; Robin Hood could have used him early on to get the goods on the Sheriff of Nottingham; and surely Lincoln would have lived had he been one of his bodyguards. Benjamin Gibson possesses a gift: a sixth sense for detecting evil, and the stamina and selflessness to try and block its deadly assault.

He is a seeker of the truth, a crusader who believes with all his heart that a free country exists only with the public's right to know. He is dynamic, meticulous, defiant, and fearless, fully complimented by innocent good looks, a disarming smile, and eyes capable of melting the most frigid heart.

He is a man who follows his own heart; time and again his journey has come near to breaking it.

Benjamin Gibson was born in 1946 on a farm just outside of Steubenville, Ohio. He was an only child and, outside of school, spent an inordinate amount of time alone. When he was eight, his dad bought him a crystal set, a present that would change the course of his life.

Ben discovered news. From the laid-back isolation of the farm—where the only news, it seemed, was about the weather—Ben could tune into what was happening out in the "real" world. By ten, he was operating a ham radio, making contacts internationally. Every morning, after milking the cows, Ben rushed to the library and read the newspaper; at night, he'd call on his radio to obtain his own information on news stories. By twelve, he was writing his own accounts of international incidents, checking his work against the next day's paper.

When Ben mustered up enough courage to show some of his work to one of his teachers, he started to receive some guidance. The school paper bored him to distraction, but he dutifully worked on it. His classmates liked him, but he remained a loner. He began fantasizing about his future, where he'd like to go (easy, *anywhere*), and what he'd like to be ("important, sophisticated, a man of the world.").

Ben's father was very much a loner himself, and it was a long time before Ben and his mother noticed that he was behaving a little more strangely each day. His behavior took a drastic turn in 1962, when Ben was sixteen. Ben was coming in from the barn one night and happened to glance in through the living room window. There he saw all the furniture piled up in the middle of the room and his father standing there, trying to set it on fire. Ben rushed in and restrained him. Sadly, Mr. Gibson didn't understand that anything was wrong with what he was doing.

When the doctors committed his father into a psychiatric hospital, Ben and his mother, Elizabeth, debated over what to do. Could he farm any longer? Would either

With the Ewings as owners of Pacific World Cable, Ben's job was not unencumbered. When Abby wasn't blocking news stories, she was harassing his newsroom staff with memos such as:

TO   P. K. Kelly
FROM   Abby Cunningham-Ewing
RE   A More Vibrant On-Camera Image

And when Ben disagreed with her policies, and tried, in fact, to quit, she surprised him by saying, "Differences of opinion are healthy. The station can only improve because of them. I don't mind a good fight. In fact, I respect you for it." (She must respect him a lot.)

of them feel safe leaving him alone on the farm? They ended up trying to run the farm themselves for a year; in that time Mr. Gibson was released and then committed again, and then did not want to come out at all. Not knowing what else to do (with staggering hospital expenses and no insurance to cover them), they sold the farm and moved to Columbus, where Mr. Gibson swung in and out of the hospital doors for the next six years. Ben, living with his mother, won a scholarship, attending Ohio State by day and working as a typesetter by night.

When Ben graduated (summa cum laude) in 1968, he was offered a free-lance assignment overseas. Since his father was in stable shape, Ben, for the first time, was free to go. He left for Southeast Asia and his string of prize-winning stories on the Vietnam War won a flood of offers, but Ben preferred to remain free-lance, picking and choosing assignments that interested him. From 1970 to 1981 he was an international globe-trotter, with a specialty in political analysis. From Southeast Asia he went to Tibet, to Ireland, to Cairo, to the Carrago Islands, to Argentina, to Peru; from the first free elections in Spain, he went to being shot at on beaches in Portugal. Finally, in 1982, he chose an assignment in the good ol' U.S. of A.—to investigate political donations from special-interest groups.

After the completion of that assignment, Ben mulled over his choices: Afghanistan, San Salvador, Beirut, Tel Aviv, the Philippines, Johannesburg. . . . After thir-

teen years of restless global travel, he was, he had to admit, a bit weary. He kept turning one offer over and over in the back of his mind; nooooooo, he said, never; but then he'd go back to it and reconsider. Well, what if he *did* take this job for a year or two? The job of heading Pacific World Cable (PWC) News, whose headquarters were in Los Angeles. Hmmm, Los Angeles. No, no, the Philippines assignment was right up his alley—but wait. . . .

On a lark, he let a realtor take him around the Los Angeles area. He listed his needs, but the realtor insisted on hearing his dreams. On the ocean, he said, a modern house—lots of glass, all view, sound of the waves, sunshine pouring in. A huge terrace, and hey—while I'm at it—a greenhouse. Orchids—I want to grow orchids. He was half kidding, but the realtor wasn't and when she brought him to Knots Landing and showed him a house—clearly *his* house—Ben, by the end of the day, was working at Pacific World Cable.

In September of 1983, Ben's curiosity was aroused by the facts surrounding the murder of rock singer Ciji Dunne. Gary Ewing had been arrested, and while all evidence pointed toward him, something smelled funny about the case. Ben ducked out of the office (as he often did for the sake of his sanity) to snoop around the County Courthouse at Ewing's hearing. It was there that he met Ewing's ex-wife, Valene, and it was there and then that Ben Gibson, for the first time in his life, fell in love. People in later years would explain Ben's staying on in Knots Landing by pointing out that he didn't need to go thousands of miles away to find trouble, drama, and violence—he had found more than he could handle by being caught in the relationship between Valene and Gary Ewing!

His relationship with Val did not exactly start off on the right foot. He helped her duck the press at the courthouse and, realizing her vulnerability and fear, did not tell her that he himself was a journalist. He "accidentally" met her while jogging on the beach, and confessed he really was no jogger, but only wanted her to have dinner with him. She agreed and he was elated. Dinner was wonderful as the two got to know each other better. There was just something about Val that touched him so. Something about her eyes, or her speech, or her heart, or maybe her whole body. The spell at dinner, however, was broken by an old colleague of Ben's who exposed his profession. Val blew up and out of the restaurant.

With his archenemy, Gary Ewing. It is not Gary himself whom Ben dislikes so much, it's Gary's arrogance concerning his effect on Valene, which in turn always affects Ben's relationship with her. Gary, in Ben's opinion, is too self-centered to even notice when he's wrecking other people's lives.

The official wedding portrait of Mr. and Mrs. Benjamin Gibson, 1985.

And so it began.

In October, they agreed to try and be friends again, and before long, Ben wanted to be in for the long run. He was in love with Valene, and no matter how he tried, couldn't shake his feelings. Meanwhile, at PWC, Ben took a special interest in the Sumner senatorial campaign and kept running into Mack MacKenzie, who was also doing some investigating. The two struck up a firm friendship, and cooperated with each other professionally as well.

Ben's relationship with Valene was getting nowhere fast because, Ben realized, of the presence of her ex-husband during the Lilimae-Chip ordeal. But then in November, suddenly, things changed. Gary was off the scene and Valene showed up at his house. They had dinner, talked for hours, and then spent an entire night together in bed. Ben was a very happy man. Everything he felt about Val already was only further enhanced by their chemistry. By January, he was pleading with Val to spend more time with him, to which she responded with nervousness. She was quite a puzzle—one minute he thought she was in love with him, the next, she was running away. Who could figure it?

Lilimae came by his house one afternoon, dropping the minor bombshell that Val was pregnant. At first unsure of what his feelings were beyond "trapped," Ben was by the next day at Val's proposing marriage, while also expounding on the joys of fatherhood. Valene responded with a confession. The child was not Ben's; it was Gary's.

GARYGARYGARYGARYGARYGARYGARYGARYGARYGARYGARYGARYGARYGARYGARY

By now, Ben had figured out that Valene's emotional state was an exact indicator of Gary's proximity. High spirits meant he was leaving her alone; far flung despair meant he was talking to her; depression meant he was seeing her. The point was not that Val had slept with Gary once more before she got involved with Ben, but that she was unwilling to get *un*involved with Gary—even now! It was a terrible blow, the whole thing, the lousiness of the timing. In five minutes his dreams of a life with Valene and his child had been cruelly denied. He couldn't ignore this, wish it away; Val had Gary's baby inside her. They could be in love, for all Ben knew.

Ben did not reveal Val's secret, letting everyone shame him for allegedly walking out on Val when she was pregnant with his children (it turned out she was carrying twins). Even Gary tried to reprimand him! Finally, miserable, hating his pain, Ben applied for an overseas assignment and picked El Salvador. Of course, as their luck would have it, he and Val reunited before he could get out of it. And so, he went off, leaving an engagement ring on her finger.

Ben and a cameraman and another journalist were in a jeep traveling to an encampment about thirty miles outside San Miguel when they hit a land mine. The other men died and Ben, unconscious and suffering chest wounds, was taken to a makeshift field hospital in a bombed-out church. Until Ben regained consciousness, no one in the States knew he was still alive.

Recovering from his wounds, Ben flew back to California in March of 1984 and surprised Val. The poor woman was a basket case; the days of thinking both Ben and Gary dead had taken their toll.

It deeply disturbed Ben how bent Val was on finding out who killed Gary. More and more it was dawning on him how much Val was still in love with him. When he found out that Gary might still be alive, he couldn't bring himself to tell Val—he wanted at least a day more of her undivided attention. When Val found out that Ben hadn't told her, she broke off their engagement.

In October, Gary and Abby Ewing bought Pacific World Cable, and Abby stepped

Holding Bobby and Elizabeth, whom Ben wished formally to adopt. Gary, however, tried to muscle in by giving the children half of Empire Valley on their first birthday. Outraged, Ben told him that giving expensive presents didn't make him a father. Qualifications he did cite: going to work with applesauce on your tie, staying up all night when one of the children has a fever, knowing everything there is to know about cradle cap, and wiping little noses and little bottoms.

in as boss. Ben tried to resign, but she held him to his contract. Reluctantly, Ben reported to Abby and immediately ran into conflict over how the coverage of the Sumner election was being handled. Meanwhile, in his own newsroom, one of Ben's best reporters, P. K. Kelly, was openly pursuing him. Ben, still pining for Val, kept his distance.

Ben was genuinely grieved when he returned from a trip to learn that Val's children were stillborn. He was right there to try and help her through the tragedy (and that creep Ewing was there too, of course), and then Val disappeared. Ben was working on the Galveston story at the time, half distracted with anxiety about Val's whereabouts. When Gary found her and brought her home (making him even more crazy—why didn't he leave her alone?), Ben was hurt when Val didn't even remember who he was. As with his father years before, Ben was patient, giving it time, all the while pushing away P. K. Kelly (who asked, "Don't you know how neurotic your situation is? With Valene I mean.").

His patience and loyalty paid off, however, and by March of 1985, his involvement with Val had increased—and so had his involvement in the search for her babies. They started spending nights together again in April, and it was more and more difficult to conceal his investigation from Val. At all costs he did not want to raise her hopes falsely.

After the babies were recovered and Val returned to an even keel, Ben's personal and professional life made great strides. He and Val agreed to get married. He was convinced that Val loved him at least as much as Gary. And at work, Abby promoted him to general manager. He was pleased, but that didn't last long since it meant he had to oversee Joshua Rush and his show; its ratings were slipping rapidly, while the arrogance of its star was climbing to catastrophic proportions. The fact that Joshua was Val's half-brother did not make it easier to deal with him.

With Abby as an employer and Joshua as an employee, things at the station were getting so convoluted and unprofessional, Ben tried to resign again. Abby convinced him to stay with the condition that under his management, all profits he generated would be channeled into the news departments. Ben agreed and, with his news eye sparkling, led Pacific World Cable into being the second largest news-gathering service in the United States.

Joshua got more insane by the day. Finally, after his constant no-shows, arguing, and lousy ratings, Ben fired him. Ben gave his time slot to Joshua's lovely wife, Cathy, from whom he was separated. Cathy was a wonderful person and terrific singer; she also became a valued friend.

In November of 1985, at long last, Ben and Val were married. Gary (of course) showed up two minutes before the ceremony to talk with Val, but since she went ahead and got married, Ben didn't think he had anything to worry about. He moved into Val's house (since with all the recent excitement, Val thought the children should stay put) and sublet his beach house to Cathy. His clothes unpacked, his piano at Seaview Circle in tune, Ben hoped for peace but got absolutely none. Gary started showing up at the house to visit the twins. Wary, Ben was angry at what felt like an impending threat. Val was worried too, Ben could tell. And Lilimae, at the same time, had waged war on Ben, claiming he had ruined Joshua's life by firing him. More and more Ben turned to Cathy, as she did to him, for support in dealing with this family they had both married into. Joshua died in December and Ben, more than ever, was crucial in keeping the family together. Cathy nearly collapsed under the strain of publicity, Lilimae never left her room she was so depressed, and Valene was scared sick when Gary started hanging around, making fatherly noises about the babies.

Ben was a rock of support. That is, until Gary decided to give the twins half of Empire Valley for a birthday present. Just what did Ewing think he was doing? It was as good as running an ad in the paper to announce that he was their biological father. But did Gary care? No. Was Gary prepared to take care of the children the way Ben was? No. Did he think writing a big check (for money he hadn't earned) made him a father? Probably. *What gave him the right to interfere in the Gibson's family life?* Ben had it out with Ewing, Ben had it out with Valene, but Valene *continued* to play Gary's game; Ben's frustration, anger and loneliness pushed him into the eager arms of Cathy Geary. Sick to death of Knots Landing and the daily pain he had endured there, in May Ben took a leave of absence from PWC to go with Cathy on her concert tour for six weeks. Only then did Valene understand that their married life, as it was, was unbearable to him.

So, that was that. But of course it wasn't. Cathy was merely a Band-Aid, applied in desperation over a gaping wound of the heart. Ben needed his family, he wanted his family, he *loved* his family, and that knowledge was impossible for him to run away from.

Ben Gibson has built a sterling career on his talents in communicating, so how is it that he has had such little success at it in his own home? Why is it, where Gary Ewing's concerned, he cannot make Valene understand how Gary affects her and, in turn, affects the stability of the entire Gibson family? Ben and Valene, as partners in life, are presumably rowing in the same boat. So why then, when Gary goes sailing by, does Valene persist in hitting Ben over the head with the oars?

Ben knows why and wishes with all his heart he didn't. Because his wife is still in love with Gary Ewing.

53

Lucy Ann Ewing Cooper

"Hey—you said Val's 'little girl.' I wasn't expecting Miss Texas!"

—Kenny Ward, 1979

The eldest child of Valene and Gary Ewing, Lucy was born in Dallas Memorial Hospital in 1961. Her father deserted the family in 1962 and her mother was driven away by her Uncle J.R. later that same year. She was brought up by her paternal grandparents, Jock and Ellie Ewing, at Southfork Ranch, and by the time she was reunited with her parents in 1979, her accustomed lifestyle as a millionairess made living with them no longer possible.

Lucy attended Southern Methodist University, dropping out to marry medical student Mitch Cooper in 1980. Her parents attended the wedding. In 1981 she was crowned Miss Young Dallas, holding the title for one year; it was partially responsible for her divorce in 1982. Lucy had a number of unsuccessful romantic relationships, but ultimately she reunited with Cooper and remarried him in May of 1985.

Lucy now lives and does volunteer work in Atlanta, Georgia, where her husband is a resident physician at the Atlanta Burn Center.

[Editor's Note: Since Lucy only lived in Knots Landing for one week, hers is but an introductory note. For her complete life story read *Dallas.*]

Bobby and Elizabeth Ewing
The Twins

"I hear them. I know when they're hungry. I wake up. I want to feed them. I can hear their crying. . . . I've accepted that they are gone. Taken away from me, but I know they are out there someplace. They are alive."

—Valene Ewing, 1985

Bobby and Betsy were conceived in a single night of reconciliation between their divorced parents, Valene and Gary Ewing. Their premature birth was induced by a drug given to their unsuspecting mother by the evil Dr. Mitchell Ackerman. They were born on the night of November 18, 1984, in Ocean Park Hospital and, right after delivery, were sold into an illegal adoption ring. Dr. Ackerman told their mama they had been stillborn, but she never believed that. They were sold to a couple who were unable to have children, Sheila and Harry Fisher. The Fishers loved the twins very much and took good care of them for ten months.

Bobby and Betsy were reunited with their mama in October 1985, and were baptized by their Uncle Joshua in a ceremony held at home. Karen and Mack MacKenzie are their godparents. Bobby is named after his deceased uncle, Bobby Ewing, and Elizabeth is named after the mother of her stepfather, Benjamin Gibson.

Bobby looks just like his mama did when she was his age; Betsy favors Gary, also bearing a striking resemblance to his mama, Miss Ellie Ewing Farlow of Dallas, Texas. Grandma Clements calls the twins "my little bunny-pumpkins."

Lillian Mae Wiley Clements
Lilimae

"Your personality, your warm friendly spirit—you know what it says to people? It says you're a survivor, that you've taken all the hard shots life's thrown at you and you're still standing there with a twinkle in your eye."

—Chip Roberts, 1982

Imagine a woman with the carriage of Mary Queen of Scots and the logic of Gracie Allen; imagine the devotion of St. Bernadette and the wanderlust trailings of Isadora Duncan; imagine the effervescent glee of Shirley Temple and the temper of Ma Barker; imagine Sarah Bernhardt with the social registry of Ma Kettle.

Imagine Lilimae Clements.

Lillian Mae Wiley was born in 1932, the youngest child of Ora Belle and Joshua Wiley. The Wileys—including Lilimae's siblings Billy, Jane, and Rosalie, and her Granny Patrick—were dirt poor. But then, so was everybody in Husky Corners, Tennessee, in or out of the Depression.

Ora Belle had a fine singing voice, which her littlest inherited. Lilimae also inherited her mother's addiction to attention, and the two of them constantly competed for Joshua's. Lilimae usually won. She was adorable, witty, irresistible, and full of life and merry song, whereas her mother's heart had become heavy with bitterness, frustration, and sarcasm.

Joshua and Granny Patrick let Lilimae get away with murder. She almost always manipulated herself out of doing chores and rarely made it to school once she left the house (she usually hid in the shed, where Granny would sneak food to her and give her autoharp lessons). With the exception of her mother, everyone told Lilimae how talented she was and how surely destined for stardom. Lilimae had no doubts about that herself.

After Granny died—bequeathing, on her deathbed, her autoharp to Lilimae— Lilimae packed her belongings in an old cardboard valise and without so much as a wave to her family, thumbed a ride to Knoxville to enter a talent pageant. Her mother sent the sheriff after her; he dragged her back home, kicking and screaming.

Three weeks later a minstrel show came to town. Joshua took Ora Belle and Lilimae, and he made a great fuss to the show folks about Lilimae's talents. Ora Belle fumed with jealousy and gave Joshua what she thought he deserved—when the show left town, she went with it. She never made it big, but she never made it back home either.

Without Granny or her mother around, chores fell to Lilimae and she responded by running away several times. Stars don't wash clothes, Papa, she'd try to explain.

Lilimae playing on her autoharp in 1981, before hostessing a little neighborhood poker game with the men.

LILIMAE Don't get riled, boys. You'll love this one. Learned it from a fiddle player in Louisiana. It's called Cajun Sneak.

KENNY Lilimae, you come up with the screwiest games.

GARY Always wins 'em, too.

At wit's end, Joshua handed her over to the care of his brother and sister-in-law, Horace and Idabelle Wiley, who were already caring for Idabelle's "problem" baby sister, Queenie.

Lilimae and Queenie got along famously. They wrote neighborhood shows together, complete plays, and songs. Everything went smoothly until Lilimae discovered a hidden batch of letters written to Idabelle from a former lover, recently killed in the war. He had been a flier and his letters were full of love and passion and drama; Lilimae and Queenie wrote one heck of a show based on the letters (Lilimae playing the flier, of course). They made a penny a ticket and the town news with Idabelle's prior love life. They also got the whipping of their lives.

Insulted at being punished for what was clearly a brilliant play, Lilimae stole the O'Reilly's DeSoto and drove (at age thirteen) to Port Arthur to enter a talent contest. She was apprehended and returned to her father, who laid down the law: either she settle down and keep house, or he would lock her up in the shed. For almost a year she complied. She learned to cook her father's favorite foods, like pig's trotters, catfish, red beans and rice, corn pone, and rhubarb pie. And she sang in the church choir (she was about the only thing you could hear, she sang so loud).

On her fourteenth birthday, Lilimae was told she was engaged to marry her father's best friend, Jeremiah Clements, a man some thirty years her senior. She was flabbergasted at her father's announcement. *What!* Was he serious? *Yes.* Two weeks later Lilimae was married and Jeremiah carried her over the threshold of his broken-down farmhouse.

Initially, it was not as bad as she had feared. Jeremiah *was* good-looking—a big, strapping fellow with a fair mane of hair and beard—and he was kind and well-meaning. Best of all, he was crazy about young Lilimae, smothering her with affection and attention. And her discoveries regarding the sexual side of life were exhilarating. For a time, Lilimae was fairly happy.

She conceived quickly and in 1947 gave birth to a daughter, Valene, "my little sweetpea." Lilimae loved her deeply, but she was jealous when Valene stole all of Jeremiah's attention. It was always "Valene this, Valene that," and never Lilimae

anymore. And worse yet, Jeremiah told Lilimae she was a *mother* now, as if this explained why he no longer had any sexual desire for her.

Lilimae hung on for four years. Without the attention she craved, without sex, without any hope of improvement in their impoverished lifestyle, only her love of Valene and music kept her going. "My music gave me lots of pleasure . . . and I needed pleasure, I needed to feel important. I needed *life.*" Many a man was captivated by Lilimae's dynamism, but she remained faithful; then one man kept coming by, a *Nashville* man, who said he would love to take her away and manage her singing career. Lilimae gave in to her fantasies and decided to go for it. Unlike her mother, she told her husband straight out about it. He didn't care about Lilimae's leaving, he just wanted to know, "Who's going to look after Valene?"

"You will, Jeremiah," she answered him. "Like you always do. You don't never let her need nobody but you anyhow so it don't matter if I'm here or not." And the next day, in 1951, nineteen-year-old Lilimae Clements set out on the road to stardom.

Lilimae's driving passion was country and western music—writing and singing it —but she also performed gospel and bluegrass admirably well. As soon as she dumped her no-good manager (who was really after one thing), she was signed by the Carter Family (largely on the strength of how much she looked like them) and performed in Nashville and in Louisville with them. Mother Carter helped Lilimae cut a record to promote while on tour with them, but then Lilimae was called home —Jeremiah had unexpectedly died.

The money from Jeremiah's insurance wasn't even enough to bury him with and Lilimae paid up the rest. She left Valene with Granny Clements, with the plan to take Valene on the road with her as soon as she was old enough. But that day never came.

Poor Lilimae would never make enough to offer Valene any kind of life on the road. Over the next seven years she did a little of everything, hoping it would lead to her big break: she was an assistant to magician Alfonso the Great (who wasn't), sang backup for a couple of records in Nashville, sold tickets at theaters, and off and on, cleaned theaters. And sometimes, *sometimes,* Lilimae was forced to depend on men for her keep, without almost all her money going home to Valene's care. She didn't have any trouble attracting suitors, but trouble inevitably arose over men wanting to own her, marry her, and she would have to move on. She never wanted to be trapped again!

And then she saw and heard the Reverend Jonathan J. Rush. Lilimae fell head over heels for him. He was such a challenge! A fire-and-brimstone preacher? Lilimae couldn't resist trying to seduce him and he, allegedly "agonized," responded with great gusto. It was not in Lilimae's plans to get pregnant, but Jonathan pointed out when it happened that God had clearly intended it.

Lilimae refused to marry him. Anyhow, that's what she says. So the Reverend Rush merely presented himself and Lilimae to a congregation on the outskirts of the city as husband and wife. The birth of their son, Joshua, elated her, but not so Jonathan. He treated Joshua as if he had some kind of contagious disease.

Jonathan was so very sure of his mission as a preacher. He emphasized performance to Lilimae, rehearsing and re-rehearsing his sermons with her. (That was what Lilimae loved most about him, his sense of divine show business). Performance, according to Jonathan, was what brought in the flock. That was what saved souls. But for all his preachings about God and heaven and sin and hell and love and goodness, Reverend Rush had a secret.

He beat his wife.

The first time it happened, Lilimae thought it was an isolated incident. After it

Chatting with Ginger and Kenny Ward in their dining room. For pocket money, Lilimae started babysitting in the neighborhood. Her favorite was little Erin Molly.

Listening to Joe Cooper discuss Valene's future as a novelist. At Abby Cunningham's urging, Lilimae let Joe read the manuscript, and he opened the door to Valene's wonderful new career.

Joshua's startling entrance in 1983. After they settled down into a comfortable mother-and-son relationship, Lilimae was proud of him when Abby offered him a job at Pacific World Cable. Refuting Val's contention that Abby shouldn't be trusted, Lilimae said, "I don't want to hold a grudge. You can do a bad thing and still not be bad. I learned that from having you [Val] here. And from you [Joshua]. If you can forgive me, I'm no one to throw stones at anybody else."

happened again, and again after Joshua was born, she fought back and got hurt worse for the effort. And so, in time, she learned the best response was simply to endure it. But why? In some strange, unconscious way, Lilimae believed Jonathan when he said she deserved it for all her sins. And he didn't even know the half of her life! She thought if she was better, could be good, he wouldn't hit her anymore.

She was thrilled when he put her in charge of organizing a church choir, though what she had to work with left a lot to be desired. "Oh, they were a sorry bunch. Most of them were half hungry. It's amazing they had the strength to sing at all." But Lilimae, carrying Joshua on her hip, made them practice and practice in preparation for the big Easter Sunday gathering. Jonathan sat in on the final run-through and they sang their hearts out for him, but he just sat there, expressionless, and then suddenly left without a word.

"It wasn't good enough. *I* wasn't good enough. I never forgave him for that. For the way he made those people feel that day. For the way he made *me* feel. I could never live up to his expectations. He always wanted more than I could give—more than anyone could give. I couldn't live with that, that constant disappointment in everything I touched." She also couldn't live with the beatings any longer, and in 1961, signed with Teddy Keener's act and left town. And left Joshua.

Lilimae didn't know what to do except keep running. She never made a success, never earned much money. With only her driving ambition as company, she was horribly lonely. In late 1962, temporarily staying in Husky Corners, Lilimae was reduced to sleeping with a prospective business manager. While in bed, Lilimae heard Valene screaming at the door. Now Lilimae had told the man that she was nineteen (at age thirty), so how could she suddenly explain not only a daughter, but a granddaughter at the door? So Lilimae pretended not to know who Valene was. And Valene hated her for that. But Lilimae tried not to dwell on that.

Seventeen years later, in 1979, Lilimae was tired and broke, and even she had to admit she wasn't nineteen anymore. Passing through her sister Jane's, she was informed of Valene and Gary's new life together. Not having a single place left to go, not a cent to get there even if she did, Lilimae went to Knots Landing and threw herself on her daughter's mercy. About thirty years overdue, Lilimae had a heart-to-heart talk with Valene, trying to explain her life in a way that made sense, but Lilimae herself was bewildered about why she was the way she was. Valene, at least, understood that no matter what her behavior, Lilimae loved her and always had. Unfortunately, Jack Horner Records offered to cut a demo record for her in Nashville, and chucking her good intentions, Lilimae "borrowed" the money from Val and was off again.

By October of 1981, Lilimae was truly one tired lady. Her life, at this point, was down to sheer survival: how to skip out of welfare hotels, how to obtain food. She landed in Los Angeles, where she stopped a purse snatcher by ramming him with her shopping cart and made the evening news: BAG LADY BAGS MUGGER! (Lord, could it be? Lilimae wondered. A *bag* lady?) Proud of her actions, she dropped by to see a hostile Valene. The next day Lilimae was arrested for shoplifting and was released into her daughter's custody. Lilimae was home to stay.

In time, Valene responded to Lilimae's sincere efforts to be a part of the family. Lilimae cooked her heart out, cleaned, did the laundry—in short, she did everything Valene didn't feel like doing. Lilimae didn't mind. It was a lovely home, a lovely neighborhood, and since Lilimae had never really had a home before, it was rather exciting. And Valene, her baby Valene, how wonderful it was to be close to her, to *help* her, after all these years!

Lilimae did some volunteer work at the Senior Citizens Center, where in Decem-

Laughing with Valene and Karen MacKenzie at the opening of Lotus Point, 1984. Searching for fame and glory all her life, Lilimae, just by living in the cul-de-sac, was able to brush elbows with all kinds of important people. And have a great time, too!

ber she was courted by Jackson Mobley. The romance was a bust, however; his proposal to marry Lilimae and be her manager was contingent on the assumption she was rich. A little wiser, Lilimae clung more tightly to her new lifestyle in Valene's household. Oh, every once in a while, the old fever biting, she'd harass Kenny Ward down the street a little about listening to her music, but she never really followed up on it.

In the spring of 1982, when Valene and Gary's marriage fell apart, she knew Valene needed her support, which she readily gave. That skunk Gary, bolting with that breezy blonde—but, perhaps, it was just as well since Valene, with her book, needed a new life. Lilimae might not be famous, but Valene would be!

The publication of *Capricorn Crude* in the fall of 1982 led into a terrible period of Lilimae's life. It began with a charming young man, Chip Roberts, who, in the course of handling Valene's book publicity, won Lilimae's heart. She wasn't seriously in love with him, but enough to want him to move into the house when he didn't have a place to stay. Lilimae bought Chip presents, such as a blazer, because she thought he had a great future ahead of him and wanted to be a part of it. It wouldn't be until early 1983 that she would get uneasy about him. When pages of Valene's new manuscript were published in the *Global Gossip*, Lilimae knew, deep down, that Chip was the only one who could have been responsible. But she gave him the benefit of the doubt—initially. By February, she could no longer ignore what was staring her in the face: That Chip, supposedly dating Diana Fairgate, had had an affair with the murdered Ciji Dunne. That Chip had released the pages of Valene's novel. That Chip was more than just a little sleazy. In March, she threw him out of the house.

A private investigator, tracking down an Anthony Fenice, filled Lilimae in on a little more of Chip's character. His name was an alias; he had wooed and used and beaten up a socialite in Seattle, and had been hiding here in Knots Landing. Lilimae was sickened by the news. Here she had thought him so wonderful, and it was turning out that he was the worst kind of human being—if human at all! And as if that were not enough, she learned that he had murdered Ciji Dunne in cold blood, and that October, was being released by the police on lack of evidence. Lilimae, outraged with the injustice, blinded by anger for the hurt he had inflicted on so many, drove to the police station on the day of his release. She was sitting there

with Karen Fairgate, watching Chip's smugness with reporters, and she just snapped. She pressed the accelerator to the floor and ran him down, nearly killing him.

Admittedly, Lilimae didn't feel quite herself during all this, but she was highly indignant when she was evaluated by a psychiatrist. It was ridiculous, questions like, "Which would you rather do, chop down a tree or give a dinner party?" Max Eisner, her lawyer, put in a plea for temporary insanity and after Val posted $100,000 bail, pressured her into committing Lilimae to a sanitarium to bolster the plea.

Lilimae begged and pleaded not to be taken—to be locked up, dear Lord, that was her greatest fear in life! Valene committed her to Lakevale Hospital for thirty-four days, the first two weeks of which she was allowed no visitors. Lilimae was despondent, barely stirring. But hard to keep down for long, she started to bounce back after making friends with Mr. Herschelman, who had played violin for the London Philharmonic (now whether he really had or not Lilimae didn't know, nor did she care). When her court date came up, she received a three-year suspended sentence on the temporary insanity plea.

When she arrived back home, Valene did much to revive her spirits. First, she had finished a new novel, *Nashville Junction,* which was dedicated: "To My Mother. Whose courage and spirit and love guided me through the pages of this book." And the other, most wonderful news in the whole wide world was that Valene was pregnant!

October of 1984 brought a combination of pain and joy and guilt and hope to Lilimae's front door. Standing there, asking to see his Aunt Lilimae, was her tiny son Joshua—now over six feet tall. He had come to ask about his mother. Lilimae, unable to tell him the truth, bitterly said, "Your mother was a vicious, wicked tramp. She was selfish and spiteful and thought of nothing but herself. She was going to be a singing star and nothing else mattered. Not family. Not husband. She deserved everything she got. . . . Be grateful you don't know her. You're better off she's dead."

Valene, however, after a while put two and two together and confronted Lilimae—

With statements such as, "We're so lucky to be together. In a way, it's good we spent all those years apart, because now I really appreciate the loyalty only a mother can give," it was not difficult for Lilimae to become obsessive about Joshua, in an attempt to make right her wrongs of the past.

With Gary at a party at Westfork Ranch, 1985. Gary has always fallen in and out of favor with Lilimae over the years, but both have nonetheless retained love for one another with a transfer of affection through Valene.

With Joshua in the Mission District of Los Angeles. Lilimae could suddenly see how very sick her boy was and felt helpless to stop the course of his insanity.

Agonized, emotionally isolated by her guilt over Joshua, Valene and Ben could not help Lilimae with her grief. Lilimae came close to killing herself in February of 1986, but the thought of her grandchildren stopped her.

was Joshua Lilimae's son? She admitted it and then slowly, painfully, told Joshua. The poor young man was so shocked and frightened, it took some time to explain and reassure him that Lilimae did indeed not only love him, but wished with all her heart that he would stay with her and Val so she could make up for lost time.

Joshua was a source of enormous pleasure in the months ahead. Lilimae nearly burst with pride as his work at Pacific World Cable led to a television ministry and marriage to Cathy Geary. When Joshua brought his bride home to live in April 1985, Lilimae believed that the Ewing household had finally been delivered from heartache. She was wrong.

Lilimae's son began to go mad.

She didn't see it for the longest time. She caught on to Joshua hitting Cathy one night, but in her mind, it was just an isolated incident. After all, Joshua was a man of God. But then Joshua was fired from PWC and he became violent again, to the point that Cathy left him. Then Valene threw him out of the house; Lilimae, desperate to help him, followed him around the city.

Her last dinner with Joshua was in November of 1985, where he flat out accused Lilimae of having been responsible for all his problems. He described how Jonathan had beaten him, demanding of her, "Why weren't you there to stop him?" Lilimae sobbed, overwhelmed with guilt.

In December, Lilimae intervened when Joshua tried to kill Cathy and himself. The truth about her son's madness had finally dawned on her, on the evil it had wrought, and she would forever regret her last words to Joshua, screamed in a moment of anguish: "I don't care that I was a bad mother, that Jonathan beat you. I only care that you've grown into a monster! Don't call me Mama. You're no son of mine!" And then, moments later, Joshua, her son, was dead.

Burdened with grief and guilt, Lilimae made it her duty to protect Joshua's memory as the man he had intended to be—a warm, sincere, loving man of God who brought peace, faith, and hope to the world. Unfortunately, the truth began to emerge in the newspapers in spite of her, and Lilimae had none of those memories to cling to, only the deeply sad, quiet agony of a son found, a son forever lost.

Lilimae was filled with despondency and despair over all the years she spent on the road instead of with her children. In February, the pain became so unbearable she drove to the building where Joshua had been killed, planning to throw herself off. Just as she was about to jump, a blinding thought came to her: *She couldn't do anything for Joshua, but she could do something for the babies.*

Where the thought came from, Lilimae didn't know, but she suspected it came from Joshua. Yes, the babies. And Val. And Ben, poor Ben, whom she had blamed for so much. Yes, there was a lot she could do to make their lives happier. . . . Love, yes, and caring. Support. Joy.

Lilimae returned home to her family on Seaview Circle.

The last word on Lilimae best comes from the great lady herself:

> "When all the adventures—all the strangers met, all the experiences had— are over, there's really nothing to hold on to. . . . At some point, you've got to be able to look someone in the eye and know that they know you. That they have known you for years, and understand you and care about you.
> This is the best part of my life."

Joshua J. Rush

"Jonathan, you've done a wonderful job with Joshua. I see so much of you in him."

—Lilimae Clements, 1984

Well, he tried.

He tried to be a religious leader (though carrying no allegiance to any power higher than himself); he tried to be a compassionate family member (though deliberately breaking their hearts); he tried to be a loving husband (in between mentally and physically abusing his wife); and most of all, he tried to be true unto himself (in the odd moment he wasn't lying).

A lot has been said about Joshua Rush—admittedly, mostly in the form of threats —but he never, *ever* meant to be a bad person. And he wasn't. Joshua was very, very sick. And now, Joshua is very, very dead.

Joshua Rush was born out of wedlock in 1959 to Lillian Mae Clements and the Reverend Jonathan J. Rush, a fact he himself did not know until 1984. Joshua did not remember any of the niceties of his babyhood, that his mama adored him, sang him lullaby after lullaby, fed him, bathed him, nursed him, and smothered him with "bunny snuggles" of kisses and hugs.

All Joshua remembered was that he didn't have a mother as other children did. He remembered thinking his father was a god, hearing for hours his thunderous ovations of the Bible, cowering in the corner, afraid to breathe. He remembered his father telling him he was a sinner, born in sin, and that he would burn in hell for eternity if he was not good. He remembered cleaning the house and church, being forbidden to play. He remembered, more than anything else, that his father, on the slightest provocation, would beat him black and blue.

Joshua learned never to ask about his mother; the times he tried, his father "would get so angry, he'd whip me." Reverend Rush never had a kind word for him; in fact, he rarely spoke to him, instead directing Joshua to the corner to talk to God. And Joshua did. He'd talk and talk and pray and cry and ask for forgiveness of whatever it was he had done that made Pa hate him so much.

Adolescence was even more painful and confusing. Jonathan made it clear that it was a sin to dance and to talk to girls, so one can only imagine what his doctrine on sexuality was. Joshua did his best to please his father; never was there a more beaten-down, obedient son. Handsome, painfully shy, insecure, and uncertain, Joshua tottered into manhood. "No matter what I did or said," he related years later, "it was always the same—he was right, I was wrong. I could count on it. I could believe in it. . . . I only wanted to be good. I only wanted to always be good."

He did not attend college, studying under his father instead and assisting him in the preparation of sermons. Reverend Rush often clipped out newspaper articles

69

Trying to sort out his feelings at the beach, 1983. Joshua had no idea that his Aunt Lilimae was actually his mother.

pertaining to the sins of mankind and kept a trunk full of them under his bed as a ready supply for sermon ideas. One afternoon, when Joshua was twenty-four, he went to get the trunk out for him and found a carved wooden box under there he had never seen before. His curiosity burned and he peeked inside.

He found a letter. It was from a woman named Lilimae Clements, some lady in California, who apologized for something awful she had done to the Reverend. What the wrong was, the letter didn't say. As Joshua said later, "When I asked Pa about the letter, he nearly went crazy. I had never seen him like that. He told me you [Lilimae] were my aunt. I said, how come you never told me Ma had a family and that I had relations?" As a reply, Jonathan gave him a violent tirade/sermon on *turning your back on evil,* accompanied by a beating.

The letter, however, had done its damage. Joshua became obsessed with this untried door concerning his mother. And so, at the age of twenty-five, in 1984, he withdrew his meager savings, stole out in the night, and bought a bus ticket to Knots Landing, California.

Joshua had no way of knowing what this trip would bring. Thus far, there hadn't been much stimulus in his life beyond fear. He hadn't read much of anything but the Bible and his father's sermons, had never watched television, listened to the radio, danced, or even gone to the movies. So there was a lot to come at him, and everything carried the heady spice of newness.

When Lilimae broke down and confessed to Joshua that *she* was his mother, it was almost an emotional overload for him. At first he wanted to run back home to his father—an unpleasant but known entity—but his mother's obviously generous heart, her genuine love, her desperate longing to make things up to him, touched him in a place he had thought long dead. Frightened, but trusting, Joshua agreed to stay on with his mother and half-sister, Valene.

Right off the bat he met a beautiful young woman named Cathy Geary, who was living with Laura Avery down the road. He liked her at once, but her rather razzle-dazzle exterior made him nervous. She looked like one of those fast girls his father had forever warned him about. But when he thought about it, his father had also warned him against *all* girls, so when Cathy invited him to come hear her sing, Joshua timidly accepted. The nightclub atmosphere disturbed Joshua. It was dark, smoky, full of young people drinking and carousing; he was, however, thoroughly impressed with Cathy's voice—certainly a gift from the Divine. He confided in Cathy about Lilimae and found her to be one of the gentlest, sweetest people he had ever met. She was *good,* pure somehow, though Joshua couldn't figure it, given her lifestyle. She was also alluring, and his sexual attraction to her scared and shamed him. But little by little, he grew accustomed to these feelings, so long as they stayed in control.

At the Ewing house, he mowed the lawn and washed all the dishes, trying to be helpful. He and his mother were getting closer and closer, and Joshua began to believe her when she said he had everything to offer in his new life: he was bright, handsome, sincere, *good.* She beamed with pride when Abby Cunningham-Ewing hired him as a production assistant at Pacific World Cable. Joshua was appreciative of the chance and worked hard, earning Abby's respect and the tutelage of Reverend Kathrun, who had a weekly ministry show on PWC.

Jonathan arrived in November to bring Joshua back home with him. The Reverend made it no secret how horrified he was at Joshua's environment—living with the mother who had abandoned him, under the same roof with a half-sister who was pregnant and not married, keeping company with a saloon singer—but Joshua found himself standing up to his father, defending his new family and friends. The Reverend's visit only confirmed Joshua's desire to stay in Knots Landing.

The evening's ordeal also pushed him into making love with Cathy, and although the act was breathtaking for an incredulous Joshua—*this* is what he had been denying himself all these years?—it also racked him with guilt. Cathy was patient with him, encouraging him to discuss his feelings, and a talk with the Reverend Kathrun reassured Joshua that perhaps it was all right for him to follow his heart, so long as it was filled with love.

Reverend Kathrun saw a spark in Joshua and urged him to try his own hand at

Watching Cathy Geary performing at Isadora's. Joshua had never been in a "saloon" before, and he hated the idea of Cathy's working in one.

Joshua resents Valene's advice about how to improve his relationship with Cathy. He didn't think her being an unwed mother was a terrific endorsement of her expertise.

With Cathy at their engagement party at Westfork Ranch. The first time they'd made love, Joshua had said, "It was a mistake," to which Cathy had responded, "A pretty enthusiastic mistake!"

With Abby Cunningham-Ewing, the woman who launched his television career. Joshua thought she was wonderful, and had she not been a married . . .

Surprising Cathy with a horse-drawn carriage after their wedding in 1985.

Upset over Cathy's refusal to get pregnant, her insistence on moving out of the cul-de-sac, and his declining ratings at PWC, Joshua's anger and frustration started distorting his thinking. Permanently.

With no place left to go, Joshua took to the streets to preach his message.

sermons. When Valene disappeared in December of 1984, Joshua, at the Reverend's suggestion, wrote an appeal to Val to come home and went on the Reverend's show to deliver it himself. The station switchboard was jammed with calls of praise, and the following day was deluged with fan mail, saying things like, "He touched our hearts," "Put me in mind of Will Rogers," "Reminded me of a very important promise I made myself long ago," and "Joshua's voice is nice; does he ever sing?" Abby had him run another appeal, and the even bigger response prompted her to slate him in a regular segment on Kathrun's show, to which the Reverend gave his blessing.

Initially, Joshua carried out his segment at the end of the show with great humility, but constant praise began to affect him, change his view of himself. Abby bolstered his confidence by continually citing his huge ratings and by doing things like sending him to *Gary Ewing's* tailor. Fans barnstormed the station daily, hoping to catch a glimpse of him. Girls threw themselves at him. Lilimae assured him that it was all just the world's confirmation of what she already knew, that Joshua was surely God's gift to humanity. Past self-confidence, Joshua started believing his own publicity. He began worrying about his public image, and then about Cathy's since she was his girl. They began having fights when Cathy criticized him, accusing him of things like running the Reverend off his own show. But since Joshua loved Cathy, he felt it was his duty to change *her,* so she could stay in his life.

In March of 1985, Abby gave Joshua his own show (and the heave-ho to Reverend Kathrun). Lilimae was thrilled and supported her son all the way. She also agreed with Joshua that Cathy's singing in a nightclub was not quite fitting, nor were rock 'n' roll tours on the road, and spoke to her on Joshua's behalf, with little effect. Joshua could only hope that changes would occur with time; his first step was to get Cathy to appear on his show and sing something appropriate—hymns. The morning of the show, outside on the cul-de-sac, while watching Cathy play with little Daniel Avery, Joshua experienced a revelation; he knew how he could save Cathy—by marrying her and making her the mother of his children! After she sang on the show, Joshua was so moved by her voice that he joyously burst out with the announcement that he and Cathy were getting married.

Cathy resisted, but Joshua knew he was right. He, Joshua Rush, who had virtually every female in the offing; who generated donations of thousands of dollars to the Home for Special Children, St. Agnes', and the Missing Person Fund; he, who was a messenger from God—he was not to be refused! And he wasn't. They were married in April 1985, in a lovely ceremony conducted by the Reverend Kathrun. Joshua returned from the honeymoon in high spirits. Ensconced with his mother on Seaview Circle, his lovely new wife at his side, his heart was full of gratitude. For about a day. Cathy wanted to move into their own place. Joshua didn't want to and his mama agreed with him; it was best they stay with her, with family. Then came a devastating blow to his plans—Cathy refused to go off birth control, saying she wasn't ready to have a child yet. And then, most distressing of all, his ratings started to slip.

Everything he had worked so hard to acquire was coming apart and nobody would help him get it back on track. Cathy was impossible, Ben Gibson was a monster, and Valene was forever conspiring with Ben or Cathy; only his mother understood his pain.

In October, Ben delivered Joshua an ultimatum: Get Cathy singing on his show to up the ratings or he was out of a job. Joshua got her to appear and was stunned when the station was deluged with fan mail—for *her.* He panicked; his star wasn't falling—Cathy was stealing it. Insanely jealous, he wanted her off the show, which she agreed to, but then Ben threatened to cancel the show altogether and Joshua

Despite Joshua's having threatened just about everyone on Seaview Circle, all the neighbors attended his funeral out of respect for Lilimae, Valene, and Cathy.

was forced to bring her back on. His temper turned foul, complaining to Abby about the sensitive nature of his show: "My work is a calling, not a career!" She stood by Ben's decision, however, including the one to fire him.

He was devastated. Scraping together what pride he had left, he looked for a job at other stations, only to find that no one wanted him. Joshua blamed Ben for blacklisting him. Then Cathy moved out on him. With no job, no wife, Joshua started teetering on the edge. Ben turned Val against him—and then even his mother was looking at him strangely. Desperate, he tried to get Cathy back, but she shunned him. Since Ben had given her Joshua's show, of course she didn't want to see him! Billboards across Los Angeles were going up, featuring Cathy in disgustingly scanty outfits. To calm his soul, Joshua took to preaching on the streets. Valene threw him out of the house, and he moved in with a kindly waitress named Linda.

It was inconceivable to him that he had lost everything.

His heart ached most over Cathy and night after night after night of torment, of wondering what to do, the answer came to him. In early December of 1985, he kidnapped Cathy, took her to an industrial building in the Mission District, and dragged her up to the roof. Joshua meant to push her off and then jump after her, together falling to death and "a rebirth of our spirit in heaven." His mother, however, came charging onto the scene, screaming at Joshua. The anger and hatred in her voice stunned him, and as he backed up in disbelief, crying, he stumbled and fell to his death, alone.

Joshua's funeral was held in Knots Landing the following week. His father conducted the graveside ceremony until he could continue no longer and broke down in grievous tears. Joshua's mama, Lilimae, finished the service; she closed the eulogy by placing her hand on Joshua's coffin, praying, "May you have the peace you never had on earth."

Catherine Geary Rush
Cathy

"My son is going to marry one of the nicest girls in the whole world. Oh, it's God's blessing."

—Lilimae Clements, 1985

Hers is the kind of beauty that can last forever. No amount of time can fade the spirit, the inner glow, the abundance of life behind it; only heartbreak can do that. Whether Cathy will find a life she can lead without agonizing pain is up to her. Up until now, she has chosen to have everything happen *to* her, opting for outside influences that vault her from pain to deceptive temporary bliss, only to kick around and strike her back down in deeper despair and grief.

Cathy's choice in men is not good.

The heart of the matter is that Cathy, her entire life, has been in search of a man who can make her feel complete. Alone, she feels paralyzed, unable to move. The irony is, if she just once looked to herself, just once really looked and saw the light and goodness and talent there, she might not be so eager to offer her wings to those who wish to clip them.

Catherine was born on the way to Fort Worth, Texas, in 1963. Her father was a cowboy on the rodeo circuit and, feeling bogged down by his baby-toting wife, deposited the two of them on an Arkansas horse ranch and went back on the road. Cathy's mother was a beautiful, caring woman and Cathy loved her a lot, but obsessively loved her ever-absent father more.

She had an extremely active fantasy life early on. The adventures swirling in her head always included horses, the wide open spaces, and her dad. She clung to the belief that one day her father would take her (his "Little Jigger-Jogger") on the road with him, and she worked hard to be ready. She was brushing down horses, cleaning out stalls, and cinching her own saddle by age eight; and by twelve, she was an assistant to the county vet. Despite her efforts, her father had no intention of exposing his little girl to his rough-and-ready lifestyle.

Cathy shot up six inches in one year, earning the nickname of "Stick" from her classmates. She was well-liked, and when it was discovered that she had a marvelous singing voice, she was respected as well. Cathy easily won the lead in her junior high musical; and on opening night, in the audience, a man named Ray Geary sat mesmerized. Others may have called her Stick, but Ray was a man of vision and recognized a blooming beauty when he saw one. Cathy was befriended by Ray, some fifteen years her senior, never suspecting his motives. The first was sexual, although Ray at least held off until she was fourteen before seducing her completely. The second was to manage her singing, and he did.

Cathy when she first arrived at Westfork Ranch to work for Gary, and secretly for Abby as well.

In the ranch exercise room, Cathy—at Gary's request—pretends she is Ciji Dunne.

Restraining Gary from killing her husband, Ray Geary. The Wolfbridge Group would accidentally do it later.

Although Cathy hated the idea of Abby's giving her and Joshua an engagement party, she was nevertheless impressed. Held at Westfork, the mayor and the archbishop attended. Here Abby introduces the couple to Senator Buchanan.

Cathy and Joshua are married by the Reverend Kathrun, 1985. Her matron of honor, Laura Avery, was unenthusiastic about the wedding; the best man, Ben Gibson, was positively against it, calling Joshua a "sanctimonious little weasel."

Cathy's favorite photograph of the two of them, surrounded by their friends and neighbors.

When Joshua invited Cathy to sing on his show in 1985, neither had any idea of the overnight sensation she would become, eventually leading to her own hit show, "A Better Tomorrow."

At sixteen, Cathy lied about her age, married Ray, and hit the road to support him. He booked her in the lowest roadhouse joints he could find, with the rationale that since she was underage, they'd be the least likely to object. More often than not, they slept in the back of the car, since Ray had a habit of making money disappear at the bar and the poker table. But to Cathy, Ray was a life-long love, a man full of drama and passion and excitement. Being married to Ray was an adventure!

In 1980, the happy-go-lucky couple ran aground. Ray got drunk in a small town and ended up shooting its leading resident. Cathy was there when it happened and, believing Ray when he said the authorities would go easy on her because she was a minor, agreed to take the rap for him. She was found guilty of second-degree murder and sentenced to eight to fifteen years; and so from the age of seventeen to twenty-one, Cathy's address was P.O. Drawer 32, Pine Bluff, Arkansas. Prison.

Cathy was let out in 1983 for good behavior. She never doubted her love for Ray all those years, but when she was released four days before Ray was expecting her, she was suddenly frightened at the prospect of getting back with him. What it might be like. The life they had led before had been fine when she was younger, but she was different now, older, yearning for freedom. And she didn't think Ray would give her any freedom. And so with $20 in the pocket of the dress she had worn when she first went to prison, Cathy took off, hitchhiking across the country. She chose Southern California as the place to make her new shot at life.

Cathy had been waitressing in Marina del Rey for only about two months when, in October of 1983, she was approached by Abby Cunningham-Ewing with a job offer. Some job! Apparently she looked just like someone Mrs. Ewing's husband used to know, and she would pay Cathy to "distract" her husband. When Mrs. Ewing wouldn't say who it was she looked like or from what her husband was to be distracted from or how she was supposed to distract him, Cathy turned her down. Mrs. Ewing's offer upped from $200 to $1,000 a week and Cathy accepted.

Once Gary Ewing caught sight of Cathy, he made her job easy. He was frantic to know her, and after he uncovered her background with horses, hired her at $400 a week as a hand and moved her into a bunkhouse on Westfork Ranch. The problem was, however, that Cathy was smitten with Gary from the start. He was kind, understanding, crazy about horses, and heaven knew, as good-looking as they come. By January of 1984 she was in love with him and wanted out of her deal with Abby, who in turn threatened to bring Ray to Westfork if she didn't continue. Cathy was amazed that Abby even knew about Ray, much less where to find him, but then Abby seemed to know every sordid detail of everybody's life. . . . Reluctantly, Cathy carried on with the charade.

As time went on, she felt ever more compelled to confess to Gary who she was, from where she had come, but he beat her to it. In February he started cross-examining Cathy about her past. When she evaded the truth, he went to Abby, who panicked and tried to fire Cathy. But Cathy refused to leave the ranch; she would risk provoking Abby's wrath to stay near Gary. Abby was true to her word and Ray showed up on the scene, forcing her to sleep with him at his motel by night and to get closer than ever to Gary by day. It was all such a mess, Cathy didn't know what to do, whom to turn to. Finally she told Gary about prison, and then later, about Abby hiring her and why. He was livid with rage, but kept her on as a hand. Cathy, disgusted with herself, wanted to leave, but Ray at this point was using physical threats to make her stay.

At the end of the month, Gary threw Abby off Westfork and moved Cathy into his bedroom. In love with Gary, Cathy immediately confronted Ray, handed him $5,000, and told him that if he didn't leave her and Gary alone, she'd tell the police who really had killed that man in Arkansas. Ray turned back up at the ranch, trying to threaten her again, only to have Gary knock the stuffing out of him. Vowing revenge, he returned in March; a gunshot rang out and Mack MacKenzie told Cathy that Gary had been shot dead. Grief-stricken, Cathy went to stay with the kind Laura Avery.

Say it ain't so, or so the song goes. It wasn't. Cathy was brought to the police station to see a very alive Gary, only pretending to be dead; it was Ray who had been shot, mistaken for Gary by a mobster hit man. Joyous over the reunion, Cathy

Cathy waits for any kind of plausible excuse from Joshua about why he again failed to show up at an apartment viewing, while Lilimae pretends not to exist.

Still in shock, Cathy numbly moves toward the limousine after Joshua's funeral.

took it to mean—since she was the only person whom Gary wanted to see—that they would spend the rest of their lives together.

In October, without so much as a hint to Cathy about his change of heart, Gary took Abby back. Stunned, hurt, a dazed Cathy quit the ranch and moved in with Laura Avery. Starting anew, she landed a regular singing job at Isadora's, a hot Knots Landing nightclub.

Some track record, she thought; first Ray, then prison, then Gary. Cathy vowed not to repeat the errors of the past. No more falling for men who wanted to use her, no more men who were never there when she needed them. So when the terribly shy, terribly earnest young Joshua Rush moved into the cul-de-sac, Cathy made an effort to get to know him. She was not amused by his virginity or innocent ways; in fact, they made her take him to heart without fear or apprehension. Their courtship was not without difficulties, many of which Cathy wrote off to Joshua's inexperience with relationships of any kind. Sexually, however, he proved to be an avid and quick learner, and for a while his magnetic hold over her screened some of the changes that were occurring within him.

To this day Cathy blames Joshua's mental illness on his career as an evangelist on Pacific World Cable. What started out to be an honest, humble apprenticeship with the good Reverend Kathrun ended up in routing Kathrun out of his own show. Suddenly Joshua was on air five days a week. The catapult to fame was too quick; Joshua stopped preaching the word of God and starting thinking he *was* God. Cathy cited Abby again and again as the source feeding Joshua's egomania, but Joshua would hear nothing of it. In fact, he would hear very little of anything. Full of starts and stops, their relationship staggered on.

In January of 1985, Cathy was offered a music tour, which, in deference to Joshua, she declined. The process was in motion but Cathy didn't see it—the worse Joshua became, the more unreliable, the more she fell in love with him, convinced she was the only one who could bring him back to his old self.

Joshua did not approve of her career and started in on her about quitting Isadora's. ("You're not willing to mend your ways.") She was stubborn on that point, however, and resisted his solution: "You could sing in church, if you need to sing in public." Fine, he said, if she didn't quit, the relationship was off. Joshua stopped speaking to her, which must have been a sign since her band was immediately featured on "Night Tracks." They made up though, when Joshua deigned to need her, and the next thing she knew he was making deals: Joshua would not complain about her singing at Isadora's if she sang hymns on his show once. Well, that was fine— Cathy actually found it quite refreshing—but when Joshua, on the air, suddenly announced to the world that they were getting married, that was a bit too much. He could have at least *asked* her.

Lilimae and everybody were so happy about the news that Cathy had to drag Joshua in private to hash this out. Reverting to his lamb-like former self, dangling his affection in front of her, he persuaded her to get married. That concession, however, gave Joshua the notion that he was now running her life—and his first decision was that she quit Isadora's. Val caught on to what was happening and tried to help Cathy stand up to her brother, which only turned Joshua sour on Val. The tension escalated on Cathy's part and she broke off the engagement, only to be coaxed back into it by Joshua and Lilimae. Joshua gave his word that their marriage would be an equal partnership, that they would share in all decisions, and Cathy, holding her breath, believed him.

The day of the wedding Cathy was not so sure. Laura helped her dress for the event and ran through the list: Something new? The gown. Something old? The earrings. Something borrowed? Lilimae's handkerchief. Something blue? "Me." Laura told her she could still back out; Cathy almost gave in to that plan of action, but went ahead anyway, hoping for the best. The wedding was beautiful, the honeymoon too, but the marriage, well . . .

The first of many fights started over Joshua's refusal to leave his mother. The second: Until Cathy agreed to get pregnant, there would be no sex.

Ray. Prison. Gary. Marriage to Joshua.

The insanity began. When Joshua failed to show up at an apartment showing and she reprimanded him at the television station, he twisted her arm until he nearly broke it. Then, changing his tack, he politely asked that she sing on his show again, and if she did, they would move out of his mother's house. She sang on the show and then, grim, Joshua told her that they couldn't move because Lilimae had an incurable disease and was dying. Upset and worried about her mother-in-law, Cathy held her end of the bargain regardless and continued to sing on his show, made aware by Ben Gibson that her performances were bolstering Joshua's sagging ratings. In response to her popularity, Joshua tried to get her off the show, but succeeded only in getting himself fired. He then got violent with her at home, but Cathy excused it on the premise that it stemmed from his severe distress about his mother's gradual demise. But when he arrived home late one night, smelling of cheap perfume and sex, she had had it and moved out. Joshua chased her all over town, alternately pleading and threatening her to come back to him. She refused; he got violent. Joshua had gone crazy.

Ben offered Cathy a television show of her own, and at first she refused, but then changed her mind and accepted, thinking it best if she got on with her life, alone. Joshua terrorized her, damaged the set, tried to beat her up in the alley, and several other charming things, but the real clincher, the thing that broke her ties to him, came when she found out that Lilimae's "incurable disease" was, in fact, a touch of bursitis.

In November, Val banished Joshua from her house because he was so violent. Cathy didn't know where he was living, but he seemed to be everywhere. He got

into her motel room and so she gratefully took Laura's offer and moved back in with her, only for Joshua to find her there too. At this point, all of the neighbors were terrified of him, and Cathy felt in fear of her life.

Meanwhile, her music show, "A Better Tomorrow," had become a huge hit, bringing new affiliate stations for PWC. Ben was an absolute godsend to her, and she leaned heavily on him for support during these difficult days.

After taping at the studio one night in December, Cathy got in her car and felt a knife at her throat and Joshua hissing in her ear. He made her drive to the Mission District, dragged her up to the roof of a building, and was just about to hurl both of them off when Lilimae showed up, saving Cathy's life. Watching Joshua's body fall that night, Cathy was not sure what she felt. She may have been scared to death of him, she may have once loved him, but she knew he had gotten sick and she had never wanted him to die. But she was relieved, too. It was over.

Leave it to Joshua, however, to continue to harass her from the grave. In January of 1986, the police accused her of conspiring with Lilimae to murder him. Once cleared, life was getting back on track when one of the scandal sheets started publishing the truth about Joshua, about his being a wife beater, among other things. When it turned out that the source of the stories was her trusted sax player, Sonny, Cathy felt completely at a loss. Lilimae herself was no longer all that rational on the subject of Joshua; only Ben seemed to offer reliable support.

That liaison, however, turned dangerously alluring to Cathy in March and April. Perhaps it was her loneliness; her dependency on Ben, her proximity to him at work; or her grief over Joshua, over Gary, over Ray that made her so vulnerable. Or maybe Cathy just would have fallen in love with Ben anyway. Whatever, Cathy began an affair with Ben and, by the middle of May, was pleading with him to come with her on a concert tour. To her amazement he agreed. But then Cathy's head began to speak to her heart. After everything the Gibsons and Lilimae had done for her, how could she break up their family?

She couldn't.

Cathy left Knots Landing on an indefinite national concert tour—without Ben.

In Knots Landing, Cathy found the first real home she ever had. Despite all the trouble and heartache, for the first time in her life she made friends and was accepted by others as family. It is a testament to her loyalty that she was unwilling to sever those ties for what may or may not have been another mistake of the heart.

Who knows what she'll find out there on the road. . . . Stardom? Undoubtedly. Happiness? Maybe. Herself? *Oh, we hope so.*

Because then she could come home for good.

The Fairgates

KAREN   I love Sid Fairgate—as much now as ever. Only now, he's not here. So instead of love feeling wonderful, it hurts like hell.

DIANA   Don't you think it hurts me?

KAREN   Of course I do! I know how much you miss him. I know how much you need him. We're in this nightmare together.

—Karen and Diana Fairgate, 1981

KAREN   I don't know. Probably.

MACK   Probably. . . . I was hoping for a yes, and I think I was ready for a no, but I'm not sure I can handle a probably.

KAREN   I'm sorry, but it's more complicated than it seems.

MACK   It's not complicated. It's simple. You either love me, or you don't. If you do, it's yes, and if you don't, it's no. Do you love me?

KAREN   Yes.

MACK   See? Simple. We're getting married, right?

KAREN   Probably.

—Karen Fairgate and Mack MacKenzie, 1983

William Sidney Fairgate, Jr.
Sid

"He's a saint. Good-hearted to a fault. Moral—I mean *really* moral. How many people do you know who actually make moral decisions in their everyday lives? Sid's the only one I know."

—Karen Fairgate, 1980

He will always be remembered for the family he left behind—his wife, Karen; their children, Diana, Eric, and Michael; his sister, Abby—but Sid's real memorial to the town is one he built himself. Knots Landing Motors. KLM, as it's known, represents many of Sid's personal traits: fairness, reliability, excellence, pride, a firm hand-shake, and a warm hello. KLM has serviced the area for twenty years, and people still come in asking for "that nice man Sid I heard would take care of me."

Sid was a man of great personal ethics and courage, and his protection of those he loved was legendary. As a father, husband, brother, neighbor, or businessman, his resounding gift, cited again and again, was his ability to foster trust and place it wisely in others. He thrived on life and its challenges. In fact, his joy was never in attaining his goals, but in the process of achieving them. And as for the difficult times, times of trouble, he was the kind of person who met them head-on, never considering defeat as an option. And he never gave up. Not even at the very end.

William Sidney Fairgate, Jr., was born in New York City in 1936. His parents were solidly working class, he had an older brother, Paul, and his early life in their mod-est Queens apartment was happy.

Sid was a little charmer, with beautiful dark good looks, an easy going disposition, a restless body, and an extremely bright mind. School bored him dreadfully, but he loved athletics and was always captain of the football and basketball teams. But what made Sid's life bright with wonderment, brimming with excitement, was the world of mechanics.

At three, he dissected an alarm clock to see how it worked; at four he learned how to put it back together. At five, he could fix the family's appliances. At seven, he was building bicycles from scratch, scrounging up the parts from junkyards around the city. At nine, he was cleaning a Manhattan filling station for the honor of peeking over the mechanic's shoulder. At twelve, he had a paying job there pumping gas and doing minor repairs. Sid was simply obsessed with cars, and uninterested in any-thing or anyone who didn't have anything to do with one. As he said in later years, "All I wanted to do was build model cars or work on my brother's engine. Everyone figured I had a nut loose and they laughed at me." Did he care? Not a bit.

In 1950, when Sid was fourteen, the family was handed a surprise in the form of a

Sid and Karen. When his first wife, Susan Philby, visited the Fairgates in 1979, she said, "I expected middle class, and middle class it is . . . emphatically. But I have to admit I'm more impressed than I thought I'd be. You know why? Because it's all so stylish. Your house has style, and your wife has style. . . . And you, well, of course you always did have the potential."

baby. His mother was in her late forties and suffered a partially debilitating stroke during labor. Since his brother had moved out and his father had to work, most of the baby's care fell to Sid.

At first Sid was terrified of this screaming tiny bundle called Abby, but when he lifted her in his arms and she stopped crying, already directing her unseeing blue eyes toward his, Sid's heart skipped a beat. He was won over. He fed her, changed her diapers with ease. He learned how to cradle her small body in his big brawny arms and soothe her to sleep, or delight her into little laughs and squeaks of joy. For anyone who knows Abby today, it is hysterically funny to envision her at a gas station, but she spent a lot of time there. Having to take her to work, Sid just piled blankets in a file drawer in the office and let her sleep while he worked.

Sid's mother died in 1952, and his father, missing her desperately, lost his spirit. Abby truly became Sid's child then, and he cared for her well. When their dad died in 1957, she was his total financial responsibility as well. His hard work kept them comfortably in a small two-bedroom Manhattan apartment.

In 1960, Sid met the very beautiful, very rich, very spoiled Susan Philby. Sid was normally pretty laid back in his approach to women, but since Susan liked fast cars and fast men, he took a shot. It was a whirlwind romance, and a highly passionate one too. As Susan said years later, "If we could have made love every minute of every day everything would have been fine." On Susan's suggestion, they married quickly, each convinced of love at first sight.

Susan was from a very wealthy, old main-line Philadelphia family. Her mother was outraged at the marriage, but her efforts to break it up were unneeded; Susan would do it herself, and quickly. She was, to be candid, a spoiled brat who never had to do so much as make a bed in her entire life, and Sid, terribly proud, wanted them to live off his income. Susan, hating Abby from the beginning, demanded that she be out of the house, and so Sid put her in a top-flight boarding school, though he could ill afford it. And then Susan, only two months married, found out she was pregnant. When Sid told her that it didn't change anything, that no, they would not

take up Mrs. Philby's offer of servants, Susan threw a tantrum and went home to mother. She didn't come back; in fact, she filed for divorce before their child, Annie, was born in 1961.

Sid was utterly heartbroken. Blindly, not quite aware of what he was doing, he reached out to the next available woman. Lucky for him, it was the lovely, dynamic Karen Cooper, who was on the rebound herself. He wasn't in love with her at first, but she kept him so busy and off balance that his pain began to lessen. She was everything Sid wasn't: educated, a sheer fireball of energy, an outspoken, zealous demonstrator. There was one place he could match her impulsive energy—in bed— and after a brief separation period, they got back together, and then Karen found out she was pregnant.

There was no hesitation on his part; he wanted to marry her, though while he did love Karen, he was still in love with Susan as well. But everything pointed in their favor: Karen was willing to be a homemaker on his income; though Abby was, by this time, nearly impossible, Karen readily agreed to having her home from school on weekends; and she was completely committed to Sid and building a life together.

He got more out of the marriage than he had ever dreamed. Not only was Karen a partner in life, but he could—for the first time in his life—lean on someone else without fear. And her brains and her zaniness and passion and dedication filled his home with laughter and love. In 1963, she gave birth to a beautiful little girl, Diana.

Professionally, Sid was doing well. He had been managing the gas station and, on the side, building up quite a lucrative business restoring antique cars and selling them. He and Karen dreamed of moving out of the city one day, finding a yard for Diana to play in, finding a lot where Sid could open a dealership.

When 1965 brought his first son, Eric, Sid found further incentive in his work. He expanded into repairing racing cars. He didn't spend much time at home in those days, and Karen would pack up the children and take them to the garage for a "picnic" lunch or dinner; Sid and Karen would sit cross-legged on a blanket on the floor of the garage while Eric snoozed in "Abby's Drawer" and Diana bounced up and down in her playpen.

Sid in one of the Knots Landing Motors television commercials, 1979. As Laura Avery would say later, "He was the only one who made the automobile business sound like a mission."

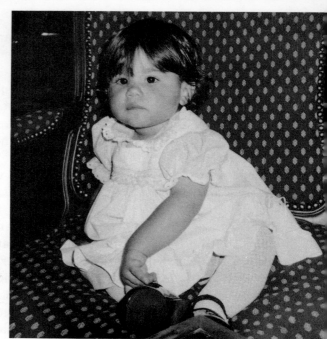

Sid's daughter by Susan Philby, Annie, in 1964. Susan dragged their daughter all over the world; the only time Sid ever saw her was in snapshots Susan would occasionally send, like this one, taken in the lobby of the Savoy Hotel in London.

Trying to talk things out with Annie in 1979. At eighteen, Sid's daughter was under the impression that Sid had not seen her over the years because he didn't want to. It couldn't have been farther from the truth.

Sid and Karen stare at their son, Eric, after finding a marijuana cigarette in the pocket of his jacket. Sid felt betrayed by him, saying to his wife, "It's like rowing your family through life, bailing like mad to keep them afloat, and then you discover one of your kids chopping holes in the bottom of the boat." It turned out, however, that Eric really had only been holding it for a friend.

By the end of 1966, the Fairgates had enough seed money to try and make their dream a reality. After years of discussion, Sid and Karen knew exactly where they wanted to move—the new community of Knots Landing, California. Sid flew out, put a down payment on a lot, rented a house, and in January of 1967, they made the big move.

Knots Landing Motors opened its doors on Labor Day weekend. It was a small operation at first, primarily a repair shop with a small line of cars. Karen did the books from home and Sid worked night and day to build up the business and word of mouth. As the population climbed in Knots Landing, more employees were hired and more cars rolled into the lot. A showroom was built; Sid bought the lot next door, and then the next and the next lot, KLM becoming the biggest, boomingest show/business in town. The end of the year brought another gift: a second son, Michael.

Sid was a founding member of the Jaycees and the Knots Landing Chamber of Commerce. In 1970 he instituted what is almost a national holiday in Knots Landing: The Annual Soap Box Derby. In 1975, KLM started a college intern program, offering part-time work to graduate students in mechanical engineering.

After waiting and waiting for the right kind of house (for the right kind of money), Sid and Karen had almost settled for buying and adding on to their rental. Then Sid heard about some Ewing Construction houses going up on the ridge. They met with the architect, looked at the plans, and gleamed at one another. Here was the house, *their* house. The Fairgate House. Five bedrooms, a huge living room, a spacious kitchen, a laundry room, a basement that could be turned into a rec room, and best of all, a 1½-acre lot with lots of lawn, trees, and a view of the ocean. The Fairgates made a cash down payment, took out a mortgage, and in June of 1979, moved to Seaview Circle.

It was not the most peaceful year Sid had in terms of family—"first" family, that is. Annie was allowed to visit from Philadelphia in September. At sixteen, after years of being dragged from Istanbul to Paris to Alexandria by Susan, Annie had a lot of problems and acted out in every way to impress them upon Sid. (As Karen said to him, "She's not here to visit. She's here to punish you.") Her visit was followed by one from Susan, on the pretense of some legal problem. Sid didn't believe it for a second, and nearly had a stroke when Karen invited Susan to stay with them. She made a big play for Sid *(now,* for heaven's sake, Sid thought), but he remained entirely loyal to Karen. There was absolutely no question in his mind about whom he loved with all his heart.

Business at KLM was a little slower than usual in 1980; people didn't seem to know what they wanted to buy, if they wanted to buy a car at all, and Sid was glad to bring Gary Ewing on board. Gary did a terrific ad campaign that helped business, and came up with other ideas Sid would never have thought of.

In the summer of 1980, Sid drove up to San Luis Obispo to help Abby pack for her move. Sid felt sad about her marriage ending so badly, but he was, as always, behind her 100 percent. Driving home, Sid was approached by a young woman for the ride. He refused, but when he saw her being harassed by another man, he let her in the car. The girl then demanded he give her money or she would scream rape; Sid pulled over to let her out and the girl went screaming to the police that he had attacked her. Stunned, and then furious, Sid was taken to jail by the police.

Sid called neighbor Richard Avery, who, acting as his attorney, proceeded (without Sid's permission) to try and bribe Pam Messinger into dropping the charges, which only served to strengthen her case against Sid. The headline in the paper

Driving home for the last time, 1981.

read, KNOTS LANDING AUTO DEALER CHARGED WITH ASSAULT ON TEEN and the scandal affected every member of the Fairgate family. Karen got another lawyer for Sid; with Abby, who had just arrived in town, she tracked down the young man who allegedly had threatened the girl when Sid picked her up. He testified that the whole thing had been a setup to extort money and Sid was cleared. Other good news at the time: Abby decided to move into the cul-de-sac!

In October, Sid took on at KLM the young, immensely attractive Linda Striker, who was taking time off from her Ph.D. program in engineering at MIT. Amused at this whiz kid, Sid gave her the hands-on experience she wanted by working with her on an experimental engine. Other cheering developments included Gary engineering a deal for class-A auto parts at an incredible discount.

In December, Sid hired Abby as the KLM bookkeeper. She got along with everyone well—particularly Gary—and her presence helped boost morale after Sid had to fire Linda for wanting her hands-on experience to include him. Sid and Gary also grew very close, giving Sid his first best friend outside of Karen.

Sid was badly shaken when in February of 1981 he found out that Gary had been involved in a stolen parts ring in order to make money for KLM. But being the kind of friend he was, after he made Gary go to the FBI, he volunteered to help catch the crooks so Gary would be pardoned. He met with Roy Lance and Frank Kolbert and placed a bogus order with them for a stolen sports car. The FBI nabbed them at the point of delivery, and Sid, asked to testify at the trial, was kept under round-the-clock protection.

It was not good enough.

In September of 1981, Sid and Agent Salmaggio climbed into Sid's car after work. On a steep highway incline on the way home the brakes failed and the car crashed through a guardrail, smashing down into a ravine. Salmaggio was dead and firemen had to cut Sid out of the wreckage with a blowtorch; paramedics rushed him to Cliffside Hospital.

Sid's head had slammed into the steering wheel, breaking his nose, lacerating the side of his head, and causing internal bleeding. The doctors had to drill a hole through his skull an inch above his ear to relieve the pressure. He had also severely compressed vertebrae C-5 and C-6, with the latter splintering and perforating the casing around his spinal cord. Sid was paralyzed.

The doctors told him the paralysis would be permanent if he didn't go into surgery, where they could try and alleviate the pressure on his spine. On the other

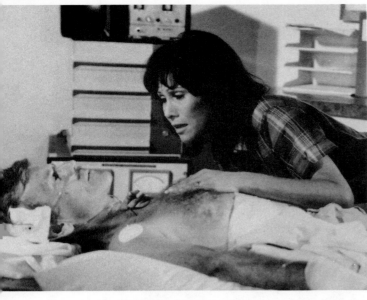

KAREN   Promise me you'll be all
     right.
SID   I'll never leave you.
KAREN   I love you, baby.
SID   Me too.

hand, they couldn't recommend the operation because it was far too risky, the odds
in no way favorable to Sid. Sid opted for the operation. Karen pleaded with him not
to—what if he died? Sid told her that to be paralyzed for life would be worse than
any death imaginable. Finally, understanding and yet desperately not wanting him
to take the chance, Karen went along with his decision.

Abby and the children came to see him, and Karen was at his side right up to the
doors of the operating room. Her face was the last thing he saw; he died on the
operating table.

Before his operation, Sid had made a tape for Karen, which he left with his nurse
"just in case."

Seeing you here with the kids a moment ago brought back so many memories. More than anything I wanted to hold you. I could see how scared you
were, and I wanted to comfort you with my body. That's why I hate this
damn accident so much. It's taken away my body's greatest pleasure—
holding you, touching you, feeling you next to me. . . .

Being able to sleep with you each night, and wake with you each morning, living with you, making a family with you, has been my life's greatest
joy. There are no words that can tell you what it's meant to me. My love for
you is strong, and whatever happens to me, my love for you will never die.

The Fairgate children he left behind: Diana,
Eric, and Michael.

Karen Cooper Fairgate MacKenzie

"She's our street corner shrink. Like the little girl in the comics. You know—Psychiatric Help, five cents. Only Karen doesn't even want the nickel."

—Richard Avery, 1979

She would be horrified to hear herself compared in any way to her sister-in-law, Abby Cunningham-Ewing; however, no one but Abby can match the willfulness and determination that course through Karen as life's blood. And since, like Abby, Karen is beautiful, charismatic, and newsworthy, and has a brilliant head for business, it is no accident that both revered and were revered by the same man, Sid Fairgate— Karen's husband, Abby's brother. And a comparison between the two women throws the most accurate light on Karen. While Abby has rocketed and crashed and zigzagged through life on whatever appeared to be a shortcut, Karen was born on the high road and has never, ever compromised the ideals that have kept her there.

She is a woman of unparalleled drive for what she believes is right. Her zeal and boundless energy, her passion to undo and correct man-made injustice, oppression, and exploitation of innocent people, have made her a savior to many, and a pain to those not so inclined.

What does she believe in that makes her so unusually strident? Karen believes that her children are entitled to breathe clean air, to drink clean water, to have oceans to swim in and fish from and sail on, fertile land upon which to live, to cherish as their own. She believes that her daughter should have the same rights under the Constitution that her sons were born with. She believes that free enterprise means exactly that and any underhanded infringement on the system should be met head-on. She believes in the freedom of the press, coupled with the country's duty to teach its citizens *how* to read and write in order to gain access to that right. She believes that children should be educated about sexuality before it is upon them. She believes in the arts and their availability to the public. She believes in working hard, playing hard, paying taxes, and protecting the bonds of familial love. She believes in the separation of church and state, the right to vote for the candidate of one's choice, and the right to impeach. She believes the United States of America is the greatest country on earth, with the P.S. that there is vast and urgent need for improvement.

She is a woman with great vision who has yet to learn her limitations as an individual. She keeps saying she *used* to want to change the world. Funny thing, she still does, every day, every breath of her life.

Karen Cooper was born to Dorothy and Joseph Cooper, Sr., on Manhattan's Upper West Side in 1943. Her father, an English professor at Columbia University; her mother, a former high school teacher; and her older brother, Joe Jr., already a book-

Karen says a neighborly hello to J. R. Ewing, not realizing who he is. Although J.R. would end up seducing her sister-in-law, Abby, Karen was actually his first choice. Whenever Gary Ewing went home to Dallas, J.R. always asked about her.

worm; comprised a rather retiring intellectual family, but one full of love and quiet affection. The Coopers were a bit at a loss to explain what it was they had given birth to. Karen was, like them, acutely bright, but unlike them, she had a 10,000-horsepower engine that kept her little body in step with her racing mind. And race she did. With large, sparkling brown eyes, she zoomed around, curious about everything, and with her fearless nature in combination with an uncommonly strong physical constitution, she even put Peter Pan to shame.

By the time she was six, she was (with a sincerity that made her parents chuckle) telling her parents how they should live their lives. When her parents failed to take her advice as seriously as she felt best, Karen expanded her horizons to the neighbors in their apartment building, and in later years, to kindly lost souls on the New York City streets. She made friends easily and without prejudice (well, on the condition that they listened to her). She was so bright, so witty, and so athletic, to be the most popular at school was a cinch for her. Her senior year of high school she was the business and circulation manager of the school paper, editor of the literary magazine, student council treasurer, and head cheerleader. Oddly enough, her competitive nature attracted primarily boys, rather than girls, into close friendship, and that would remain true for years to come. Many of the boys fell in love with her, but Karen was slow to regard anyone not as bright as her family as romantically appealing. And so, up until college, she didn't take any boy seriously *that* way.

In 1959, at the age of sixteen, Karen entered Barnard College as a freshman, she

Karen and Jason Avery try to assist Laura Avery, who was being toyed with by the leader of a motorcycle gang. The gang later hurt Karen's son, Michael, and she had them arrested, only to have the remaining gang members terrorize the cul-de-sac. They didn't leave Knots Landing until the entire neighborhood ganged up on them one night at the beach in 1979.

With Sid, 1980.

moved into a dormitory, and her life took many exciting new turns. The first was with her gorgeous man-killer roommate, Victoria Hill, who had the personality to match her dazzling wardrobe of her own design. Karen briefly copied Victoria's style, for the sheer fun of it, and the two had more than their share of Columbia boys wildly competing for their attention. In the classroom, for the first time in her life, Karen was challenged and pushed. All her life she had been devoted to poetry, savoring, lingering over her favorites—Wordsworth, Dylan Thomas, Dickinson, Edna St. Vincent Millay—but her teachers pushed Professor Cooper's daughter into new realms, new centuries; Karen discovered Milton, Virgil, and others. She found art and art history—ancient, renaissance, modern—and they utterly captivated her. By the end of her first year, Karen and Victoria "were planning to be household words," and, shunning sorority life as "much too bourgeois," Karen fancied herself to be a connoisseur of world culture. *That* would be a nice career.

Enter Theodore Becker. Teddy. Her first true love. Teddy was brilliant; he was rich; he was an activist extraordinaire. For the first time, Karen met someone with her energy, her drive, and her intellect, who so bedazzled her, she let him teach her something. As she recalled, "Teddy opened a larger world to me. . . . God, it was exciting. Civil rights. Ban the bomb. Peace rallies." And part of that larger world included the exploration of a seventh heaven called sex. Whether Karen fell in love with Teddy, with activism, or with sex, didn't really matter—all she knew was that she was in *love*.

With her youngest unmarried, 1980. "Michael, my little innocent, you remind me of all the things I hope I never lose."

Alone, terrified, exhausted, Karen during her vigil at the hospital after Sid's accident. She refused to leave.

With her brother Joe in 1982. He was a [god]send in the Fairgate household during his [brief] stay. It cheered Karen enormously to hea[r] [her] big brother calling her Cookie as in the [old] days. And, as when they were children, [they] paid each other to tell their secrets.

With Mack right after their wedding in 1983. Originally, the wedding had been set to take place at Daniel, with Valene as the matron of honor, Michael as best man, Diana leading the procession, and Eric as head usher, but then it got so complicated with the guest list (how could they invite Gary with Val there; Diana refused to be in the wedding unless her Aunt Abby was invited, etc.), they just drove to Las Vegas and stopped at the first chapel, "The Bridal Veil Wedding Chapel—24 Hour Service." Mrs. Grace turned on recorded organ music and cried for them, while Mr. Grace performed the four-minute ceremony.

They were inseparable for the next two years, working in the deep South on voter registration drives, in Washington to protest nuclear testing, in Boston picketing racial discrimination, and on many, many street corners in New York, demonstrating and petitioning for signatures for a variety of causes. Even the liberal Coopers lifted an eyebrow when their daughter, on occasion, was handcuffed, dragged in a police van, and taken to jail. But Karen was driven, exhilarated by the sense of being able to *do* something about the way the world was, of seeing the great vision of what it could be.

Despite her hectic life, she maintained an accelerated college program with the intention of graduating with Teddy in 1962; they were talking of joining the Peace Corp together and working and traveling around the world. They had everything figured out, Karen thought, but the plan did not include Teddy losing his heart to fellow activist Sarakay. Karen was devastated.

When Karen first met Sid Fairgate in the spring of 1962, it was like—nothing. No fireworks, little interest on her part; he just seemed so utterly lackluster in comparison to Teddy. He was a high school graduate, a mechanic with terra firma ideals, quiet, shy. But on second and third look—when he persisted in taking her out—he became more intriguing, or at least his life did. His wife had left him while pregnant —why? She had divorced him—why? He was the guardian of a twelve-year-old brat, Abby—why? And oh, after a while she thought, Let's face it, Karen, Sid's gorgeous, kind, gentle, sexy, reliable, smart, and the most down-to-earth man I've met outside of Dad.

They were both on the rebound and readily admitted it. Once that was established, something clicked between them, something akin to love, something that had to do with licking each other's wounds. And, Karen had to admit, sexually speaking, she and Sid seemed made for each other in a way that she and Teddy never had— there was something almost spiritual between them at those times. So while Karen was in marches, Sid worked on cars; while she was at museums, he was off fishing; while Sid read detective stories, she read Shakespearian sonnets; and Sid would go with Karen to a movie when John Wayne was in it. As Karen said years later, "Since the day we met, I knew we were an odd couple. Straight, sweet, street-smart Sid; caustic, cause-oriented, overanalytical Karen."

And then Teddy had a change of heart and came sweeping back into her life, begging Karen to go with him to Atlantic City for a weekend to sort things out. She was overjoyed, at first. Then came telling Sid, which she did. He said he understood and wished her a great deal of happiness.

The weekend was a bust. The second Karen went to bed with Teddy, she was overcome with the sense of having made a terrible mistake. Early the next morning she came back to New York, knowing the truth. She was in love with Sid Fairgate. With a deep breath, she went straight to the garage and told him everything. He said he understood, because he was in love with her too.

Their courtship radically changed. It became serious. Karen landed a job with the city's department of health, education and welfare, but two days before she was to start, she found out she was pregnant. Really pregnant—three and a half months along. Sid promptly proposed marriage, and Karen accepted.

Diana was born in 1963. While Karen's pregnancy had been an easy one, childbirth was another story. She had been exercising and practicing with Sid for weeks in preparation for natural childbirth, but she was in heavy labor for over twenty-four hours, with no end in sight. And then—half hysterical in pain—she looked up and who should she see in the delivery room but Abby! Leave it to her not to be left out of anything. The doctors were forced to do a cesarean; Sid never left her side, Diana

99

Mr. and Mrs. MacKenzie make their social debut at Assemblyman Sumner's campaign fundraiser.

was safely delivered, and Karen to this day laughs at the memory of Abby's expressions of horror throughout.

Karen started doing the books for Sid's business, something she would continue to do for him over the next ten years. In 1965 came son Eric, another treasure, and in 1967, the year they made the move to Knots Landing, Michael was born.

Karen loved Knots Landing and did much to realize her dreams in the kind of community she wanted her children to grow up in. She was instrumental in founding the Knots Landing Community Center, the Family Planning Center, the Day Care Center, Senior Citizens Center, and Volunteers for the Public School. She was many times an executive officer of the PTA; she was—and is—a Friend of the Public Library, Public Broadcasting, the Symphony, the Zoo, No-Nukes Coalition, the Whales, and the Earth.

The Fairgates' lives were ones full of hard work, happiness, and increasing prosperity. As KLM and their money grew, Karen and Sid were able to share new things with their children. They *all* learned to ski and sail; they went regularly to the beach, to car races, on picnics, and on weekend trips to Mexico and Nevada. Karen started sewing and taught Diana (and would have taught the boys, had they agreed). They took loads of home movies, played basketball in the driveway, and cooked out and ate outside at every opportunity. In short, by the time the Fairgates moved out of their rental house and into the cul-de-sac, they were the kind of family, neighbors said, that belonged on a Norman Rockwell *Saturday Evening Post* cover. And Karen's married life with Sid was still as close as ever; mutual trust had only increased over the years.

Karen's attractiveness was apparent to many men other than Sid. Even in suburbia men were smitten with her, but she always responded gently, firmly, that she wasn't interested. And she never was, but in 1979 one of Diana's extremely attractive teachers, David Crane, caught her at a vulnerable time. As she explained at the time:

> Lately I feel like a wife, and a mother, and a good friend, and committed citizen, but less and less often like a lover. So when I look at myself and see a line that wasn't there a year ago, and feel a little droop where there used to be firmness, I feel scared . . . because midlife is coming—how I hate that word—and that implies more endings than beginnings.

She resisted the temptation, however, knowing that her feelings would pass. But nonetheless her attitude changed a bit, because *she* had changed over the years and needed her life to change a bit as well. She put more effort into her private relationship with Sid; for the first time, she took care to make time for *herself*—separate from being a wife and mother; she allowed herself the pleasure of cultivating a best friend in Valene Ewing, her first outside of Sid; and took up exercise with a happy vengeance.

In December of 1979, Karen was surprised to learn she was pregnant. She wrestled with the implications of how her life, and her family's, would change with a new baby after all these years, but in time she came to accept and welcome the event. It was not meant to be, however; she suffered a miscarriage. The experience, after the initial sorrow, served only to make her more appreciative of her life and that of her family's.

Life went on as usual in the hectic Fairgate house, and Abby's arrival in the neighborhood in the fall of 1980 only made it more so. As an adult, Karen could hardly tolerate her, and though she loved her niece and nephew Olivia and Brian a great deal, it was tiresome to have them constantly underfoot, as undisciplined as they were in those days. In the meantime, Michael was being more unruly than usual, and for a while Karen wrote it off to the general chaos of family, but then he began to do things not like him at all: interrupting people, disrupting games with overzealous energy, doing badly in school and seemingly misbehaving on purpose. Karen wanted to take him to a psychologist; Sid disagreed angrily, arguing that Michael only needed more attention to straighten out.

At KLM one afternoon, Michael fell and cracked his head open. After he had been stitched up at the hospital, the Fairgates agreed to let Dr. Karl Russelman run some tests on Michael concerning his progressively odd behavior. They discovered that Michael was suffering from hyperkinesis. The problem wasn't psychiatric, but physical. For years "hyperactivity" had been treated by doses of stimulants—a thought Karen could not bear—but Dr. Russelman recommended the treatment of simply changing his diet and literally wearing him out each day. Eventually, he promised, Michael would outgrow it.

Easier said than done, and Michael's new lifestyle fell largely to Karen to enforce. First to go was all the sugar in the house, which immediately threw Diana in revolt. Just because Michael has a problem, why do we all have to— *Because,* Karen answered, as she wracked her brain for substitute goodies for the Fairgate house. Now,

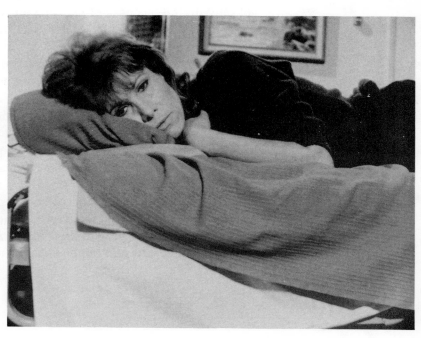

Lying in her room at the drug rehabilitation center, contemplating the reality of what another patient had just said to her. "The drugs I use are illegal. I have to go to the streets to score. You get yours from a doctor—for now. You can deduct them from your income tax. But we use for the same reason. Because life is tough, and we want out . . . and somehow, deep down, you feel that, on your own, your best just ain't enough." Her words were key in shattering Karen's denial about her addiction, and prompting Karen's willingness to work at recovery in group therapy.

Explaining to Mack how important it was for him to give up the Wolfbridge case before something happened to him.

about wearing him out; Karen got in the best shape of her life. She jogged with Michael, swam with Michael, bicycled with Michael. She assigned Eric to provide basketball and football in the yard. Gymnastics, long walks, calisthenics, all became daily outlets. Fortuitously, even within a week, there was improvement. And Michael, poor lamb, took it like a trooper. Karen loved her youngest so very, very much and it lightened her heart to see him adapting so beautifully.

Later that year, reminiscent of the good old days, Karen temporarily helped out at KLM. She stumbled on to Abby's bookkeeping system and was the one who blew the whistle on the stolen car parts ring. She had no idea of the consequences of her discovery. Sid's death in September of 1981 left her numb with shock and grief. For the first several weeks after his funeral, Karen was unable to be there emotionally for her children, but she finally snapped out of it. She was terrified without Sid; she felt as though someone had ripped her skin off. And the children, the household, KLM—every aspect of their life—had been created on the foundation of Karen and Sid's being together. Without him, their dreams, their future as a family, was scarier than hell. But Karen mustered up whatever strength she could find, whatever faith in the future she could find, and relying on the understanding and love of her children, got on with the business of carrying on without him.

Her first major decision was to take over the management of KLM herself. Her second was to fire Abby.

In November Karen received a visit from Teddy Becker, who had been divorced from Sarakay for some time. Teddy was not so interested in seeing Karen as he was in meeting Diana. With no children of his own, Teddy jumped to the hopeful conclusion that Diana was the product of their night in Atlantic City. Knowing all along Sid was Diana's father, Karen left the issue ambiguous out of feeling for Teddy's loneliness and sense of rootlessness. He made no attempt at fatherhood; he wanted only to be in friendly contact with Diana from time to time, to see how she was doing.

The same month the IRS notified Karen they were coming to KLM to audit the books. Frantic at Abby's bizarre bookkeeping system—which no one could make head or tail out of—Karen was forced to mend fences with a friendly luncheon and a request that Abby meet with the auditor. After Abby ordered a $110 lunch of champagne cocktails, caviar, a bottle of Chablis, lobster, and a Grand Marnier soufflé, she smiled and said no. But at the last minute, Abby showed up and saved the day; in appreciation, Karen offered her her old job back, which Abby accepted.

Just after Christmas, Karen was pushed by her neighbors into accepting a date from Charles Linden, a stockbroker friend of Richard Avery's. Karen was unnerved and broke down and confessed her feelings to Diana:

KAREN   What do I know about *dating?* I'm no date. I'm a
mother . . . a wife . . . a businesswoman.

DIANA   But, you're also single now.

KAREN   No I'm not. I'm not single. I refuse to be single. Alone,
maybe. Not single. A widow. Widows date, don't they?

DIANA   Eventually.

KAREN   Why aren't you against it?

DIANA   You seem to be doing fine without my encouragement.
(After a minute or two . . .)

DIANA   What's the guy like?

KAREN   Nice looking. Tall. A little pompous. Square. Boring. A
drag.

DIANA   In your state of mind, he sounds like a perfect date.

When, God help him, Charles showed up, it wasn't Diana, but the boys who gave him a hard time. After Eric told Karen not to let Charles drive too fast, he and Michael greeted Charles.

ERIC   Do you like being a stockbroker?

CHARLES   Very much so. It's fascinating work.

ERIC   It's awfully risky, isn't it?

CHARLES   Not if you know what you're doing.

MICHAEL   Do you know what you're doing?

Karen bade good-bye to Charles when she realized he didn't like her children. That became a main criterion for her to go by in the time ahead: whoever cared for her must also care for her children.

In January of 1982, Victoria Hill swept into town to do a benefit fashion show for one of Karen's pet causes, the Battered Wives Shelter. Victoria was ecstatic to be with Karen again, absolutely adored Diana, and ended up trying to convince Karen to come to New York City and work for her. Karen seriously considered it—to the point of having Laura Avery put their house on the market—but then just didn't have the heart to move the children and herself across the country, leave KLM, leave Knots Landing, and somehow leave Sid.

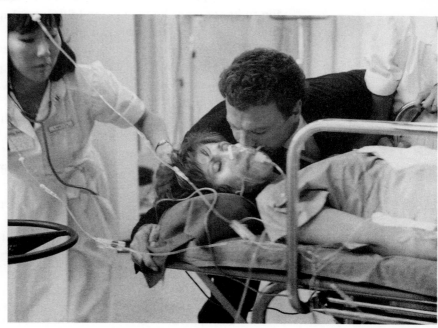

Mack kisses Karen as she is wheeled into emergency surgery after being shot by the Wolfbridge Group.

Meeting Mack at the opening of Lotus Point, 1984. It became harder and harder to pretend that she did not love him.

Karen's brother Joe, a professor now like his dad, moved in with the Fairgates while conducting the Neiman lectures on a visiting professorship at the University of Southern California. It was wonderful to have a father figure in the house and another adult to confide in.

Karen dated Larry Wilson—one of Abby's ex-boyfriends—until he asked her to go away with him for the weekend. She explained she couldn't do anything like that as long as she still felt like a wife; although she stopped seeing Larry, it sparked a turning point for Karen. Visiting Sid's grave, she made the decision to take her wedding band off and wear it on a necklace which Sid had given her the Christmas before he died. To Sid—his grave—she said, "I think that taking it off my finger will mean that I'm starting to let go. Not of our love, or our marriage—not of our beautiful, sacred memories. But of . . . fantasy. The one that hovers around, telling me it hasn't really happened, you aren't really gone, it's all been a horrible nightmare."

In September of 1982, Karen was jolted by the morning paper's lead story that Roy Lance and Frank Kolbert had not been convicted for Sid's murder, and that while they had been convicted of auto theft, interstate transportation of stolen goods, and wire fraud, the convictions were being dismissed on a police procedure technicality —Lance and Kolbert were being set free! Outraged, Karen flew into the U.S. Attorney's office and screamed her head off at Assistant DA Mack MacKenzie, demanding to know what he was going to do about it. Not much, at first. Later he gave her the thousands of pages of trial transcripts to read.

At KLM, on a short fuse to begin with over Lance and Kolbert, Karen was more than a bit vexed with Gary Ewing. He wasn't paying much attention to his work and for good reason—he had run out on Val and was shacking up with—who else?— Abby. Gary protested her criticism.

GARY   I'm getting pretty sick and tired of you riding me, okay?
If I'm not doing my job, that's one thing, but my personal
life is none of your business. If you can't separate the two,
then fire me. Otherwise, get off my back. (He stormed off.)

KAREN   Gary?

(Gary turned around.)

KAREN   You're fired.

Meanwhile, Karen's unlikely friendship with Mack MacKenzie (unlikely, because they fought *constantly)* was growing. She had him over for dinner. They had a

wonderful time, full of laughter, and the boys absolutely loved him. He got Karen to dance the Lindy Hop to old 45s and she happily agreed to another date. Every night through this, Karen was diligently plodding through the trial transcripts, searching for anything that might bring her husband's killers to justice. She kept a legal dictionary at her side and called Richard Avery something like nine times to ask technical questions. And then she reached the point where she read that it had been *Mack's* wiretapping methods that had gotten the case thrown out of court. Livid, she vowed to go her own way after Lance and Kolbert. In the course of her snooping and tracking, Karen found out that one of her very own KLM mechanics, Wayne Harkness, had been the one who had tampered with Sid's brakes that fateful day. Terrified, but determined, Karen masterminded a setup to get enough on all three to at least put them behind bars, but when it all came down, it backfired, and Karen was nearly killed. Mack, fortunately, had kept her under constant surveillance, and at the eleventh hour, stepped in to arrest Harkness. As for Lance and Kolbert, whom they still couldn't arrest, Mack handed them on a platter to angry underworld leaders whom they had double-crossed; they'd have a trial all right.

Joe moved back to New York in November and Karen started seeing Mack very seriously. They went on a fishing trip together, which ended in unmitigated disaster with Mack's assuming they'd have sex. Karen was freaked out by his cavalier attitude, that he didn't seem to understand that yes, it *was* a big deal. They came home early, leaving their relationship in a hazy status. Then there was the little problem of Mack's girlfriend, Patrice, but no matter how much Karen wanted to turn her back on this relationship, she couldn't. She was in love with Mack; really in love.

In January of 1983 Mack proposed, but the timing was not very good. Teddy Becker was back in town, here to convince Karen to marry him. It didn't take long for Karen to know in her heart that it was Mack whom she loved, whom she wanted. At the end of the month they eloped to Las Vegas and married.

Life with Mack was exciting, to say the least. He was so unlike Sid that Karen couldn't even try and compare them; that, in fact, was why their marriage had a good chance. Mack was loud and pushy and a show-off, but he was also full of laughter and joy and playfulness. And their sex life was wonderful, different. In the marital department, Karen was one happy lady.

Karen was outraged when Abby tried to talk to her about her divorcing Mack.

KAREN This isn't your business, Abby.

ABBY The hell it isn't. Every time you have a fight with someone, it winds up in my lap.

KAREN In *your* lap.

ABBY You make it impossible for me to stay neutral. Do you remember where your daughter lived while you two were feuding? Do you know how many times your arguments with my brother wound up with me in the middle? I've heard every side of every argument you've ever had!

Mack asks what's wrong, after Karen dropped a plate while preparing for the Thanksgiving feast. Her hand was completely numb—the first sign of descending paralysis—and she was hard-pressed to keep the truth from Mack.

Problems, however, started with Diana. She was mixed up with the Roberts boy next door, whom Karen liked all right, but whom Mack abhorred from the beginning, which gave her pause for thought. When Diana announced her intention to leave for New York with this guy—whose character had come into question—Karen put her foot down. In response, Diana ran away with him. Then the news came out: Chip Roberts was very likely the killer of Ciji Dunne. Karen took off immediately, tracking Diana, and Mack joined her in Oklahoma, where they caught up with them. The police arrested Chip, and Diana defiantly announced to her mother that she was married to Chip—whose real name was Anthony Fenice—and even though she *knew* Chip had murdered Ciji, she was determined to protect him in any way she could.

Karen was sick over the daughter's misplaced loyalty and told her so; in retaliation, Diana declared she hated her mother and refused to talk to her; seeking protection, she moved in with Abby.

Karen was agonized. In the weeks ahead, as it was more and more evident that she had "lost" Diana, her baby, her worry and anxiety over Diana's well-being took its toll; Karen began to lose weight, suffer back problems and insomnia and crying jags. Diana with a murderer, dear God in heaven! After months of running herself down, in November Mack forced Karen to see a doctor, who insisted on prescribing tranquilizers for her so she could get some badly needed rest from her jangling nerves. She resisted, but the doctor sternly told her, "If you're sick, you take medicine," and reluctantly she took the prescription and had it filled.

Suffering from blinding tension headaches, Karen starting taking the pills. A commonly prescribed tranquilizer, Karen took them exactly as prescribed, but when troubles with Diana and Chip escalated, so did her intake of pills. Meanwhile, her other physical symptoms had grown much worse, and she was additionally prescribed sleeping pills, and for her back and neck pains, muscle relaxers. Soon she couldn't sleep at all without pills; soon Karen found herself bolt awake in the middle of the night, desperately needing more to knock herself out. She took them. During the day her back and head were killing her, and so she began mixing the tranquilizers with the muscle relaxers. After a while, the only thing Karen knew for sure was that she needed pills to cope, and without them, she was a basket case. And since this was no time not to function, she pressed onward, relying heavily on the tranquilizers to get her through each day.

Her cheerful calls to doctors were met with prescription renewals, but as she started to run out more frequently, she got caught in the humiliating act of—for example—rummaging through Valene's medicine cabinet in search of Lilimae's tranquilizers. Valene tried unsuccessfully to talk to her about the pills; Mack was busily tied up in the Wolfbridge investigation; Karen strongly denied her addiction; and so it wasn't until the end of January of 1984, when she accidentally overdosed, that she received help.

She was released from a hospital drug rehabilitation ward a month later, and continued therapy as an outpatient for the next year. She was just in time to help Mack through his damaging frame-up in the Wolfbridge case. When Mack was nearly killed, when the Fairgate-MacKenzie house was ransacked, Karen fearfully pleaded with Mack to give up his investigation before something happened to him. He promised.

After Gary Ewing's mock death in March, Karen learned that Mack had been behind the whole scheme in an attempt to crack Wolfbridge once and for all. Despite all his reassurances to the contrary, he had been working on the case all along! Karen, feeling betrayed and hurt, threw him out of the house. But whether she liked it or not, the Wolfbridge Group got *her* involved in the case, and when it came to a head in April, in the course of trying to warn Mack of impending danger, Karen was shot in the line of fire and nearly died.

Surgeons operated on her to remove the bullet from her spine, an operation which was only partially successful. Her doctor explained that there was one fragment they could not reach; the fragment would eventually work its way into her spine, causing paralysis and ultimately, death. Karen could have a very risky operation now or take her chances, which would be eventually fatal. The news was so reminiscent of Sid, Karen had to think it over carefully before making the decision. Karen, swearing the doctor to secrecy about her diagnosis, declined the operation, determined to get her family's life in order before she died. She refused to leave her family unprovided for, unprepared for what lay ahead. And as a part of that decision, she resolved not to reconcile with Mack. There was no point in bringing him back into her life, only for her to die, leaving him with the obligation of her children. If he wanted to help her children, that would be his choice.

With the nurse, Carrie Wilson, who had assisted Dr. Ackerman in stealing Valene's children after they were born. Karen and Mack convinced her to confront Ackerman at a bridge tournament to see if it would spark a confession from him. Ackerman's response was one they had not expected—he shot himself.

Taking photographs at Lotus Point.

After finding out that her partnership with Abby in H & O Management—which she had inherited from Sid—in actuality meant a partnership in mighty Lotus Point, Karen told Abby that not only would she not sell out her half, but that she would now be working with her. Moving into the Lotus Point offices, working side by side with Abby and Gary, Karen pressed for speedy developments she wished to see finished before dying. With Eric out of high school and unwilling to go to college, she appointed him Manager of KLM, and had him employ Michael after school. Diana, who was now living with Joe in New York, was already settled. The remaining pressing, painful concern was to rebuff all of Mack's desperate attempts at winning her back.

Oddly enough, it was Abby who made Karen reconsider her stance with him. Abby, off base as usual, assumed Karen had *lost* Mack because of her excessive stubbornness. And Eric and Michael were also impatient with Karen, not understanding what they saw as abusive behavior toward Mack. Tentatively she made motions toward reconciliation, but was unable to bring herself to tell him the truth about her future. Mack moved back home before Thanksgiving of 1984, and Karen started losing her motor control in one arm, the first sign of descending paralysis.

In January, with Mack at her side, Karen opted for the operation. She took time to spend what could have been the "last" with Eric and Michael; she talked to Diana on the phone for hours, insisting she need not come; she said a tearful good-bye to Val and the neighbors; and she even made peace with Abby, thanking her for things she had done for her children in the past.

The operation was a total success.

Karen resumed her career at Lotus Point with full steam. At home, however, in the neighborhood, what really started tearing at her heart was her best friend's loss of her babies. Karen came to believe that Val wasn't crazy—that the twins *were* stolen at birth. From February through October of 1985, Karen did not rest in her investigation of Dr. Ackerman, and with the help of Mack and Ben Gibson, was able to deliver Valene's children back into her arms for keeps. With the exception of the births of her own children, Karen had never experienced such joy.

Work at Lotus Point was going extremely well. Karen undertook, with Gary's approval, revising Abby's vision of it as a hangout for business people hungry for a little action away from home. Instead, Karen would make it into the kind of resort that lovers and families would look back on with fondness. She hired Laura to help her, handing her $11,000,000 for improvements. Laura, delighted and amused by the amount of money, asked, "Is this the same MacKenzie family? The one who lives in Knots Landing and does their own laundry?" Karen merely beamed in response, basking in the fun of it all.

In January of 1986, Karen learned she was up for an appointment by the governor to the State Planning Land Use Commission because of her work at Lotus Point and her track record as an environmentalist. She was thrilled to have the nomination and was furious when suddenly *Abby* was nominated as well. Abby, who'd convert the Grand Canyon into a nuclear waste dump if it meant she could sell it! And then Abby got the appointment. Disappointed, smelling a blond rat, Karen shrugged it off and plunged her energies back into Lotus Point.

Prompted by Laura Avery's idea, Karen went to work with her in planning a 32-acre expansion of Lotus Point. Gary signed over to the corporation the acreage from his own Empire Valley holdings, and Karen put Eric to work on surveying the property. What had looked like gorgeous rural acreage, however, turned out to be an environmental bomb. Unknown to all, Galveston Industries in prior years had used the site to bury manufacturing waste by-products. Years of corrosion of the waste receptacles caused leaking and, like Love Canal, acid and arsenic mixed to produce lethal gases and contaminated water.

Being both a strident environmentalist and an architect of Lotus Point was enough to drive Karen to any lengths to find the criminals responsible and to take any measures to clean up the site before the danger spread, but when her son Eric nearly died from his exposure, it became more than a cause, more than outrage at her livelihood being threatened. It became a mother's obsession to see that no other family would have to go through the kind of ordeal the Fairgate-MacKenzies had with Eric.

In May of 1986, Lotus Point employee Charlie Lee died from arsenic poisoning and Karen shut down the resort complex. The following day, Karen disappeared without a trace.

Long gone are the days when families existed, generation after generation, in the same communities, sometimes even in the same house. Karen was a part of "The Nation of Strangers," the transition into family mobility in the quest for economic opportunity. But unlike her neighbors, Karen brought with her to Knots Landing a deep sense of tradition and family. Some say she has outright adopted the neighborhood as the large family she always wanted. But it is more unconscious than that, and much more practical. The fact is, she is the only one on Seaview Circle who has a stable, loving childhood upon which to draw her life experience from.

Karen learned early on that you get back from life pretty much what you put into it; her inexhaustive supply of love and support and camaraderie for others is evidence of how strongly she believes it to be true. And while she doesn't understand why other people haven't learned that lesson, she is nonetheless quite willing to teach them.

So long as they listen, of course!

Marion Patrick MacKenzie
Mack

"A commission needs . . . guys who know the streets and know the courts. Guys who talk like people, not like social workers. Mainly, guys who are absolutely one hundred percent whistle-clean. So far, the only guy I know who qualifies is Mack MacKenzie."

—Gregory Sumner, 1983

The glint in his eye is the tipoff he's the good guy.

This is a man of extremes. That's what makes him so exciting. He's got a temper that kicks like a Magnum 44, but he possesses a gentle side that can make a lamb look mean. He's a tough guy, making big-time racketeers quake in their limos; he's a nice guy, making big time with giggling kids. His spirit and drive are like iron; his frustration can tie him up in knots; his love for dear ones makes him teary-eyed; his temperament turns "No, Mack" into the declaration "Then I must." He's a deadly earnest, extremely funny, icedly determined, warmly affectionate man of deep voice, hearty laughter, and hushed whispers of blatant, earthy sexuality. He is Mack MacKenzie, longtime playboy turned devout family man, glitzy Wall Street lawyer turned kick-ass crimebuster.

Marion Patrick MacKenzie was born on New York City's Lower East Side in 1941. Pat's (as he was called then) earliest memory of home was of his parents and relatives screaming at the top of their lungs, and so he just joined right in. His mom, Anna, was first-generation Italian-American, and his pop, Peter "Mack" MacKenzie, was first-generation Scots-Irish-American. His father would start yelling first and then his mom would start screaming in Italian, and before you knew it, Pat's uncles Angelo, Dominick, and Santino would be barreling up the stairs, followed by uncles Mike and Shawn, and then there would be a good old-fashioned brawl, furniture and oaths flying everywhere.

Pat never did understand why his mother married his father. The only thing he could figure is that when she met the strapping, handsome Pete at a neighborhood church dance, it was before he had started drinking. Or maybe she had just gotten in too deep, making life with her vehemently disapproving family impossible. Or maybe she was only able to see with her heart and not her eyes and head. As for his father, Pat knew well why the bully married her; she was a dark, radiant beauty in those days, and Pop, Pat grudgingly had to admit, did have an excellent eye for the ladies.

Pat's father was a salesman and, had he ever drawn a sober breath, probably

Valene Ewing said about Mack, "Mack looks very rugged and handsome. I never realized what a nice smile he has. And his eyes are so sensitive and alive."

would have been a good one. But, he never had and so he wasn't. He had a big mouth backed up with an ego the size of the moon, and cheated on his wife every chance he got. When cornered by her, he'd let her have it. None of this won the heart of his only son. Pat hated him and, from the time he could walk, would take on his father in defense of his mother. As a result, he often sported a bruised and swollen face.

As for Pat's relationship with the outside world in his early life, that wasn't too great either. Although he greatly favored his father in looks, he was used to speaking Italian at home, making him a kind of cultural oddity. The Irish kids ethnically slurred him as Italian, while the Italian kids slurred him as Irish, and since the MacKenzies lived on the border of Italian and Irish neighborhoods, "the only way to stay out of fights was to stand on the corner and beat myself up." His younger sister Meghan, a shy, pretty girl, was his playmate at home, and on the streets Pat was her guard dog.

Like his father, Pat was born with the gift of gab, and he was known as a smart aleck at school, though very bright as well. Adolescence and teenage years brought wonderful new things to Pat. He was a gifted athlete in basketball, track, baseball, and handball, and it won him the respect he had always craved. Girls—as they do to this day—swarmed around his charismatic smile, manly good looks, and easy manner. And Pat gladly accepted all that the girls were willing to give.

The honors he earned as an athlete also made him somewhat of a hero on both sides of his family; acceptance by his uncles and cousins meant a lot to him. His favorite time of year was Labor Day, when all the MacKenzies would wear their kilts, just as their fathers and *their* fathers had done before them. Pat liked tradition, and it was the only similarity with his father that he wasn't ashamed of.

Pat always worked part-time at night and all day on Sundays, giving almost all he earned to his mother since his father rarely managed to get past a bar to pay bills. When Pat finished high school, although he didn't want to leave his mother and Meghan (who his father constantly accused of being "loose," which was utterly ridiculous and cruel), Pat couldn't bear to live in the same house with him and enlisted in the Army. The minute he left the house, Pat became "Mack." He served three years overseas and did some hard thinking about what he wanted to do with his life. He decided: to be so distinguished and so stinking rich he could make up to his mother for everything his father had robbed her of.

He entered New York University in 1962 on the GI Bill and graduated in 1966 with honors. He then entered the School of Law at Fordham University and there made his first best friend, disinherited rich kid Gregory Sumner. Sumner was as competitive as Mack and as athletes and "brains" they matched head-on. They shared an apartment and studied together.

Mack landed a job as a conductor on the Long Island Railroad to support himself and pay his tuition. While punching tickets one evening, he caught the flirtatious attentions of a beautiful young socialite, Pamela Matheson, and they started dating. With her Locust Valley "lockjaw" background, Mack was quite a departure from Pamela's usual boyfriends and her parents were aghast when they met him. They forbade her to see him again, but Pamela was falling in love (as was Mack) and they continued to see each other on the sly. And then, in 1967, Pamela told Mack she was pregnant. Mack wanted to get married and she said yes, but after she went to tell her parents, she disappeared. Her parents would tell him nothing, and despite his frantic attempts to locate her, all he could find out was that she was somewhere in Europe. It would be a mystery and heartache he would carry for years.

By 1968 he had a spanking new law degree and a big fat job as a tax attorney on Wall Street. He dressed in pin-striped suits and wing-tipped shoes, and gloated every time he looked out his office window. He made piles of money and gave a great deal of it to his mother and Meghan in the form of their-name-only bank accounts. He assured his proud mother he loved his job, but inwardly he grew restless, uneasy with the "easy" life. In 1973 his mother died and Mack lost his appetite for the job. As he said years later, "I loved the job, I loved having it, *the fact that I'd gotten it.* It wasn't easy to give up." But he resigned and went to where his heart led him—the Legal Aid Society.

How he loved it! He was exhausted and vastly overextended, but defending people who would otherwise be helpless appealed to Mack's sensibilities. In an odd way, they all reminded him of his mother. And the more he defended people without money, without clout, often without a friend in the world, the more Mack got a hankering to see the *real* criminals have their day in court. He wanted to get at the *bullies* of the world. Stick it to the *big* guys for a change. So in 1976, Mack switched over to the State Prosecutor's office and raised Cain. That same year, his Uncle

Dealing with Karen's denial of her drug addiction was the hardest thing Mack ever had to go through. His strong, idealistic partner in life was acting no differently than the drug addicts he knew from the streets. Here she pleads with him to get her out of the rehab center, saying that Dr. Wilson will take care of her. Mack refuses, saying, "He has no understanding of drug problems, or he wouldn't have overprescribed in the first place."

Overwhelmed with guilt and worry, Mack waits with Val at hospital while Karen is being operated on for gunshot wou.. sustained when she tried to warn Mack that St. Clair had him up for a hit.

Mack, having been badly beaten the night before, and Karen, having just been released from the drug rehab center, grimly realize that the Wolfbridge case will get them before Mack gets *them*.

Mack pleads for Karen's forgiveness for deceiving her, Karen refuses to let him back in her life.

Hours later, Ben arrives to support his friend.

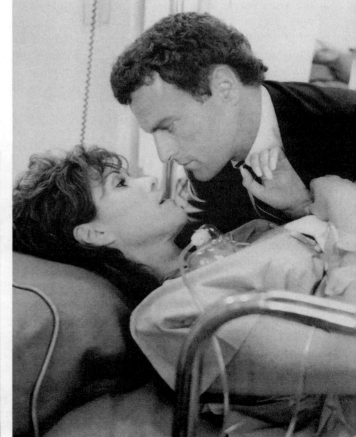

Shawn died of cancer and Uncle Mike was diagnosed with the same. In 1979, when Mike finally died and Mack's father disappeared, Mack thought about moving on to start a new life.

Meghan got married and moved to the West Coast, giving Mack some ideas. He snooped around a little out there and some folks snooped around about him too. In 1980 Mack accepted the post of Assistant U.S. Attorney, specializing in fighting organized crime in Southern California. He moved into a nice apartment in sunny Los Angeles, started a regular, nonemotionally committed "thing" with his next-door neighbor, Patrice, and settled into a happy, but strangely empty, new life.

In September of 1982, Mack's office door slammed opened and standing there was the beautiful, fiery, wildly angry Karen Fairgate, who demanded to know what was going to be done about her husband's killers. He liked her on sight—as he did all challenges, in whatever form—but their first meeting did not end very well:

> KAREN   Look, I didn't come here for a civics debate. Are you going to help me or not?
>
> MACK   I'm on your side, Mrs. Fairgate. We lost. That's it. Finished. I wish I could help you but I can't. Nobody can. I'm sorry. (pause) However, I *would* like to take you to dinner.
>
> KAREN   You really are a creep.
>
> (Slam!)

As the two worked to catch Sid's killers and they saw each other socially, Mack was more and more taken by Karen. She was just so . . . such a fighter! Mack wouldn't ever consider himself a bully, although he did know he was obstinate and controlling. Karen, however, never let him get away with anything unless he had earned it. Clearly this would be a fifty-fifty proposition in terms of leadership and aggressiveness, something Mack had never experienced before with a woman.

Karen's brother Joe liked him right off, and Mack really enjoyed Karen's two boys, Eric and Michael, who were as sports crazy as himself. Diana, however, presented problems, but Mack assumed they'd straighten out in time. And the neighbors—oh boy, his first time at a cul-de-sac party he was *nervous.* As Karen said, just as they were walking into the Averys' house, "Just remember, they're only here to judge you." But it went well, and Mack liked Karen's best friend, Valene Ewing, enormously. In fact, he liked most everyone Karen liked.

By late October, Karen was worried about how much Diana apparently disliked Mack and she asked him to discuss it with Diana. Mack knew how important it was to Karen that her kids accept him and so he tried. Diana was quite open about her not liking him, not exactly sure why, but willing to say, "Your style maybe. The way you're always so sure of yourself." Mack tried to explain, honestly, "actually, that's a symptom of lack of confidence in this particular situation." They did not, however, come to a resolution.

All this family stuff was beginning to scare Mack. He wanted Karen to go away with him for a weekend and now he felt as if he was being interviewed as a prospective father. And frankly, it unnerved him about how he was feeling about Karen. If she were anyone else, he'd *never* go after her, not with a ready-made family! There were just too many attractive single women in Los Angeles to begin a new family with.

After their nasty spat on the fishing trip in November, Mack was miserable. Karen had made it more than clear she was not yet ready, or willing, to have sex with him. Misinterpreting it as a lack of caring on her part, Mack pushed the relationship back a few stages in his mind and resumed sleeping with Patrice. Unfortunately, Diana arrived unannounced one morning and saw Patrice. Mack raced to the Fairgates to

Home for the holidays. Mack and Karen reconciled in time for Thanksgiving, 1984. All the neighbors came over, and all in all, it was one of the happiest days of Mack's life, having no idea of Karen's pending paralysis.

tell Karen about it first, stressing that Patrice meant nothing to him, but Karen didn't understand his reasoning and broke off with him.

Sad, angry, Mack confided in Patrice about Karen: "When I can't see her, I want to see her. When she gets close, I run away. She scares me." Patrice thought it meant a lot of love as well and pressured him to tell Karen his feelings about her. He did. Rushing into Daniel Restaurant, he humbly declared his love. Karen cooly turned away from him.

Though Karen wouldn't see him, she posed no objection to his ongoing relationship with her sons, and Mack was grateful for that. No matter how much he hated to admit it, he was longing for a big rowdy family like the Fairgates. It wasn't only Karen he loved.

Mack and Karen reconciled after Mack came to her side through the ordeal of Diana's failed kidneys. Diana too, in this period, did a turnabout on Mack; she was enormously grateful for his supporting her mom. Mack and Karen's relationship was on more solid footing than it had ever been, and in the middle of January, with great nervousness, Mack proposed. Karen hemmed and hawed and finally, days later, said yes. They started to plan the wedding—which at the Averys' invitation, was to be held at Daniel—but the wedding got so complicated that Mack and Karen finally said to heck with it and eloped to Las Vegas. After a brief honeymoon, Mack moved into the cul-de-sac.

Mack's assistance in cracking the Ciji Dunne murder case was complicated by the investigation's being led by an old flame, Janet Baines. She still had a lot of feeling for him, but Mack resisted any involvement, and stood like a rock for Karen to lean on throughout the nightmare of Diana and that scumbag Chip Roberts.

In November of 1983, Assemblyman Gregory Sumner appointed his old friend the head of a new Crime Commission, one whose presumed success would help Sumner win the Senate campaign in '84. Mack accepted the position, stating at the press conference, "Some of the dirtiest jobs are done by guys in white collars. And I don't mean priests. I want to find out why some of the most powerful corporations in this state break laws continually and never pay. Why law enforcement and the courts and government turn their backs and close their eyes. I want to find out who and what is behind it. And who profits by it. And how it can be stopped."

The first target for his commission—The Wolfbridge Group. "Their own banks finance their operations. Their own contractors build sub-standard buildings, which their own insurance companies insure. They've got enough politicians on the payroll to make sure the right inspectors inspect—for the right price. They've got plenty of local union leaders in their back pocket and three at the national level. They use mob tactics to wipe out competition . . . and they're good at it because they're in bed with the mob."

The first thing his investigation turned up was that *Sumner* was somehow connected to Wolfbridge. Mack suspected campaign money was at stake, and sadly realized that his friend could not be trusted. By January Mack had enough evidence to get a warrant from the DA and the federal prosecutor to go after Wolfbridge on some of its construction projects around Los Angeles. Meanwhile, at home, Karen was acting increasingly erratic and strange under the weight of her undetected drug addiction. She accidentally overdosed and Mack committed her into a drug rehab program, despite her cries and pleas that she was all right. Clearly she was not and Mack's heart nearly broke at what had happened to his strong, vital partner in life. While trying to cope with all this, emotionally exhausted, Mack was stunned to hear Sumner announce at a press conference that he was demanding Mack's resignation,

Checking to see if Karen is okay, 1985. Mack and Karen cornered Dr. Ackerman at a bridge tournament when he bolted and tried to make a getaway. Mack chased him on foot, and when Ackerman tried to drive out of the parking lot, Karen backed up Mack's jeep to block him. He smashed into it and then shot himself.

because Mack had allegedly used his position for financial gain. *What?* By morning there was a new Commissioner Saxon, Mack's Wolfbridge files were all missing, and the DA wouldn't act on the evidence given to him.

Mack came very near to buckling under. It wasn't so much losing his job as it was the implication that he was in some way not clean. The accusation was based on Karen's having inherited a partnership with her sister-in-law, Abby Cunningham-Ewing, in oceanfront property of some kind. The charges didn't make any sense; what did an apartment building have to do with Mack? When Karen was released from the rehab, things started to fall in place, the upshot being that Karen was unknowingly the partner in the gigantic Lotus Point development with Abby. The whole thing stunk to high heaven. Hot on the trail of Wolfbridge and its connection to Abby and Sumner and Lotus Point, Mack was jumped and severely beaten, prompting a hysterical Karen to make him promise he'd stop working on the case. But then the governor himself called, requesting that he take Sumner's reinstatement offer and secretly continue the investigation for him. Mack agreed to it, not liking to deceive Karen, but feeling it was his duty.

While pretending to be investigating the judicial system, Mack continued his Wolfbridge investigation by making them believe they had succeeded in killing Gary Ewing. Mack convinced Wolfbridge of that, but it also meant deceiving his family and all his friends, including Valene Ewing. When word got out in March that Gary was alive, Mack arrived home to have Karen hand him back his wedding ring. No amount of explaining or begging would sway her, and under a lot of stress and deeply depressed, Mack moved in with Ben Gibson at his beach house.

When Mack brought the Wolfbridge case toward its conclusion, its end and the aftermath were deeply disturbing. The pieces had come together for him: that Wolfbridge had supported Sumner in his senate bid with millions of dollars, that in exchange for some coastal variances arranged by Sumner, Wolfbridge had forced itself on Abby as a construction partner. And whatever control Sumner and Abby had had over Wolfbridge was long gone. When Gary Ewing had frozen the assets of

Gary Ewing Enterprises and hence the progress of Lotus Point (which he didn't even know he owned), Wolfbridge leader Marc St. Clair had ordered Gary's death; St. Clair knew Gary would leave his estate to Abby, who could then unfreeze Lotus Point. Gary cooperated with Mack, and in the end Abby herself did too, but the end of the trail was destroyed. Sumner shot and killed St. Clair—the only person who could have testified as to the extent of everyone's involvement, including Sumner and Abby—and the only witness at the shooting was Abby, who backed up his story that he had shot him in self-defense. But of course.

When Karen was shot and hospitalized, she still refused to reconcile with Mack. Mack pleaded with her, opened his heart to her, but she was adamant and he was miserable.

Job offers flooded in from all over the country and Mack accepted the job of special investigator to the governor. In the meantime, Jane Sumner, who was in the process of leaving Sumner, surprised Mack by declaring her love for him after he had confided in her about Karen. Jane said that she had *always* been in love with him. Mack shared a kiss with her, but did not pursue it as it was obvious that, lousy marriages or not, they were both still obsessed with their legal spouses.

In December of 1984, Mack began an investigation of the Tidal Basin murders—crimes that involved the huge conglomerate, Galveston Industries—another case that would go on and on and be equally frustrating in the end, since its conclusion was also shrouded in Sumner/Abby mystery. It was amazing how those two names kept "accidentally" popping up in connection with organized crime. . . .

Just before Thanksgiving, at long last, Karen had a change of heart. Mack, all this time, had known that she loved him, and knew there had to be something else going on. Finally, she told him; she told him about the bullet fragment lodged near her spine, her probable death, her unwillingness to bring Mack back into her life under the circumstances. Mack was there for her 100 percent through the operation and also in the hospital chapel, praying his heart out. His prayers were answered by her recovery.

Meanwhile, wading in the filth of the Galveston case, Mack, with Ben's help, had pieced together an ugly story. It began with a chemical spill in Wesphall, California; residents there got deathly ill from contaminated water, some of the older people actually dying. Galveston Industries, to keep it quiet, paid off the residents of the town, but when two secretaries—Mary Farnsworth and Lila Maxwell—learned how deadly this spill was and were going to go public with the story, they were murdered.

The investigation led back to Paul Galveston himself, a man who was partners with Gary Ewing in a huge new community development called Empire Valley. Empire Valley was the new name for old Wesphall acreage. Gary swore up and down that nothing funny was going on out there, but Mack after a while didn't believe him. There *was* something funny going on out there. When Paul Galveston died in March, and Gregory Sumner—announcing that Galveston had been his real father—stepped down from the U.S. Senate to run Galveston Industries, Mack knew Sumner wouldn't do it unless there was something more than money involved—it had to mean *power*.

Was there ever something going on. . . . Sumner and a syndicate of other covert world corporate powers were secretly building some kind of communications complex that was capable of intercepting electronic signals anywhere in the world. However, in December, Mack's investigation stopped when Gary blew the whole complex up to kingdom come to stop assassins from killing him and Abby. So much for Empire Valley. At least for the moment.

Literally putting the pieces together on the Empire Valley case. Mack wanted to know exactly what kind of electronic parts were being shipped there.

After Mack, Karen, and Ben located and retrieved Val's babies, Mack did the follow-up work to bust the illegal adoption ring and ensure Val's possession of the children. The governor sent down one of his special aides, Jill Bennett, to assist. Mack did nothing but fight with the pushy young dynamo from the beginning. Karen liked her a lot (saying Jill reminded her of herself when younger) and Mack started to be attracted to her. She *was* a lot like Karen, but younger, single. . . . When Jill told him that she was in love with him, however, he gently sent her back to Sacramento, which was no easy thing to do.

In January of 1986, Jill was reassigned to work in Los Angeles with him and she immediately made another play for Mack, giving him one of her hotel room keys to visit her, should he change his mind. Mack didn't go, but he held on to the key—not because he would use it, but like his job on Wall Street, he loved just having been able to get it. To him it meant he was still attractive, still desirable in middle age, a time when he was feeling too old to realize many of his dreams. Unfortunately, Karen found the hotel key and immediately jumped to the conclusion he had used it. He explained that he hadn't, why he had held on to it, but Karen persisted in blowing it out of proportion. That made Mack angry—here he hadn't done *anything* and his wife was boycotting him! He had tried to be honest about his fears of being middle-aged and, instead of understanding, Karen insisted that she didn't feel that way. Even after they worked through their misunderstanding verbally, Karen couldn't respond to him sexually for almost two months. Mack suspected that she too was having her own fears regarding middle age, but didn't bring it up; he only waited it out, hoping that her usual drive would return. In March, it did—and in Karen's usual way, it did not return subtly. After having lunch with him at the Markham Hotel, she had a love note and room key sent to Mack at the table. They checked out some eight hours later.

Meanwhile, at the office, Jill Bennett (who was now having an affair with Gary Ewing) insisted on reopening the Wesphall case. When Mack persisted in finding out her motivation, she finally confessed to him that, yes, her real name was Dorothy Simpkins, and that she had grown up in Wesphall. In fact, much of the Empire Valley land had belonged to her father, and Paul Galveston ruined him financially to get it. Her father had killed himself, and Jill had vowed to one day even the score with Galveston, and even though he was dead, she still wanted to bring Galveston Industries to justice. Mack tried to help her, but the case came to a dead end in March, shortly before Eric nearly died from exposure to a chemical dump in Empire Valley.

After having accepted the fact that he would never have a child (biologically) of his own, Mack was in for quite a shock in May of 1986 when Page Matheson showed up in Knots Landing. After all these years, Mack finally found out what had happened to Pamela. She had gone to Europe and given birth to his daughter.

But nothing, not even a newfound daughter, could save Mack from the greatest despair of his life. Karen vanished. Simply vanished. And Mack couldn't find her.

Slowing down? Mack? *Never.* The good guys always win? Mack wishes it were so. And so long as the bad guys are around, Mack MacKenzie will be around trying to stop them.

Diana Fairgate Fenice

"There is something about her I've always admired. . . . A wildness, almost, a freedom of spirit."

—Karen Fairgate, 1982

"Where there's a will, there's a way." In Knots Landing there is a slight variation on that old saying. "Where there's Diana, there's a willful way."

She's an awful lot like her mom. Her high-driving energy, fearless defense of what she believes is right, and high-spirited, heartfelt passions will make you smile in recognition. But Diana's judgment is something she created on her own. For every direct path, there have been many more wreckless ones. For every pang of love there have been as many incidents of misplaced trust. And for every moment of acting out, there have been less moments of *thinking* things out. But—give her time, more experience, and more consistency, and never a more dynamic and likable young woman shall you meet. She is a Fairgate (as in Abby), she is a Cooper (as in Karen), but she'll always be Diana, an unusual mix of both.

Diana Fairgate was born in 1963 in New York City, the first child of Karen and Sid Fairgate. As a newborn, her parents stayed up with her for endless nights with the colic. When she was one year old, she came down with roseola and nearly died after a two-day temperature of 105 degrees. Between illnesses (whooping cough, chicken pox, and measles), however, she was alarmingly healthy.

She was a veritable fireball, this little tyke, a show-off too, and stubborn and precocious to boot. She was talking her head off by age two. A favorite tale of the Fairgates is that when Diana was three and had strep throat, Sid asked her, "Do you have a temperature?" and Diana answered, "No, Mommy took it."

When the Fairgates moved to Knots Landing in 1967, Diana was in child heaven with a grassy backyard to romp in, a big wonderful beach to zigzag around on, a two-year-old brother to boss around, and a newborn brother to play mommy with. She adored her daddy, who'd let her do everything she wanted; fought with her mother, who wouldn't let her do *anything* (according to guess who), and she simply worshipped her beautiful Aunt Abby, who let her do anything and everything.

Karen had Diana reading before first grade, and Diana fell in love with it. Another talent emerged early under her mother's encouragement as well—she was clearly talented as an artist. Never did the Fairgates have to ask what Diana had drawn. She took to school like a bird to air and made friends in the course of her flight. Maybe too many friends, her parents thought, since it seemed Diana was already including the wrong kind. When her class took a field trip to the San Diego Zoo, classmate Jimmy Crane spiked the Kool-Aid. Diana thought it very mature for first grade and was impressed; by the time she got home, as Karen described, "she looked like the world's youngest bag lady."

Diana in 1964. Her mother said once, "She didn't learn to walk, she learned to run. Even when she was crawling, she was always in a hurry. Then she'd get up on those little legs and even when she could barely keep her balance, she was always so determined to get where she was going . . . no matter how many times she'd fall down, she'd get up and go for it again."

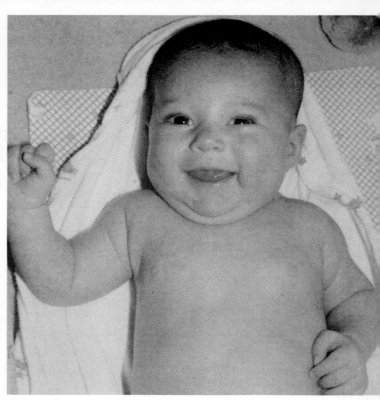

Diana found it impossible to win arguments with her mother, but didn't stop trying. One of their better ones in 1979:

KAREN   I'm not exactly a medieval relic.

DIANA   I'm not saying you are. Exactly.

KAREN   That's exactly what you're saying. And you don't know. Why as recently as 1960—

DIANA   Nineteen sixty is not exactly recent. I wasn't even born in 1960.

KAREN   Don't be silly. Nineteen sixty was the day before yesterday. Everybody was born by 1960.

DIANA   Not me.

KAREN   Don't argue with your mother.

DIANA   What did Grandma tell you about handling boys?

KAREN   She said don't.

As she grew older, still more talents emerged: she had a flair for dance, she had a lovely voice, and like her parents, she was very athletic. In fact, Diana's only problem seemed to be that she had *too* many talents, too many interests. When it was clear she could write well, then she dug into that for weeks, at the expense of her art and music and sports. When an acting talent was uncovered, she moved into that, dropping everything else. She was always flying about from one thing to the next, with obsession her only guide.

Diana learned to cook well and to sew, and what a flair she had for the latter. After Karen showed her how to follow a dress pattern, they didn't see her for three days. When she emerged from the sewing room, she explained that patterns were too boring and she had made her own creation—ta da!—a sizzling strapless black dress that only Abby would dare even look at.

All in all, the Fairgates had a gifted, temperamental child on their hands, but with her interests being so varied the potential problems seemed to diffuse themselves. She was generally unruly, in harmless ways, and Sid frankly didn't help by constantly encouraging her to take on any challenge.

And the drama she wrought! By fourteen, the Fairgates were so accustomed to her "Camille" scenes that they wrote off her complaint of stomach pains as an attempt to get out of doing the dishes. She disappeared into the bathroom and, when she came out, solemnly slid to the floor, clutching her stomach, swearing Eric had put ground glass in her dinner and she was going to die. Fortunately Karen felt her forehead and realized that she was indeed very sick and they took her to the hospital in the nick of time—her appendix had ruptured. She liked the long recovery; Eric said it was her crowning achievement, starring as the Queen of Sheba, ordering everyone around at her slightest whim.

Diana was quite popular in high school and went through the usual experimentations of her age group—first encounters with boys, first loves that turned out to be skunks, episodes of drinking beer with the gang at the beach, trying pot once—and the Fairgates were relieved that Diana proved to be surprisingly level-headed about it all, showing no signs of self-destructing like some of her classmates.

The death of Diana's father in October of 1981 hit her extremely hard. She was very supportive and helpful to her mother (who had gone to work full-time at KLM) with the cleaning, cooking, and running of the household, but Diana was lonely for her dad, his talks, his warmth, affection, fun, his love. She was a vulnerable target for Chip Roberts, the handsome young PR junior executive who appeared to have the same traits as her father. Though Chip had his peculiarities—funny moods and brief disappearances—Diana was positive she had met her man.

In December, while staying the weekend with Abby and Gary, Diana got very ill and was rushed to the hospital. At nearly 2 A.M., the doctors told her mother, "Her blood pressure is extremely elevated, and her potassium is very high. She is showing signs of early heart failure and her kidney function tests are very abnormal. She is in what we call renal failure." As it was explained to Diana, her kidneys had failed and the damage was permanent. If Diana wanted to live, then she would have to go to the hospital and have a painful four-hour session on a dialysis machine three times a week *for the rest of her life.* Diana thought she'd rather die. Who could live like that? There was one more possibility, a kidney transplant; she hoped against hope. Her mother, Eric, and Michael were eagerly tested, but they did not match. Diana's blood type was O, which she had inherited from her father. There was only one other relative to try—Abby. Abby was a perfect match, and God bless her, she came through for Diana by agreeing to give her one of her kidneys.

Over the course of Diana's recovery, her relationship with Chip intensified and he

"Chip and I have a love that nobody will ever understand. And they think that finally death will separate us, but it won't. We had the love that will never die."

Diana hugs Mack at the hospital, after her mother was shot by the Wolfbridge Group. It was only two years since Diana had been on death's door at the same hospital for kidney failure. She had been hooked up to an IV, catheters, a Jackson-Pratt Drain, and a heart monitor, prompting Eric to say that she looked like the ultimate video game.

Diana in one of her fashion designs, 1985. She sent this picture to her mother from New York, prompting her mother to remember a morning Diana refused to eat breakfast.

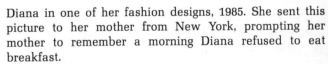

DIANA   I'm not hungry. I'm fasting.
KAREN   For religious reasons?
MICHAEL   For her thighs.

made declarations of love. In February of 1983 Diana agreed to move to New York with him. Her mother hit the roof, and Diana bitterly resented her forbidding her to go, basically because her mother kept hinting that Chip was somehow not good enough for her. They postponed their departure after the murder of Ciji Dunne, but in September Diana withdrew her savings out of the bank, loaded her car up, and they left to drive cross-country.

Diana left Knots Landing with very bad feelings about her mother and stepfather, Mack MacKenzie. They did not approve of Chip and yet never explained their reservations; they treated Diana as though she were a child. She was wildly in love with Chip at this point; she had never felt like this before, not ever. She was overjoyed when Chip proposed on the road, and they spontaneously got married in Las Vegas.

In a motel room one night, Diana was flabbergasted to hear an all-points bulletin out for Chip, who was wanted in connection with the murder of Ciji. Chip confessed to her, admitting that he had slept with Ciji once before he had met Diana; and that Ciji had been jealous of Diana, to the point of threatening to tell her that the baby she had been carrying belonged to Chip. "All I could think of was how much I loved you," he declared, "how I had to be with you. Ciji and I had a fight. I got mad, crazy, and I hit her. I didn't mean to kill her! Don't you see, Diana, I did it for you. I killed Ciji for you so that we could be together." Diana believed him, and she tried to help him elude the authorities. They were cornered by the police, however, led to them by no less than Diana's mother and Mack!

She refused to talk to her mother after that. Diana was sick of her interference, her insinuations, her lack of support, her hysterical threats and accusations. She moved in with Abby at Westfork Ranch.

Diana refused to testify against her husband; in the eyes of the law, she didn't have to. Chip was released on insufficient evidence, only to be nearly killed by Lilimae Clements. When he slipped into a coma and it looked as though Chip would die for sure, Diana finally told the authorities that Chip had killed Ciji. No sooner had she finished her statement than Chip came out of the coma. With the police having enough to convict him, he escaped from the hospital and hid out at Westfork. He and Diana planned to flee as soon as things cooled down. But then, Chip was killed.

Diana's world caved in. Somewhere, deep down, her greatest fear had been repeated—she had been left behind, alone. Her rage at being abandoned in death was directed almost full force against her mother, whom she held responsible for wrecking her chance at happiness with Chip. Eric tried to bring her around, but Diana was in too much agony to hear him; besides, lately her mother had been acting like a lunatic and no one could deny it. Diana *wanted* her mother to hurt over this. Even Abby—who had little or no use for Diana's mother—tried to put Karen's responsibility in the matter into some kind of proportion, but Diana couldn't break out of her fixation. "As long as I'm in pain, I won't forgive anybody who did anything to make this happen. I don't want to forgive; I want to hurt and hate and keep him with me. . . . I cherish the pain. It's all I have left of Chip, and I don't ever want to let go."

She went to New York in January of 1984 and, in the care of her Uncle Joe, slowly started to come out of it. She came back to Westfork in February and met with her mother, who had just been released from the drug rehabilitation center. Hurt, tired, needing each other desperately, daughter and mother forgave each other, and Diana moved home for a while.

In April of 1984, Diana moved to New York, where she is currently attending college and working part-time, illustrating fashions for her mother's college roommate, Victoria Hill.

Anthony Fenice aka Chip Roberts

"You ought to be against the law."
—Ciji Dunne, 1983

Sometimes one wishes that certain people *wouldn't* put their best foot forward and just be the rotten SOBs they are outright, so that they can be identified and thus avoided. Such was the case with Chip Roberts. Because of the mayhem, heartbreak, violence, and murder he brought to Knots Landing, it is understandable why many a resident maintains that his most charming social asset to date is that he's dead.

Anthony Fenice was a "mistake," born in 1957 in Syracuse, New York. In the first cold snowy winter of his life, his parents were killed in an automobile crash, leaving Tony in the care of his sister, Angela. Tony grew up obsessed with the idea that the world had an obligation to take care of him, and he would spend his life perfecting a facade to encourage exactly that. To be fair, in certain ways his emotional survival depended on acceptance by others, but once he learned how to win affection, he veered off from honest need and into more tangible kinds of greed. As Angie would describe him, "Even as an eight-year-old, he could always con a woman." He was a good-looking kid, rarely attended school, learning from the outside world what would become his most valuable tool as a con man—sex. He indulged early and learned quickly, specializing in unhappy housewives with generous allowances. By age sixteen he was notorious with the police and, after making one last score, skipped town on a bus heading West.

From 1973 to 1978, he "made" his way across the country—Chicago, Detroit, Milwaukee, Pierre—gradually working his way West. In 1978, at the age of twenty-one, he hit the jackpot with fifty-seven-year-old Dina Benson in Seattle, Washington. Dina was about the closest thing possible to American royalty; her family had been here for three centuries, her money was endless, and she was now a lonely widow. She was never considered a beauty, but her money had always drawn dozens of insincere suitors. Including Tony.

Ah yes, young, handsome, instantly love-struck Tony, who had no idea just *who* she was when he first "accidentally laid eyes on her" (like heck he didn't! He had her net value down to the penny). He was ardent, convincing, fabulous in bed, and the next thing Dina knew, he was living in the mansion.

What a life . . . the clothes! The cars! The parties! The girls on the sly!

Everything went along smoothly until Dina found out that if he didn't get his way, Tony'd threaten her with violence. And the more he demanded money and the more strings Dina put on it (thinking, and thinking correctly, that with too much money in hand he'd bolt), the more threatening he became. And then one night in 1981, he blew up and beat her. Badly. Very badly. He hightailed it out of there fast, a servant discovering Dina's unconscious body and rushing her to the hospital.

Chip bolstered Diana's dreams by describing their life in New York as living in a town house in Sutton Place, overlooking the East River. There would be a bakery on the corner that made the best fresh croissants. The doorman would tip his hat every morning and say, "Good morning, Mrs. Roberts." Chip would be a vice president of the largest public relations firm in New York, but only until he started an agency and stole all their clients away. The Robertses would be invited to all opening nights on Broadway; would have a box at the opera; and would be known at all the finest restaurants . . .

He arrived in Los Angeles with the new name of Chip Roberts. In a matter of days he had spotted and landed newly divorced Bess Riker, a public relations executive. Chip pulled the same "love at first sight" scam with the vulnerable lady and moved in with her. Within a couple of months, however, Bess demanded that he get a job. When he was slow to do so, and when she suspected he might be playing around, Bess said that since Chip was such a fast mover, he could come and work for her as a messenger.

And so began the career of Chip Roberts.

In October of 1981, he conned Lilimae Clements and Valene Ewing into believing he was Val's assigned publicist for *Capricorn Crude.* After Bess threw him out of her house, he sweet-talked Lilimae into letting him stay at the Ewings "temporarily." There he met Diana Fairgate from next door, who seemed interested in him, so he flirted his way into having her "loan" him a brand new car from Knots Landing Motors.

He continued to romance Diana—liking her country club friends and connections around town—and actively sought to woo Lilimae platonically, so as to ensure his residency in the house. With those two on a string, he met aspiring rock singer Ciji Dunne and convinced her to hire him as her PR agent, based on his account of a long and distinguished history in the field. By the middle of November, he was sleeping with Ciji, steadily dating Diana, and toying with the affections of Lilimae to the point of winning himself presents and services reminiscent of an indentured servant. He was fired by Beth Riker, of course, but Lilimae even stood guard for him while he stole files from her office.

He gave Ciji a marvelously concocted explanation of how he, not Gary Ewing, got her singing career off the ground, and persuaded her to sign over 25 percent of all her earnings to him as her business manager. Meanwhile, applying for a job at Thornwell Public Relations, Chip ripped off two chapters of Valene's private manuscript and gave them to his prospective boss, who in turn published them in the *Global Gossip*. Denying any involvement with Val and Lilimae, he recruited Diana to try and pressure Valene into signing up with Thornwell, explaining that they could *protect* her from this kind of horrible thing. Racing back to his promising financial future with Ciji, Chip was outraged in November when Ciji got pregnant and refused to have an abortion. She wanted to get married. Chip's argument ran, "Munson thinks he signed a hot number. Not just your voice—your whole look. The way you dress, your style, your body . . . he didn't sign some pregnant housefrau to waddle on stage." When Ciji put her foot down, declaring she was going to have the baby with or without him, Chip decided to cover his tracks and quickly spread the rumor that Gary Ewing was having an affair with her.

In February, Ciji stumbled on his past and threatened to expose him as Tony Fenice if he didn't leave her and everyone else alone. In response, Chip beat her to death, wrapped her body in garbage bags, and dumped it into the ocean off the Vernon Beach pier. Revowing his "love" for Diana, he happily took her, her car, and her money on the lam with him. He married her in Las Vegas, and tried to make their flight away from Knots Landing as romantic as possible, while tearing up Diana's postcards home, cutting off her phone calls, and trying to keep her in the dark. Finally, with an APB out on him, Chip had to make up a story about how he had killed Ciji to be with Diana and, silly girl, she bought it. Chip knew a good thing when he found it.

When he was caught and taken in custody back to Knots Landing, he smugly knew Diana would never testify against him, and was soon released on insufficient evidence. Lilimae, whom he had unwisely scorned and ridiculed, ran him down in a car, coming close to killing him. He suffered two fractured ribs, a broken arm, and internal hemorrhaging. He slipped into a coma in November and came out of it to find that Diana, thinking him dying, had spilled everything she knew to the cops. After trying to take a swing at her (he was restrained from doing so), Chip escaped from the hospital and hid out at Westfork Ranch, where good ol' Diana snuck him food and arranged for airline tickets to make their escape. Just before they were to leave, Chip was hiding in the stables when in walked Ciji Dunne. Shocked, scared down to his boots, Chip gasped, "My God," stepped back in terror, and impaled himself on a rake.

Poor Cathy Geary just stood there, wondering what had just happened.

The final word about Chip best belongs to the end of the eulogy written by Diana, which the minister read at his funeral. His sister, Angie, flew to Knots Landing to attend the service.

MINISTER He was a diamond in the rough. Those who loved
him know that that roughness would have been polished
away, and had he lived, the beautifully cut diamond within
would soon have burst through, full of color, crisp of edge,
radiant.

ANGIE Did you ever hear such garbage in all your life?

Eric Fairgate

"He's like Daddy. Very . . . laconic. He doesn't say much—
about his feelings, I mean. Then he goes ahead and does something."

—Diana Fairgate, 1981

It isn't as if Eric is forgettable in any sense, but with all the high-flying passion
around the Fairgate-MacKenzie household, Eric is rarely the focus of attention. He
is, as the neighbors will tell you, the eye of the temperamental storm, the gentle lull
that eases in a breather before the next front hits. First comes Diana, wham-zang-
screech! And from the other end of the sibling line, bam-flash-zzzzz-
zoooooommmmmm Michael! And from the east and west, sweeping in simultane-
ously, Tornado Karen and Hurricane Mack coming head to head. And there's Eric,
sitting in the middle of it all, calm, rational, determined, careful.

It's as if Sid Fairgate himself has returned in the legacy of his son.

Eric Fairgate was born in 1965 in New York City to Karen and Sid Fairgate. His
delivery was easy, and his initial spank to life prompted the only cry of protest his
parents would hear from him for some time to come.

He was Sid's child all the way; even at two he was playing the stoic, silently
bearing up amid even the wildest hysteria. Diana loved to play with him, especially
as Pocahontas, tying him to a tree in the backyard and wandering off, forgetting all
about him. Hours later Karen would find him still tied to the tree, smiling sweetly,
his warm, gentle brown eyes blinking a happy hello.

It was evident early on that he was extremely athletic, but while everyone clamored for him to play on their team, he was already displaying a craving for solitude.
He best loved helping his dad work on cars; not talking really, just observing, reading Sid's silent signals and handing him tools, just being together, working together,
each lost in his own thoughts.

He wasn't exactly shy (he really just didn't like to say much), but of course in
comparison with Diana it seemed as though he never spoke at all. At the beginning
of the school year, teachers would scan their pupil list, stop at the name Fairgate,
and roll their eyes, thinking, "Uh-oh, here we go again—another motor-mouth whiz
kid," but instead of a streak appearing in the room, in Eric would amble, everything
organized to a T, sliding unobtrusively in the back row. He was smart, in fact a B+
student, but unlike Diana, Eric worked for his good grades.

Sometimes it was difficult to believe that Diana was the eldest, since Eric spent an
inordinate amount of time looking after her. When she was broke, Eric always had
money on him; when Diana was hurt, Eric was always there to comfort her; when
Diana's temper flew, Eric always knew how to calm her.

The only problem Eric ever presented his family with was in the form of compari-

Leaving for school with his high-flying sister, Diana, 1981. She was his best friend while growing up, and his biggest responsibility.

Greeting neighbor Lilimae Clements at Thanksgiving, 1984.

In 1985 Eric seriously dated UCLA student, Whitney. Nervous about his family's reaction to Whitney being black, Eric pulled Mack aside and asked him, "Surprised?" Mack smiled and said, "Yeah. I'm surprised that someone so lovely and charming would go out with you." The family never seemed to notice.

son. Everyone—including his siblings—looked like a dead-end kid next to him. He dressed nicely, talked nicely, played fairly, never lied, never cheated, never did anything but try to mind his own business, and that of others if they asked him. He possessed a deep sense of fairness and any time he lost his temper—maybe once a year—you could bet your bottom dollar it was because someone had hurt someone he loved. And an added pleasure—Eric is a bashful charmer, knows it, and can use it to good advantage. Just like his dad.

The death of his father in the fall of 1981 hit him extremely hard, but Eric found solace in taking on some of his father's responsibilities. He helped his mother by doing yardwork unasked, helped out at KLM, did things such as carve the family roasts, and not only did his actions help him adjust, but they made him feel close to Sid as well. He also switched from a college prep program in high school to work-study, in preparation for working full-time at KLM instead of going to college. His mother argued on that point, but when he kept citing Sid's background, his success, Karen eventually backed down and gave her permission. He started dating once in a while, but under pain of death wouldn't bring a girl anywhere near his nosy family.

In the fall of 1983, his mother formally hired Eric as assistant service manager, a position he would work at for twenty hours a week over the course of his senior year of high school. He was nervous: "I don't want the other guys to think I'm getting an unfair advantage." To which his mother replied, "You aren't. That's the lowest position in the shop." The other employees had no problems working with him—it was clear that Eric had won the job on his own hard work, and not as the boss's kid.

Throughout the dreadful, painful break between his mother and Diana over the next six months, Eric was the sole member of the family to be in touch with both. His sister's behavior infuriated him, but on the other hand, his mother's behavior was bizarre. And with his brief romance with Mary Frances Sumner (who was living at the Fairgates') and his volunteer work for Assemblyman Sumner's campaign, Eric had his hands full.

He graduated from high school in June of 1984 and started work full-time at KLM. In October, when his mother left for her partnership in Lotus Point, Eric assumed all financial responsibilities for KLM in addition to his service job. A few weeks later, Karen made him manager of the whole shop. The employees were enthusiastic, but Eric secretly was not. He was thinking what he had always thought unthinkable—that maybe, after all these years, he really didn't like the car business. That maybe, he had for so long equated KLM with his father, that he had too quickly assumed that KLM was him too. It wasn't that he wasn't good at the work; it simply did not make him very happy or satisfied. He longed to be outdoors more, longed for something other than cars. Construction maybe. But he said nothing and ran a tight, reliable, friendly shop in the Fairgate tradition.

In the fall of 1985 Eric cautiously hinted to his mother that KLM was not really his dream of life's work. After a long discussion, he admitted to her he was interested in the kind of thing Karen was doing out at Lotus Point; he yearned to be out and about and around, working on something as big, beautiful, complex, and ever-changing as Lotus Point. After Karen conferred with Aunt Abby, he was surprised by their offer to come to Lotus Point as assistant manager of operations. Grinning from ear to ear, he accepted and plunged right in.

In April of 1986, Eric was hospitalized after unknowingly working in a chemical waste dump that was under a Lotus Point expansion area. He nearly died of arsenic poisoning, but his sturdy constitution pulled him through to complete recovery.

Michael Fairgate

SID Why are you trying to make an exception with Michael?
KAREN Because he *is* an exception.
                    —Sid and Karen Fairgate, 1980

Every parent with a daughter in Knots Landing says a silent prayer of thanks for Michael's being a Fairgate. With his alarming good looks, heaven only knows what a young man with a different upbringing would be charming out of his female class-mates. He was born with attributes that men dream of possessing: an athletic prow-ess that borders on the supernatural, a body of a young god, a face of divine cre-ation, and the spirit of wild horses.

But guess what? If you told him that, he'd smile, shrug his shoulders, and not have the slightest idea what you were talking about. He's just Michael Fairgate. You know, just a guy. If pressed, he might admit, well, a nice guy.

Michael's birth in 1967 was more like flying a kite than it was delivering a baby. Although having done it twice before, Karen Fairgate couldn't anticipate how easy or difficult it was going to be, but apparently the wind was just right because Mi-chael came sailing out. He was never still, not for one minute, making Diana's babyhood look like passive submission. And was he ever a screamer too! He was never sick like Diana was; Michael just liked to remind his family of his presence—like every five minutes.

There were predictable inheritances for Michael—his energy, his athletic gift, his high IQ—but the intensity of each was a bit startling. And so was his coloring. Just *where* had this little towhead come from? (Beaming, Sid had said, "He looks just like Abby did at that age," and Karen silently prayed, "Oh Lord, you wouldn't really do *that* to us, would you?")

Michael loved attention and never had much trouble in getting it. With his quick mouth and his fearless feats of physical prowess (standing on one hand, riding backward on a bicycle, parachuting off the garage roof), he not only got attention, but often applause as well. He was a restless student in school, but did well aca-demically, and teachers and students both liked him a lot.

With the new school year in 1980, Michael started feeling and acting a bit strangely. He was, well, kind of fidgety, jittery, restless beyond the norm. He was incapable of sitting still for half a minute, was reprimanded for misbehaving in school, and his parents often found him up in the middle of the night, zooming around in circles in the living room dark. And he couldn't explain to anyone why he was doing these things because he didn't know himself.

His parents finally sat him down and asked him directly about his schoolwork. Michael tried to explain, "I'm trying, Dad, but there's so much to remember, I get bored. Pretty soon, I'm all confused. The teachers start treating me different, and the

Michael's class picture from the sixth grade.

There is no mystery about how Michael developed the nickname "The Hunk," given to him by the girls at Knots Landing High.

kids laugh and so I feel lousy. I hate it, Dad! I just want to be like everyone else." And breaking into tears, he sobbed, "What's wrong with me?" His mother's suggestion to see a psychiatrist met with Michael's horror—the only kid in the class who saw a shrink was Herbie Franklin "and he's definitely a weirdo!"

Michael was so relieved to be told by Dr. Russelman that his problem—hyperkinesis—was physical and not mental, that he tried his best to follow his no-sugar diet and hard physical regimen. The difficulties paid off, and it was not long before he started feeling like himself again. His grades soared, his record cleaned up, and he felt good. To this day, Michael still largely adheres to his old regimen (he has grown out of the condition), resulting in A1 physical condition and near straight A's in school.

His father's death was a hard blow, from which Michael was slow to recover. For months he would read the obituary column every morning, searching for people younger than his father who had died. To find one gave him a sign of it somehow being okay. He was terrified that something might happen to his mother too, and he doggedly followed her around out of fear, until, gradually, the pain of loss subsided, and with it, many of his fears. He was very happy when his mother married Mack MacKenzie, and found a new kind of father in him. Not a replacement—Mack would never try to be that—but a father figure all the same. He's even come to call him "Dad".

High school life is currently treating Michael well, a life well earned. He is on the student council, is captain of the basketball and baseball teams, and is the most sought-after guy by girls on campus. He is also, his mother is proud to point out, the most outspoken advocate in his school for the ERA and the reduction of nuclear arms. And in the spring of 1986, he played a crucial part in making his cousin, Olivia Cunningham, face up to her addiction to marijuana.

The Averys

RICHARD I don't like this master-slave relationship with Scooter. He says jump, and you jump.

LAURA You're describing what my relationship used to be like with *you*. You're just upset it isn't like that anymore.

—Richard and Laura Avery, 1981

Richard L. Avery

"I could say Richard isn't as bad as he seems, but I've been wrong before."

—Laura Avery, 1980

He's the kind of person you wish you hadn't given your phone number to.

At first meeting, he *seems* sincere, helpful, smart, confident, and interested. And he has this way of using his eyes to seductive advantage; for women, it is a mischievous little boy look, for men it turns to the cocksure glint of a winner. But then, later, when you've known him awhile, it's like—oh dear, what to *do* with this guy? This guy to whom hints are meant to be ignored and tact is something one does in a sailboat.

He is a social climber and the worst kind of player of angles, mainly because he never pulls them off. Oh, yes, to be fair, many times Richard means well, but then, a second later, there he is careening off the path of good intentions in pursuit of easy money, prestige, or sex. Even when Richard got honest with himself in 1983—realizing that the charade was over, that he could no longer pretend the way he lived his life worked—he couldn't face the changes life demanded of him. There was nowhere for him to hide in Knots Landing anymore, no one left to make excuses for him. Not even himself.

Richard Avery was born to working-class parents in Washington, D.C., in 1943. He had one older brother, Philip, but never gave up the notion that he was entitled to the rights of an only child. And his mother didn't help matters. Philip was very much like Richard's father—silent, hardworking, extremely independent—and Richard's mother felt shut out by them both, neither displaying much emotion, and so in Richard she found an eager recipient of her attention and affection.

Mrs. Avery smothered him with love and assured him twenty times a day that he was God's gift to humanity. In return, Richard was cocky, arrogant, and contemptuous of anything or anyone who did not agree with his mother. He never cleaned his room (or even hung up a shirt, for that matter), never washed a dish, never mowed a lawn. He was an unbelievably bad sport and had virtually no friends; but it didn't bother him since he always found something terribly wrong with everyone. He was small for his age and hated the fact, and grew a ten-foot mouth to compensate. He ignored homework assignments, attended classes at his leisure, but invariably aced exams. Although his teachers found him insufferable, they begrudgingly had to admit to Mrs. Avery that, yes (sigh), Richard was extremely bright.

When Richard was fifteen, Philip died in a motorcycle accident. Richard didn't talk about it, but inwardly missed his brother terribly. Philip had never had any patience with him, but the brothers had loved each other. Mrs. Avery's devotion to Richard became even more obsessive, and Richard was content to allow it.

Exercising before bedtime, 1979. Although on this night, as on most others, Richard told Laura he was too tired to have sex, he seemed to have a miraculous burst of energy a few days later with Sid Fairgate's ex-wife, Susan Philby, while she was visiting Knots Landing.

By the end of high school, Richard had great grades, but an absolutely abysmal track record in every other regard, resulting in—to his shock—no scholarship offers. He applied to Georgetown as a paying student and was accepted and, without so much as a passing thought to the extreme financial hardship it would put on his parents, tossed them the bills. He continued to live at home, majored in business, and graduated with honors in 1965. Fearing the draft, Richard enlisted in the service.

As Richard tells it, he was in active combat with the Green Berets in Vietnam. The truth was he was a company clerk handling the paperwork for a regiment. How he hated the service! He was constantly in trouble, having no concept of picking up after himself; but once he demonstrated his head for paperwork, he managed to wheel and deal himself into having a couple of privates do it for him. When, after a year, it appeared he might actually have to serve somewhere closer to his fighting regiment than from a thousand miles away, Richard paperworked himself into the Coast Guard.

He finished his hitch in 1968 and returned to D.C., where he took his law boards. He was accepted at Georgetown, but then after taking advantage of the GI bill, the government descended on him, investigating his rather peculiar tour of duty. True to form, Richard told them what they could do with their bill, that he didn't need their help, and presented the tuition bills to his parents. Heartbroken, his mother admitted that they were still thousands of dollars in debt from his undergraduate days.

This was alarming news indeed. He told his parents off and declared he would support himself. And he was moving out, too! When he actually did move out, he instantly regretted it. It cost him a fortune. He took out a number of loans to cover school, but his living expenses, yikes! He *had* to eat all his meals out, he *had* to send his laundry out, he *had* to have a cleaning person, and he *had* to, well. . . . There was so much wrong with girls in those days, according to Richard, that he *had* to go to prostitutes.

In 1968, at a fellow law student's party (which Richard had crashed out of loneliness), he met the most incredible woman—Laura Murphy. It wasn't that she was beautiful (which she was); it had something to do with her personality. To Richard, she was extraordinary; to anyone else, *she was just like his mother.* There was nothing she wouldn't do for him. She never disagreed, always complimented him, smothered him with affection, waited on him hand and foot, and also gave Richard sex of a caliber he had never dreamed of. Over Mr. Murphy's stern objections, Richard moved quickly and married her in 1969.

Laura and her father put Richard through law school, and he worked hard at his studies to prove to her that he was worth the investment. He graduated in 1970 and, on the strength of a brilliant piece published in the law review on *Delta Cattle* v. *Illinois,* was offered a job in Los Angeles with Pincus, Simpson & Lyle, a top drawer firm. Richard was exuberant; Laura was bursting with pride. They moved into an apartment in L.A., where Richard was tickled to make Laura a full-time housewife. In 1972 she gave him the most precious gift imaginable—their first child, Jason. Richard worked like crazy at the firm to push his family ahead.

Richard was a very good lawyer, except that his demeanor, his mouth, or *something* troubled his career at Pincus. The partners there were all from old money and manners, and while they valued Richard, they did not consider him one of them. They never invited him to play golf, or even to have lunch, though other lawyers, not as good but more polished than Richard, were. It drove Richard nuts.

With Jason to care for, Richard was bound and determined to buy a house—only, with what? He played the stock market with no success, but kept trying; money just seemed to slip away. He *never* had any. He fell into the habit of borrowing here and there, using assets already borrowed against as collateral, and more than once was forced to go to Mr. Murphy for a bail-out loan.

One day in early 1979, he overheard some of the partners discussing new houses going up in Knots Landing. Richard listened, and not being able to help himself, blurted out, "Oh, yeah, Laura and I are moving in there soon." There, he had said it. Gulp. Now what? Just move and figure it out when they got there. And figure he did. And finagled and schemed and worked his tail off, his down payment done with mirrors. But boy, was it ever worth it. Laura cried when he showed her the house—four bedrooms, a tremendous yard—and Richard had to admit, he cried too because it was so beautiful.

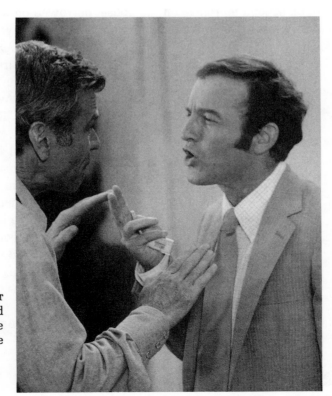

Arguing with Sid Fairgate over how he handled his attempted rape case. He insisted he had done the right thing (by trying to bribe the woman); Sid fired him.

Richard gets annoyed as Laura growls at him to stop trying to borrow money from their friends while they're eating dinner, 1979.

Richard Avery had arrived.

In October Richard ran for a seat on the School Board, a position he was convinced would show him off to the community. He wanted to win in the worst way and conducted his expensive campaign (for which the Averys were the only contributor) on a platform of condemning liberal teachers like David Crane. Unfortunately, his neighbor Karen Fairgate was adamantly for Crane and ran her own campaign, *against* Richard, hanging banners all over town that read, "Vote for *Teachers,* not Preachers. Vote *No* on Avery for School Board." Richard lost, 140 to 148, each vote costing him $18.36, money the Averys did not have.

By December, even Laura had gotten wind of their precarious financial condition, but she didn't even know the half of it. The most pressing crises came from Richard's losing $5,000 in cash and $20,000 on margin in a "sure thing" stock investment in Drilco Oil Company, the only return on Richard's investment being a bankruptcy notice. Richard was desperate for the cash to cover the debt. He had already taken out a second mortgage on the house, borrowed on his insurance policies, and owed thousands to the only neighbor who had any money, Sid Fairgate. Sid was willing to loan him $5,000, on the condition that Richard *sign* something this time; and the other $20,000, after much pleading, came from Laura's father. Only, the check was made out to Laura, who put a list of demands on it: They had to cut their expenses, Laura was getting a job, and she would do *all* the Averys' finances here on in. After kicking and screeching, his back against the wall, Richard gave in and Laura took over.

Absolutely despising Laura's working at a real estate agency, Richard pushed harder at work. He proved his mettle to an important client, Lynn Baker Cargill; Cargill made overtures about a job with his firm in Chicago. Richard gleefully told his employers to take their job and stick it. But then, oh dear, when the actual job offer was detailed, Richard was aghast to find the salary not to be the $100,000 he had been planning on, but $28,500. And he *had* been making $37,500!

Depressed, jobless, Richard stayed home and did the cooking (since *Laura* was at work), played golf in the living room, went on an occasional job interview and, *and,* started an affair with idle Abby Cunningham across the street. The latter roused him out of the doldrums.

In January of 1981, Richard landed a job as associate general counsel for Kipler,

Janson & Stearns, a brokerage firm, with a starting salary of $35,000. But leave it to Laura—she sold a house the same week and the commission on it was $36,000! Hating her success, he turned to Abby for comfort, who in turn bounced him out of her bed.

His marriage, at this point, was rocking and rolling all over the place. Richard suspected that Laura was getting it on with her boss, Scooter Warren, but hadn't any proof. Their fights were horrendous, and Laura's sharp tongue was no picnic to be around. How Laura had changed! From the sweet, kind, obedient little mate he had married and lived with for ten years to such a cold, calculating, selfish witch!

In October of 1981, Richard's boss, Andy Parkhurst, asked him to do a favor. Could he round up some "interesting" women to entertain a very important client? Richard got phone numbers from party boy neighbor Kenny Ward and came up with two gorgeous girls for the client to choose from. Parkhurst was very pleased and in November asked Richard for another "favor," a party for some Japanese businessmen. Reluctantly Richard employed a call girl, Marni, to organize the evening's festivities. The party went very well but Marni accidentally overdosed on pills and booze and Richard ended up staying up all night, throwing her in the shower and walking her around, and succeeded in saving her life. The next day at the office, he was given airline tickets and a $1,000 cash bonus from Parkhurst in appreciation of a job well done.

December brought requests from other partners in the firm to connect with "Richard's girls," making him feel like a pimp. His frustration and guilt from the situation at the office spilled over to home and he and Laura resumed their fighting with a vengeance. It was by far the worst period of their marriage. Then, in the middle of it, in January, Laura told him she was pregnant. Richard was overjoyed! This was exactly what they needed to get their marriage back on track! Laura at first did not respond, but then when she did, Richard wished she hadn't. "Oh, God, why can't I just say it?" she cried. "I don't love you anymore. I have to leave you." And she did.

That bleak, horrible February, Parkhurst forced yet another favor from him. Richard came home angry, and when Laura rebuffed his plea for her and Jason to move back, he stormed over to Marni's place, got drunk, and ranted and raged to her about Parkhurst and what he was making him do. The following week, Richard was watching a television news special, an exposé on corporate pimping. Richard suddenly bolted upright. He was hearing his own voice on the show! "Parkhurst, Janson and Stearns runs its whole business with hookers. We're always entertaining a lot of

Stringing popcorn with his neighbor Karen Fairgate. After Sid's accident, Richard brought meals and changes of clothes to the hospital for her. When Sid died, he handled the funeral arrangements and the insurance claims, and was the executor of Sid's will. Richard and Karen became best friends after that, Karen often being his sole support through his mental breakdown.

clients from out of town. The theory is, if we show the client a good time, they take our recommendations. So, we hire high-class call girls. What the hell, it's all tax deductible." Marni had taped him.

Richard arrived at work the next day to be handed an official press release: "Parkhurst, Janson & Stearns announced today that Richard Avery, an attorney with the firm, has tendered his resignation pending an investigation into alleged improprieties. It was brought to the firm's attention that Mr. Avery, in his zeal to attract clients, utilized his connection with known prostitutes. Parkhurst, Janson & Stearns wishes to assure its clients and customers that this is an isolated incident."

Richard was finished.

Grabbing for any kind of comfort, he turned to Abby, who refused to have anything to do with him. He tried to woo Laura back again, and when she refused him again, he pulled an (empty) gun on her so she and Jason would stay in the house and talk. The police blocked off the cul-de-sac and sent in a SWAT team, though Richard made it clear he didn't want to hurt anyone, he only wanted to straighten things out with Laura. Clearly having slipped over the edge, the police delivered him to a psychiatric hospital, where he stayed in treatment through March. (Because the hospital had such a wealthy, heavily medicated clientele, Richard called it "Club Meds.") Karen was the only one to visit him for a long while.

When he was released, Richard moved home, alone; he tried to keep busy by running with Valene Ewing, eating dinner with the Fairgates, and playing racquetball with Kenny. He was still in therapy, but Richard thought his best cure would be to become Laura's Lamaze partner. She refused and he got more and more depressed, starting to draft out suicide notes.

Summing up what little energy he had, Richard went back to Parkhurst to apologize and beg for his old job back. The firm—terrified at seeing him—called Laura to come and get him out of there. Richard, in the middle of his plea, was astonished when Laura suddenly came striding in, declaring, "You don't want to work here. Look around you. What do you see? Look at that degenerate behind the desk. Do you want to entrust your future to him, Richard? He's dismal, he's obsolete, and he's —*tacky.*" Richard beamed at her and then said, "Mr. Parkhurst, I withdraw my application."

Laura and Jason moved back home, and Richard, happy as could be, madly set about reading everything on natural childbirth he could find. It was a good thing, since when the great day arrived, Richard ended up delivering Daniel himself.

Richard's next adventure began when he happened into a leasing agent trying to unload a restaurant. Richard's mind filled with dreams when he saw the interior. Always having been a fine food and wine freak, he knew in his heart that this is what he wanted to do. He turned down a job offer and leased the restaurant instead. At first Laura went berserk, but on second thought, she turned around and gave him the down payment as a present. Karen came through with a $15,000 investment, and Gary Ewing pledged an investment as well. Abby, however, delivered the money to Richard with an agreement to sign, one giving the restaurant to Gary Ewing Enterprises in the case of default. Richard signed.

Daniel opened its posh doors in November and lost money every night, prompting Laura's involvement to protect their money, and the Ewings' insistence that Richard start late-night live entertainment in the form of Ciji Dunne. Richard was against it, but had no choice since he was behind in his payments to Abby.

The Averys knocked themselves out, and while Richard liked having Laura around, he didn't like her developing friendship at the restaurant with Ciji. In fact, he really started to get angry about it. Friendship was one thing, but to cut out

Opening night at Daniel, which all the Averys' friends and neighbors attended. Richard insisted that dinners were on the house, only for Laura to come swooping over to assure everyone they were *not*. Seated are Ciji Dunne, Kenny and Ginger Ward; Mack MacKenzie is on the left, Joe Cooper on the right.

attention to her husband in favor of this girl was not Richard's idea of a good marriage. And then, in January, Laura said she wanted to go back to work in real estate because, "Lately, I feel like we're stuck together with Krazy Glue, twenty-five hours a day. I think maybe the answer is that I need to be on my own more." Richard agreed, but was increasingly jealous as Ciji took up what little time Laura had outside of work and motherhood.

Richard finally confronted Laura about the time she was spending with Ciji—at their house, over at her apartment; morning, afternoon, night—and Laura refused to discuss it. Then, one night in February of 1983, Chip Roberts took Richard aside and said, "You know, if I were you, I'd keep an eye on what that broad was doing with my wife." Richard went wild with assumption and jealousy, threatened Ciji, and positively exploded when he found Ciji in his house again, alone with his wife in what appeared to him as a compromising position. He demanded to know, once and for all, what was going on, but Laura's response was not what he expected:

> LAURA Come on, Richard, you know it's over. We tried and we
> couldn't make it. It's nobody's fault—or if it is, it's *ours*.
> Why bring Ciji into it?
>
> RICHARD What's over? I never—
>
> LAURA Our marriage! Can't we please admit it, try to remain
> friends, and go our separate ways? I think you should
> move out. Soon. Now.

And then Ciji was murdered. Now that what he thought was the competition was gone, he rushed to Laura's grieving side and supported her through the aftermath. He assumed Laura would stay with him now, but he assumed wrong. She was appreciative of his support, was sorry, but she needed time to herself.

Finally accepting that his marriage was at an end, that his restaurant would always flounder—even if it survived—Richard gave up. He fixed up things around the house, cleaned out the garage and installed an electric door opener, cashed in his insurance policy, and requested that the check be made out to Laura. And in the dead of night in March of 1983, Richard Avery slipped a picture of his family under his arm, and drove out of the cul-de-sac for the last time.

No one has seen or heard from him since.

Laura Murphy Avery Sumner

"Don't run yourself down. I've watched you. You've got plenty of reasons to feel great about yourself. . . . You're smart, you're beautiful, and you're funny."

—Ciji Dunne, 1982

She was born to fly with the grace of an angel.

Well, yes, admittedly, life *has* forced her into using a broomstick on occasion. And yes, it's true what they say about the sting of her tongue making the sword of Zorro feel like kid's play. But what is equally true is that Laura Avery is Knots Landing's most widely misunderstood citizen. Her extreme self-consciousness is seen as coldness, her life-necessitated defenses as weapons, her pursuit of security as pushy, and her stunning appearance as vanity.

She is an extremely complex person and—as her neighbors will tell you—it takes a great deal of time and effort to penetrate the facade to get to the real person underneath. And while outsiders admire her loveliness but complain about her hot-and-cold temperament, her friends gather closer, trying to assist her in the ongoing struggle: Laura must break her life-long pattern of misplacing her love, and to—at long last—direct some love toward herself.

Laura Murphy was born in 1948 in Pittsburgh, the youngest of four children in a staunchly Irish Catholic family. Her sister and brothers were loud, boisterous, good-looking, and confident, whereas Laura, while a nice-looking child, was small and quiet. Her siblings were forever taking advantage of her passive disposition and by the age of seven, she recalls, "I used to feel like I was invisible. People never noticed me. . . . I kept doing things to attract attention—*any* attention. Not bad things— good things." Unfortunately, Laura could have good-girled her parents to death and still be lost in that boisterous family. But she never gave up trying.

School was difficult for her. She was so shy and self-conscious that she made few friends. It wasn't that other children didn't like her; it was just that no one really knew her. And the expectations of her teachers! What torture! Being a Murphy meant, in their book, star athletes, cheerleaders, class officers, and debaters, all of which were beyond Laura's comprehension. Her schoolwork, with the exception of math, did not come easily. "I was the kid who worked twice as hard as anyone else just to get B's. . . . It was always like that—nothing seemed to be enough. I always had to do more, or do it better, or faster."

At home she readily learned to cook and clean, do errands, and help her dad outside with the yardwork. When she was eleven her mother was diagnosed as having cancer, and suddenly Laura had a prominent role in the house. She assumed her mother's household duties without complaint and became a devoted nurse, spending afternoons and entire nights next to her mother's sickbed, reading to her,

The model housewife, 1979.

dispensing medicine, and later, feeding her and changing her bedclothes. Her mother was grateful and happily surprised at how bright and affectionate her youngest was. Despite the ravages of her mother's illness, Laura basked in the attention. Taking care of her mother gave her a sense of purpose, of worth, of importance.

She was devastated by her mother's death the following year. Somehow, despite everything she had been told, she had believed that her love and care would ensure her mother's life. Her shock turned to grief, and then to anger. When left alone with her coffin before the funeral, Laura, with tears running down her face, said, "I hate you, Mommy, for doing this to me."

Laura redirected her love to the only place it seemed likely to be reciprocated, her father. Mr. Murphy was too preoccupied to see her needs. Laura would have gladly killed herself if it had meant he would pay attention to her. She settled instead on putting her all into replacing her mother. She did all the shopping, cooking, cleaning, laundry, dishes—anything and everything to make her father happy. He wasn't. He felt lonely and alienated, and found Laura's eyes—so like her mother's—painful to look at for long. But he did notice when Laura got to be that age when he did not want to have to deal with a daughter. Adolescence.

Against her protests, Mr. Murphy enrolled Laura in an all-girl parochial school so she could spend time with other women. Laura was miserable. Most of the girls had been in the school for years, and as a newcomer, she failed all their tests. If she had been shy before, here she was downright terrified. The uniform, the other girls setting her up for trouble with the nuns—it was awful! She became absolutely obsessed with the fear of making a mistake, and in the classroom felt so awkward that her flustered attempts at participation always resulted in her humiliation.

More alarming, she shot up several inches, her body undergoing changes into womanhood. She picked up the facts of life from odd bits strewn here and there, the most important story being about how a girl had sinned with a boy (whatever that was), got pregnant, and had an abortion. The girl had her day of reckoning and bled to death, right there in the halls of St. Mary's. Well, that's what they said.

One day in class, Laura lost her temper, so much so that she forgot to be shy and shot off some back talk to one of the class bullies. The class broke up in laughter, and afterward, some of the girls said hi to her in the halls. Laura liked that response and tentatively experimented; she discovered that her mind was full of spontaneous, clever, sarcastic remarks. When she was lectured that the word "sarcasm" came from the Greek word *sarcazo,* meaning "to tear flesh," Laura thought that was just great. Just let them try to mess with her!

Her teenage years, in physical ways, were more than kind to Laura. Her uniform was unable to hide the fact that she was curving in the right places; her carriage was tall, proud; her face, once her bemoaning feature (she thought), emerged into something even she couldn't deny was pretty. High cheekbones emerged, her eyes blazed an intense blue, her teeth were perfect and her smile dazzling, and her formerly red hair darkened into a rich auburn. The boys flocked to her, though she was still too wrapped up in pleasing her father to notice.

In 1966 she left home for the first time to attend the University of Connecticut. Upon her arrival and initial stroll around campus, she suddenly realized that she was away, *free.* She didn't have to care for anyone but herself, didn't have any chores, didn't have to attend church if she didn't want to; Laura didn't know what to do. And then she did. Laura decided to major in boys.

After years of neglect, Laura initially found a sense of well-being with boys. She didn't throw herself at them; she just sort of let them do whatever they wanted with her. She adored being held and fussed over, and she was several boys along before she thought that maybe there was something wrong with this. Changing her method of operation in the name of being "good," she began to examine each boy as a candidate for marriage. The boys generally couldn't get away fast enough once they sensed that Laura's generosity was actually an overtly needy request for commitment from them. By the time she was a junior, Laura felt lonelier and more lost than ever before. Only she felt something else as well: *bad.*

Enter Richard Avery.

He was a headstrong, spoiled, hopelessly-in-debt braggart. He was no great shakes in the looks department either, but as Laura would explain later, "I kept trying to be someone special in someone's life and . . . then I met Richard. He was a loner, and lonely. He kept coming back—one of the only ones who did." After a brief scare that she was pregnant, Richard proposed and Laura gratefully accepted —besides, she was crazy about him. She dropped out of college and they married in November of 1969.

Laura worked full-time as a secretary to both support them and finish putting

Despite the problems in her marriage, Laura was, physically speaking, positively aglow throughout her pregnancy with Daniel.

Arguing with Greg at his campaign headquarters, 1983, an activity they engaged in more and more as his ties to the Wolfbridge Group became more and more apparent. At one point, Laura said, "Do you want me to stay? Does it matter? Give me one good reason." Greg replied, "I *want* you to stay. But if I were you, I wouldn't." She did.

Richard through law school; she also did all the housework, helped Richard study, and stood passively, devotedly at his side no matter how foul his mood. The fact that he was an ego-centered neurotic didn't seem to come to her notice. Never mind that he didn't pay her any attention half the time, and that when he did, it was usually by yelling about starch in his collars or something; all Laura knew was that when Richard felt like it, they would have sex, and during it, he would tell her over and over how much he loved her. Those were the times she lived for! She felt needed by Richard, protected by him; her role as his wife made her feel important because *Richard* was important.

When Richard graduated and they moved to Los Angeles for his job at a law firm, troubles started for Laura. Richard was working hard at his new job, and while she understood what he was trying to accomplish, she despaired over his loss of interest in sex. She felt unattractive and unloved, and then an alert Chip Todson came along and wished to remedy her situation. She resisted him, but finally, after ten months of no sex and practically no conversation with Richard, she gave in to what would be a two-month sex affair. Richard didn't notice a thing. But that fall, when things at the office settled a bit and Richard was feeling a little more secure, his sexual appetite returned, and Laura, stricken with guilt, immediately severed all ties with Todson. She wouldn't so much as look at another man for seven years, instead focusing her every effort toward Richard and making it up to him.

In 1972 she was given the gift of a child. She had wanted to have a natural childbirth, but Richard said, "Not if I have to be there," so she didn't. Jason was overdue, but his delivery went very well, clocking in under seven hours. He was a little godsend. He had the best traits of both parents—Richard's energy and delight and smarts, Laura's affectionate nature, sense of humor, and good looks. Laura became the model mother and housewife, to the point of self-denial. She had no friends of her own, relying on Richard for everything and making her identity an extension of his. Whenever she felt unbearably repressed or unhappy, whenever she had the urge to break free of the house, then Richard would do something wonderful and she'd be back where she started—his slave.

When Richard surprised her with the house on Seaview Circle in 1979, she thought her heart would burst with happiness. She didn't know how Richard had managed it —he had suffered so many bad breaks in business, to the point where they had borrowed money from her father more than once—but what did it matter? He had done it! This big new house! Her cleaning efforts doubled; Richard's martinis were perfectly chilled and waiting for his arrival in the evenings, her dinners were sumptuous, she kept the lawn pristeen, and by evening, Jason would be too.

There were old problems in her marriage coming back, however. Richard was always "too tired" to have sex, and once again Laura started to feel unloved, unwanted, and unattractive. In October, old friend Chip Todson came back to Knots Landing, representing the Ewing Oil subsidiary, Petrolux Oil, in an offshore drilling venture. Finding out that he was once "a friend" of Laura's, Richard demanded she charm Todson into bringing the Petrolux account to his firm. When approached, Chip gave it to her straight out: Richard could have the account on the condition Laura sleep with him. Under protest, Laura did just that, but Todson did not uphold his end of the bargain.

Having done it once, and since Richard continued to ignore her, Laura started to cast an idle eye. One afternoon she ventured into a cocktail lounge and met an artist and went home with him for a friendly drink. She had maintained the notion of having sex but, after talking with Martin a while, changed her mind. Angry at her backing off, he forced her to have sex. She returned home with her clothes torn and her body bruised, and Richard arrived moments after her, asking what had happened. Feeling trapped, Laura claimed she had been raped at home. Later she confessed to the police that she had been lying, but she never did tell Richard.

In December, Laura tried to pay for a dress at a Knots Landing shop and, right in front of her neighborhood friends, saw her credit card ripped up. The clerk explained that the Averys' credit was radically overextended. Baffled and sure it was a mistake, Laura soon learned differently. Richard had always handled all the money and never allowed her to know anything about what he was doing with it. But this time, asking her father to mortgage his house to bail Richard out was too much! Laura had her father make out the check in *her* name only, and told Richard that she was getting a job to make sure her dad got paid back. (Richard had never made the slightest effort to pay the thousands back that he already owed him.) And on top of that, from here on in she was handling *all* the Averys' finances.

She was hired at Southland Realty as the secretary to the owner, Scooter Warren. The job opened a whole other world to Laura, one where her quick mind, bright wit, and hard work were well appreciated. When she demonstrated how she could calm

Ciji look-alike Cathy Geary had an instinctive trust of Laura, although it gave the latter the creeps to look at her for a while. When Gary threw Abby off the ranch, Laura, however, gave Cathy a little friendly insight into Gary's character.

LAURA   Since I've know Gary, he's never been alone. He went from Val to Abby without skipping a beat.

CATHY   You think that's what he's doing with me?

LAURA   I think he's trying to drown his troubles in the next available woman. Gary is a binger. If it isn't booze, it's fast cars or money or sex.

Although Cathy didn't heed her warning, Laura took her in after Gary abruptly dumped her. The two became close friends.

and steer even the most difficult client, Scooter picked up on her inherent flair for the business. As a secretary, she closed a deal for Scooter, selling a $750,000 Tudor house to a customer Scooter had just given up on. Under his tutelage, Laura studied for her real estate license.

At the tail end of November, Laura received her license and was made an associate realtor, earning a fifty-fifty split on commissions. Richard reacted to her achievement with unbridled sarcasm, bitterness, and jealousy. He hated her working, and now that he was out of a job, hated the idea of her being successful. At a neighborhood celebration in honor of her receiving her license, about the nicest thing Richard had to say was, "Ranks right up there with the discovery of the Rosetta Stone."

Their marriage was a fiasco by December of 1980. Richard threw his affair with Abby Cunningham in Laura's face, but she largely tried to ignore it (since by this time she was actually happier being left alone). She was doing extremely well at work—simply thriving on every minute of it—and as always, her time with Jason was a joy. That left little room for Richard's demands. He never asked about her, about what she was doing, and since he wasn't doing anything, they had nothing to talk about. When a wealthy and *very* good-looking client, David Souther, tried to woo Laura, she reluctantly declined, explaining, "Right now, I feel about my life the way you do about your house: anxious to move in, but not really sure where to start."

When Richard landed a new job and was feeling better about himself, a major strain on their marriage was lifted, only to be replaced by another. Richard freaked when Laura sold the Sgaro house for $1,200,000—raking in a $36,000 commission—more money than he made in a year.

The New Year of 1981 brought more criticism and resentment from Richard, and more kudos at the office. As the best salesperson, Scooter promoted her to sales manager and boosted her commission rate. The jealousy of some of her colleagues started rumors that Laura and Scooter were having an affair. They weren't. They were in agreement that there was too much at risk to have sex together, including their friendship. By the end of the year, Scooter was her best friend and confidant. For Christmas she received from him not only a generous cash bonus, but a spanking new Mercedes as well; a small return, he said, for someone who had sold $5 million' worth of houses in one year.

Scooter's wife left him shortly thereafter, and he tried to coax Laura into the affair they had agreed not to have. Laura gently declined, but not because things were so great at home these days. Richard had grown more and more distant, suddenly refusing to talk about his job. As she explained, "At first I thought he was just coming off a high. He stopped talking about his work. Refused to talk about it, in fact. When I pressed him he'd snap at me, start in about my neglecting Jason—all the old stuff. Lately, we hardly talk at all except to fight and we've even lost our enthusiasm for that."

In January, Laura finally leapt into an affair with Scooter. She wasn't ready to move in with him, but she was ready to leave Richard. It had been years since their marriage had held anything good, and their constant hostility was taking its toll on Jason. When she was just about to tell Richard, Dr. Gold informed her she was expecting (Richard's child).

Richard was elated and Laura felt suicidal. Finally, not being able to stand it anymore, she told him that babies don't fix bad marriages and moved out, taking Jason with her into a condo. And then Richard was exposed as an alleged corporate pimp. Poor Richard was so down and out that all of Laura's old tapes started run-

Young Daniel gets to blow out a candle, Thanksgiving, 1984. Laura believes with all her heart, "When you have kids, they become a part of every decision you make. Your life is never the same. Whatever happens throughout the day, being with them makes everything worth it."

At Gary Ewing's funeral.

GREG   You're good for me. You remind me of myself. The best parts of me. I count on you. . . . I love you. Don't make me say these things. It embarrasses me.

With Greg and his mother at the Galveston Ranch, when Mack MacKenzie was approached to fill Greg's vacated Senate seat.

LAURA All I want to hear is, did you set this up? I'd like to hear a little honesty for a change.

RUTH That is not the issue. I think the issue is whose side you're on.

LAURA I didn't know we were taking sides. What's the truth got to do with taking sides?

RUTH What's best for Gregory is the truth.

ning: *Go help Richard, go save Richard, Richard* needs *you*. She fought hard to resist them. Her suspicions that her husband was losing his mind proved correct when he held her and Jason hostage. To talk, he said. Scared as she was, she nevertheless broke his calm dissertation with, "Distance ourselves? The house is surrounded by cops; you're sitting there with a gun in your lap and you're talking about *emotional distance?*"

After Richard was released from the psychiatric hospital in the fall of 1982, Laura was still worried about him. No matter what her bad feeling, she and Richard did share a history, a son, a child on the way, and . . . she still cared. When she found a draft of a suicide note of his, Laura ignored her weary heart and moved back in.

The frightening circumstances around the birth of her child changed her feelings for Richard somewhat. They got stranded on the way to the hospital, and only Richard was there to deliver the baby. When the little child came out and was not breathing, Laura went into the Hail Marys of her childhood while Richard resuscitated their son to life. In celebration of the baby's survival, they named him Daniel.

In gratitude, Laura gave Richard the down payment for his restaurant, Daniel, and worked there part-time. By December, however, Richard had stopped going to his psychiatrist and it was showing; he was driving Laura nuts again with his constant complaints, ill humor, and "poor me" 's. She became friendly with Ciji Dunne, a young singer who was working there. Ciji was so sympathetic to Laura's situation and unhappiness that, despite herself, Laura started opening up to her. After all, it was no secret what her life was like: "Richard and I are beyond privacy. Our marriage is a neighborhood joke."

Ciji too was enduring all kinds of problems and Laura was a willing confidante. They became devoted friends and Ciji often came over to the Averys to talk, watch TV, or play with the children. Richard, completely reverting to his bratty self, made no secret of his dislike of Laura's friendship. So used to his jealousy over the years, Laura wrote it off to Richard's intolerance for anyone else being in her life.

She underestimated him. By February Richard had convinced himself that Laura and Ciji were lovers, and actually threatened Ciji. Laura thought it was hysterical, as did Ciji, but then when Ciji was brutally murdered a week later, Laura stopped laughing . . . for a long, long time. The loss of her friend was bad enough, but this— cold-blooded murder of someone so gentle, so kind, and so inherently good. . . .

Richard was incredibly supportive during the first days of her grief, but then when

Laura told him that, no, things wouldn't "go back to normal" between them, that the marriage was over, Richard disappeared. Gone. Vanished without a trace.

Laura, convinced that Richard had murdered Ciji, begged the police to track him down. She was strangled by the sense of betrayal, of loss, and she spent many a long night hating and missing Richard, missing and mourning Ciji.

Pulling herself back together as best she could—she had a family to support now—Laura went back to work. In October she sold a huge ranch to Gary Ewing, and he surprised her by offering her an investment job at Ewing Enterprises. He wanted her also to keep him abreast of what Abby was up to there. It sounded challenging and exciting, and the money was good, so she happily accepted.

Working with Abby was quite a trip. She'd ask for one thing done to keep Laura busy elsewhere, while she secretly closed deals and buried them in the books. One of Laura's more interesting tasks was to try and buy out Karen MacKenzie's half of a beachfront apartment building. When Karen refused and Laura reported back to Abby, Laura sensed something was up—something big. Abby didn't get that funny look in her eye over nothing. So, putting on her beguiling charms, Laura seduced Abby's lawyer, Jim Westmont, into doing a little talking. He revealed that Abby was setting up a holding company to issue checks to Karen, making it appear that the apartment building they co-owned was providing a steady income when, in fact, it was being torn down to make way for something else. What the something was, Laura wanted to know.

The news broke that Chip Roberts had been Ciji's real killer, and Laura, at long last, could absolve Richard of that in her mind. She wondered where he had gone, but truly, she was relieved. Peace had finally settled on her little family. More and more she was getting used to the idea of being the boys' sole emotional and financial support, and more and more she was determined to create a nest egg for them in the event that something happened to her.

Laura learned that the new something to be built on the beach was to be a colossal resort complex called Lotus Point, and Abby bargained with her about working on it and keeping a tight lip. Before settling on Laura's percentage of the project, Abby accused her of being greedy, to which Laura responded, "Gary's got his millions. You'll get yours, if you haven't already. Karen's husband died and she's happily remarried. Val's husband left her and she has a bestseller, a new boyfriend, and more money than she had before. Well, my husband left me too. And the little I've got is five percent of profits on Lotus Point."

Laura plunged in, buying out oceanfront homeowners around Abby and Karen's property. She disliked doing it (because many did not want to move), but she offered them generous moving allowances and more than current market price for their houses, which assuaged her conscience a bit. She felt terrible about not being true to Gary, but—darn it—her kids came first!

At Lotus Point, Laura ran into a stone wall with a couple named Marcus, who absolutely refused to sell their house. After reporting this to Abby, Laura was outraged when the Marcus's house "mysteriously" burned to the ground. Abby then declared innocence, blaming her construction partners, the Wolfbridge Group, headed by Marc St. Clair. Laura started getting nervous about her involvement.

A new face seen regularly around the office those days was Assemblyman Gregory Sumner. Laura knew he couldn't possibly be very trustworthy if he knew Abby well, but his charismatic charm, rugged good looks, and sharp humor appealed to her. He was not only working with Abby, but sleeping with newlywed Mrs. Ewing as well, and Laura guiltlessly stole him away from her. Laura did not like Greg's apparent ties with Wolfbridge, but she couldn't help herself. She was falling for him.

All smiles with Karen MacKenzie on her first day on the job at Lotus Point. The two women suffered a severe breach in their friendship during the Wolfbridge affair, but now are closer than ever.

In February, when St. Clair and the Wolfbridge Group threatened the lives of her neighbors, the MacKenzies, Laura demanded to be let out of the Lotus Point project. Abby told her sorry, too late, she was in as deep as everyone else. But when St. Clair proceeded to threaten the well-being of Laura's children, she told Mack MacKenzie about St. Clair's connection to Abby and Lotus Point. She refused, however, to implicate Sumner in any way.

When Gary found out about Laura's involvement, he of course fired her, which she took as her due punishment. But then he turned right around and rehired her, saying, "You know the business. I think now I can trust you. I don't think you'll lie to me again." What she didn't expect was for Abby to come pleading to her, wanting Laura to convince Gary to unfreeze the assets of Ewing Enterprises. If Laura did that, hence getting Lotus Point under way again, she would still get her 5 percent in it. Laura refused but, seeing a new look in Abby's eyes and hearing a new tone in her voice, knew that she must be in desperate trouble with St. Clair. Laura urged Greg to do something to help her. He pooh-poohed it, denying there was anything he could do. Laura was sitting right there in his hotel room when Abby came flying in, revealing not only that Sumner was linked to St. Clair, but that he could have been responsible for Gary's (alleged) death. Greg calmed Laura with a plausible explanation of innocence, but Laura was still badly shaken. She would stick by him for the duration of the Wolfbridge mess, but not without constant demands to be told the truth.

After it was all over, in November of 1984, Greg won his U.S. Senate seat and announced to Laura that he was divorcing his wife. He asked her if she would come to Washington as his assistant. Laura was slow to say yes, even though Greg said that somewhere, down the road, he'd like to think about getting married. Their move to Washington was delayed by trouble from Paul Galveston. When Greg confided in Laura that Galveston was his biological father, Laura could only rub her eyes in apprehension at the kind of trouble that was in the wind.

After Greg stepped down from the Senate to run Galveston Industries, Laura—always wary of his sleight of hand—was desperately trying to make him an honest man. They spent long hours together, Laura often sleeping over at the ranch. Their short-lived peace was rudely interrupted by Greg's mother, and Laura instantly knew where every dubious trait of Greg's had come from. Laura and Ruth hated each other and Laura summed up the situation well: "I know the business about

Galveston's influence and money and spirit and genes, and Sumner's courage and noble ideals. I am properly impressed with the breeding you tried so hard to—breed, in your son and heir. I also know why you dislike me. I keep the Sumner side alive in him. The idealist. He apologizes to me. He explains to me. You want me to leave him to you. At least to leave him."

In May, Laura arrived at the ranch early one morning to find Abby getting dressed. Assuming the worst, and hating Greg for hurting her so, Laura walked out of his life.

Desolate, feeling emotionally ravaged, Laura wearily tried to pick up the pieces of her life and pressed onward, finding another job in real estate. She was not happy on any front; only her children could warm her heart. Sumner's attempts to reconcile with her only caused her pain. And how sick she was of that! She had had enough to last anyone a lifetime.

In November of 1985, Laura's spirits picked up when Karen and Gary offered her a job at Lotus Point as supervisor of improvements. Abby coolly greeted her, but nothing could stifle Laura's excitement to be working hands-on on the project she had helped to realize. She was outdoors a lot, out and around, and her hours were flexible, giving her more time with the children.

After Gary blew up Empire Valley in January of 1986, Laura received a phone call from Greg's assistant, Peter Hollister, telling her that Greg badly needed her. He had never seen Sumner so low, so discouraged, so . . . broken. The old sense of duty calling, Laura rushed to his side. He felt like such a failure, he said; Laura told him that it didn't matter when it came to love. By the end of the month, they were regularly spending nights together. By the end of the month, Laura was more deeply in love than ever. Greg came to her house often, offering to babysit on occasion, and together they enjoyed dinner and long talks in the Avery kitchen. Richard's ghost was finally being exorcised from the house. And as if to confirm it, her divorce came through in March.

Nonetheless, Laura was still worried about Greg. While she was striding forward at Lotus Point, planning and executing its expansion, all Greg seemed to do was sit in his office, pout over Empire Valley, and drink. In April she finally confronted him about it, urging him to *do* something with all of his money—bring water to the Sahara, she didn't care, just do something! She summed up her plea with a request for him to stop posturing and really feel passionate about something again. After a long pause, Greg responded, "Hey, what do you think about getting married?"

They were married in May.

Of all the neighbors of the cul-de-sac, Laura has undergone the most dramatic change since 1979. From a radically insecure person clinging to her (unbearable) husband for an identity, she has blossomed into an extraordinary human being in her own right. As a mother, as a friend, as a neighbor, as a lover, as a businessperson, she has all but excelled in recent times. After years of looking at herself through other people's eyes, she has simply started to live her life in the way that comes naturally to who she really is. You know. Laura. That person she had abandoned so long ago.

And you know what else? She's becoming rather fond of her.

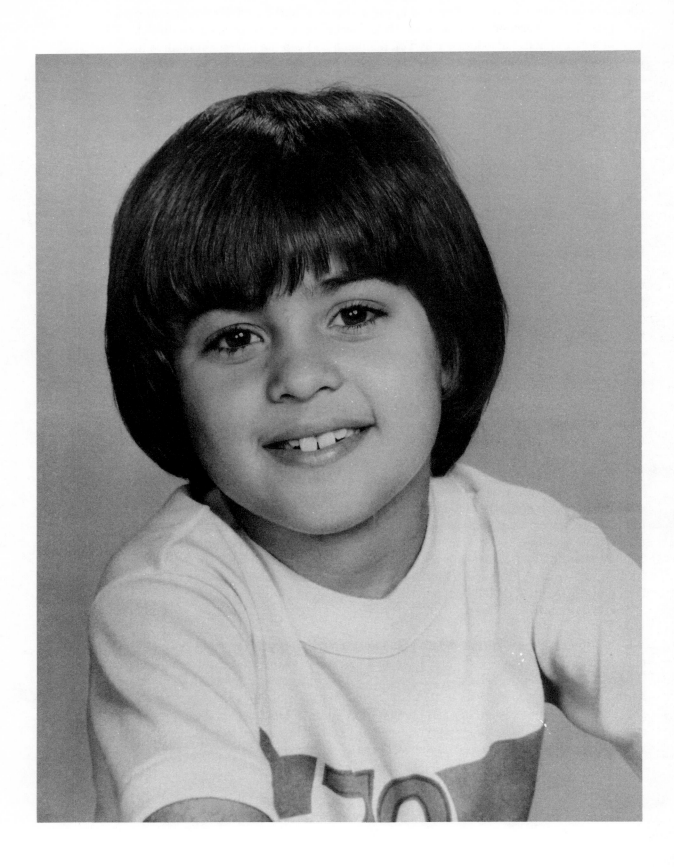

Jason Avery

"I've explained that several times, darling. Daddy and I have problems."

—Laura Avery, 1982

He's a good-looking, bright, energetic, loving young man, but it's anyone's guess what emotional baggage he'll carry into adulthood. For the first eleven years of his life, Jason adored his parents; for the first eleven years of his life, Jason cried alone in his room while his parents yelled and screamed at each other; for the rest of his life, Jason will remember that no matter how good he tried to be, his father abandoned him anyway.

Jason Avery was conceived in 1971 by Laura and Richard Avery at the Little River Inn in Mendocino, California. They were on a scouting trip for bargains in fine wines, but a cold spell occurred, keeping his parents in bed the entire weekend. Jason was born in Ocean Park Hospital in 1972.

His parents, individually, showered him with attention and love, but together all they ever did was fight. Nonetheless Jason has always managed to do well in school. He also loves swimming, snorkeling, karate, fishing, and sailing, and is on the little league team sponsored by Knots Landing Motors. His favorite hobby is computer games, and happily, he was allowed to quit his hated trombone lessons.

His dad abandoned the family in 1983, and although Jason misses him terribly, he is a little relieved that there are no more fights at home. He lives with his mom and baby brother, Daniel, and likes it when Uncle Greg, his stepfather, comes over.

Daniel Avery

"Isn't he the darlingest thing?"
—Lilimae Clements, 1982

It's hard to believe that a marriage as awful as Laura and Richard Avery's could produce such a joyous little child.

Who says miracles don't happen?

Daniel Avery was delivered by his father in his mother's Mercedes-Benz in September of 1982. His parents had been on the way to the hospital when traffic backed up on the highway, prompting them to try a shortcut; they got lost, blew a tire, and then Daniel was arriving whether they liked it or not! When all three finally reached the hospital, he was officially weighed in at a whopping nine pounds three ounces.

His father briefly ran a restaurant in Knots Landing, which was named Daniel in his honor. It was shut down when his father ran away in 1983.

Daniel lives with his mommy and big brother, Jason, in Seaview Circle. He is very fond of Cathy Geary Rush, who lived with them on and off over the years, and wishes she would come back.

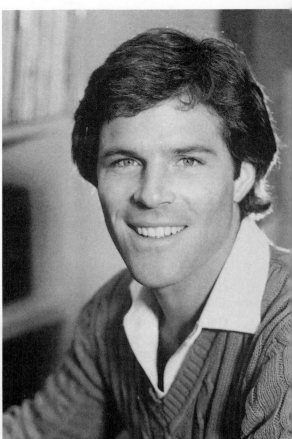

The Wards

KENNY I started to get this picture of the way we were going to live—like a normal family—and it kept getting stronger every day. Now, all of a sudden, it's all falling apart before my eyes.

GINGER I don't understand why you think anything is falling apart.

KENNY Everything was going so perfectly.

GINGER For you it was!

KENNY I'm sorry. I didn't know you had it so bad! A beautiful baby, a nice house. . . .

GINGER *You* have a beautiful baby and a nice house too, but it's not enough. You need to work, too. Well, so do I.

                                             —Kenny and Ginger Ward, 1981

Kenneth Ward and
Ginger Kilman Ward

"Snappy Ginger, the closest thing to perfection in Knots Landing or probably anywhere else. Kenny Ward is Ginger's hubby —born and raised on a surfboard. He and Ginger were married on an incoming wave."

—Richard Avery, 1979

They were the new kids on the block, the ones who didn't even have the money to buy furniture for their new home. They were both terribly young, terribly good-looking, and terribly unaware, for the longest time, of how compartmentalized their life together was. Once they recognized each other as partners in life, their life turned into something wonderful; so wonderful, neither could have ever imagined it.

Kenneth Ward was born in 1954 in Marina del Rey. His parents were the oldest children he knew, who spent all their time listening to music, painting, "communicating" on the beach, and living comfortably on his mother's family money. Kenny remembers long days on the beach, and nights awash with music. He loved his parents, he loved the beach, and he loved music.

He was a completely winning child, with exuberant good looks and a sunny disposition. All the hundreds of beatniks who passed through the Wards' home loved Kenny. He was well liked at school too, and though his attendance and homework were hit-or-miss, teachers found it next to impossible to be cross with this little charmer.

Much to his parents' disappointment, Kenny did not have any talent for playing or composing music. Nor did he have a voice. (Not that they did either.) He was, however, a fabulous swimmer and surfer, and always had a job on the beach, first at the umbrella concession, then on beach cleanup, and when old enough, as a lifeguard. He loved cars and regularly snuck off to stock car races. He refurbished his own sports car (complete with a radio not to be beat), and outfitted himself with some fifty girlfriends. With his eternal suntan, glint in the eye, *that* smile, that body, the boy was in like Flynn. He attended every party within a fifty-mile radius.

In 1976, Kenny struck up an acquaintance with a record producer, who, impressed with Kenny's informal but extensive music education, offered him a job at his recording studio. Kenny did fabulously. His temperament, his years of immersion in popular music, and his nose for star quality made him an invaluable employee. Artists—and some were as crazy as bedbugs—trusted him. A lot of the females also liked to sleep with him, which didn't bother Kenny in the least. He had no interest in settling down; he liked his scaling career in the industry, liked his car, his apartment in the Marina, and all the girls.

Ginger's first publicity photo as a country and western singer. Later Kenny would change her style to romantic, favoring silk or velvet dresses.

And then he met Ginger Kilman.

Ginger Kilman was born in San Francisco in 1955. Her conception had forced her teenage parents into a marriage neither of them wanted. It was not a particularly nice childhood. Ginger's father was a distant, unhappy figure to her. And her mother, Jane, just as miserable, took it out on Ginger. Jane had so many rules for her, that about the only thing she could do with any degree of confidence was to sit still. Both parents never hesitated on speculating how vastly different and wonderful their lives would have been had it not been for Ginger.

Ginger was, from day one, a beauty. It was clear also, by the age of six, that she had an exceptional voice and a gift for music. Her mother did not encourage her in any way. When Ginger was eight, her mother had another baby, Cindy, and two years later, still another, Jill. Jane Kilman could never say enough nice things about them. Usually her line ran, "Cindy's the smart one of the three, and Jill's the beauty," with no mention of Ginger at all; who, incidentally, was employed as a full-time babysitter.

In school Ginger got good grades and was well liked. Her teenage years transformed her into a full-fledged beauty, and as the boys circled around her, Jane's strictness got more severe. Lonely, timid, Ginger crept on. When she was sixteen, she fell wholeheartedly in love with classmate John Handelman. His love, his adoration, and his gentleness were gifts love-starved Ginger couldn't ignore. Maybe because Jane had screamed so much at Ginger about sex, or maybe because she never did tell Ginger the facts of life beyond *"Sex is bad,"* Ginger, one afternoon, made love with John outside in the Handelman's garden. It was lovely.

Ginger got pregnant. She was secretly elated, assuming that she and John would get married. Maybe her mother thought her life had been a mistake, but Ginger was convinced this would fulfill her every dream: a child and husband to love, and be loved by.

Mrs. Kilman made her get an abortion. It broke Ginger's heart and left many scars.

As she described years later, "That baby was taken from me . . . from inside me! There's been a part of me that's been empty ever since." Outside of school, she was not allowed out of the house for the next two years, except one Saturday when she was crowned Homecoming Queen by her classmates.

In 1972, at seventeen, Ginger left home to attend the University of Southern California at Los Angeles. Her freedom permitted her to soar. She majored in early childhood education, made many friends, and had several "nice" boyfriends. She graduated with honors in 1976 and landed a job as a kindergarten teacher in the Knots Landing school system.

In 1977, while sunning herself on the beach, she opened her eyes to see the most handsome man she had ever seen in her life. He was just standing there, staring down at her, smiling. He said, "Hi, I'm Kenny Ward." Ginger thought, "I'm in love."

Their courtship was glorious. They spent weekend days at the beach, followed by a movie, Mama Stelloni's for dinner, and then to Kenny's apartment to listen to music and talk and neck. For Kenny, this was a first—a woman who didn't fall into bed with him. For Ginger, it was a first—a man who didn't attack her. They both tiptoed with courtesy around each other, falling a little more in love each day.

Over the course of the next year, Kenny started dropping his other girlfriends, one by one. In 1978, at Mama Stelloni's, he asked her to marry him. She said yes, of course yes, and three weeks later they were Mr. and Mrs. Ward.

Ginger moved into Kenny's apartment in the marina, but didn't like it very much. The building was full of swinging singles, with every woman apparently some kind of "old friend" of Kenny's. And Kenny's professional life demanded attendance at countless parties, and between those and the atmosphere around their apartment, it *all* began to feel like one long party. Ginger yearned for some quiet time together and hinted and then prodded and then finally flat out demanded they move out of there. She'd have to wait.

In January of 1979, Kenny, working late and having too much to drink, slept with one of his recording artists, and afterward felt terrible about it. He never considered telling Ginger, but he did feel that he owed it to her to try and be a better husband. When "it" happened again in April, his guilt prompted Kenny to give in to Ginger and they began looking at houses.

Ginger fell in love with the three-bedroom house they had been shown on Seaview Circle. They really couldn't afford it, but even Kenny was won over by the beauty of the area, the cul-de-sac itself, and the spacious backyard. And there was also the living room to think of—in it Kenny could at long last use his $10,000 stereo system in a way he never could in the apartment complex. The Wards made the down payment, obtained a mortgage, and moved in that summer.

By November, Ginger was tired of Kenny's endless party going and throwing, and the couple started to argue over how much time they spent together. Kenny thought Ginger should understand how vital these parties were to his career; Ginger thought Kenny should understand how vital some time alone was to their marriage.

Ginger's concern was not unfounded. Kenny was being constantly approached by women; she knew that because she saw it all the time. When he took on the singing group Cosmic Steeple, the lead singer, Sylvie, was no exception. Kenny was sorely tempted by her, but resisted. For a day or two anyway. As Sylvie complained, "You come on like a swinger, but you've got a streak of latent fidelity in you." By December, however, Kenny had succumbed to Sylvie's charms—regularly.

Ginger suspected as much and confronted Kenny, but he vehemently denied it. Then Ginger dropped in at the recording studio one day and found Kenny and Sylvie

in a romantic clinch. Kenny went charging after her back to the cul-de-sac. Behind the locked front door of the house, Ginger screamed at Kenny, "Listen to this, you *pig!* Your Audio Pulse Model One Digital Time Delay!" *Smash.* Kenny heard his precious equipment being hurled against the wall. "Your D-B-X three-B-X dynamic range expander!" *Smash.* "Your electronic subwoofer!" *Smash.* Frantic, Kenny broke in the door, just in time to save his "Reel-to-reel deck!" from being destroyed, but not in time to save the situation. Ginger threw him out of the house.

Kenny moved in with Sylvie, though within the day he was missing Ginger terribly. He felt awful about what had happened, but Ginger was not interested in listening to his explanations. In October, however, for one night Ginger relented and let Kenny stay over. He was surprised when she sent him packing the next morning. Their night together had not been a signal of her wanting him back; she was just lonely, or so she said.

Ginger started seeing Karl Russelman, a pediatrician, and coming home from a date one night, Ginger found Kenny and Kristin Shepard passionately involved in *her* living room. Kenny tried to tell her that he had assumed Ginger had gone away for the weekend with Karl and—Oh, who wanted to listen to this! Ginger threw him out, and the next day Kenny was served with divorce papers.

Ginger continued to see Karl and got to the point where she felt ready to go away for a weekend with him, but then she received the stunning news—Ginger was expecting a child, a child conceived in her one night with Kenny. She told Karl about it, and reluctantly backed down from further involvement with him, though he was willing to stand by.

In an effort to prove his sincere love (without knowing about the baby), Kenny left Sylvie's and moved into his own apartment. When Ginger told him about the baby in December, he was ecstatic—but not so ecstatic when Ginger told him that it didn't necessarily mean they could ever live together again. However, when Valene Ewing had her brush with cancer in January, it made Ginger reconsider her stance a bit, and she asked Kenny to participate in her natural childbirth classes. Kenny was moved into sincerity on *all* fronts, and eventually the couple reunited.

In November of 1981, Ginger, with Kenny assisting, gave birth to Erin Molly Ward. It was an experience that brought a new bond of intimacy between the two. Once home from the hospital, however, Ginger had her hands full—not so much with Erin Molly as she did with Kenny. He was so overprotective and obsessive with Erin Molly that more care was needed to control him than to take care of the baby! But as the weeks went by, and Erin Molly fell into her routine, Ginger started getting restless. She missed teaching, or some involvement outside the house, and while she adored being with Erin Molly, she couldn't make her daughter her entire life. She yearned for something part-time, something . . . well, something.

The night before Kenny was supposed to cut a demo record, one of his singers called in ill. Kenny wracked his brain for a stand-in at this late date, until Lilimae suggested he use Ginger. Kenny thought it over, and Ginger was thrilled when he brought her down to the studio the next day. She was terrific, so terrific, in fact, that Kenny's boss, Andy Moore, wanted to sign up Ginger as a singer in her own right. Ginger's hopes skyrocketed; Kenny hit the roof. Ginger was not to work until Erin Molly was a couple of years older—*three,* at least. Ginger was stubborn and Kenny was angry. They argued and swayed in one direction and then the other. Finally, they compromised. *Kenny* would work with her; and they'd bring Erin Molly with them. In February of 1982, they flew up for her first gig in Berkeley, where she was a big hit. The audience loved her style of country and western music.

In March, Ginger went along with Karen Fairgate's brother, Joe Cooper, to a faculty dinner as a fill-in for Abby Cunningham. It was just a favor, but Joe was enormously attractive—and attracted to Ginger—and Ginger found herself being tempted by him. It wasn't love—for heaven's sake, she barely knew the man—but, as she said, "It's been a long time since I last felt this feeling. Sort of—like a teenager on a first date. A *good* first date, when you feel really good. Not just because you like each other, but because *being* liked makes you feel so special." Nothing happened, though it made Ginger realize how distant she and Kenny seemed to be lately, romantically speaking.

In October, Kenny produced a demo record for Ciji Dunne, a young singer that Gary Ewing had discovered. When Kenny's company failed to back Ciji, he quit and went into partnership with Gary, forming G & K Records. Kenny was very excited by Ciji—her vibrant voice, her stunning looks, her fresh appeal—and he just knew he had a star on his hands. Ginger, in the meantime, was hurt by Kenny's apparent abandonment of her career in favor of Ciji's. Kenny promised to record her next, but that did little to pacify her. Ginger began work on a song of her own.

Kenny was furious when, in December, he learned that Gary was thinking of selling G & K Records out to Jeff Munson, a big-time producer. Since Gary was carrying the financial end of the partnership, he could do it. Kenny voiced his vehement disagreement with the proposal, and continued working with Ciji. In rehearsal, he had her try out the ballad Ginger had just finished writing, and when Ginger arrived at Daniel and heard *her* song being sung by *that* woman, she blew up and threatened Ciji for stealing her song and trying to steal her husband. Kenny at least cleared Ciji of the charges.

Kenny got his, however, when Gary did sell the company out. Kenny, refusing to take Munson's offer of staying on as producer for Ciji's album, sat home fuming. Later, when Munson threw a debut party for Ciji at Daniel, Ginger talked Kenny into attending it. That night, when Ciji didn't show up (she was being murdered), Kenny put Ginger on stage to perform for the crowd. She was simply dazzling, and the crowd loved her. Munson too. When the Wards got home that night, Ginger shyly asked Kenny if he had liked her performance. Had he! "Here I've been running all over town, chasing after a dream, pinning all my hopes on Ciji, and everything I've been looking for has been in my own home the whole time. I'm not only talking about the mother of my baby, a fabulous wife, sensational lover—I'm talking about one hot singer."

Munson offered Kenny the huge job running his Nashville studios, which included producing records and developing new talent. Kenny had three requirements: (1) a lot of money. "Done." (2) a house. "Done." (3) most important, a contract for Ginger. "That goes without saying."

The Wards were elated by this new start in their life together; and in March of 1983, the moving van arrived, the good-byes were said, and they drove out of the cul-de-sac for the last time as neighbors.

The remaining neighbors, teary at their friends' departure, smiled as Erin Molly waved bye-bye.

Erin Molly Ward

"It's a beautiful name. She's so beautiful."
—Karen Fairgate, 1981

Erin Molly was born in Knots Landing in October 1981, to Ginger and Kenny Ward. Her mommy delivered her by natural childbirth and her daddy helped a lot! She weighed in at eight pounds four ounces, had a full head of brown hair, and sneezed when given her first bath.

Her godmother is Karen Fairgate-MacKenzie, and her babysitter for two years was Lilimae Clements, whom she loved a lot. She was a terrible sleeper until Lilimae showed her parents how to move her crib "head to the moon, feet facing the North Star." Every time they did it, she slept soundly through the night.

Erin Molly is always called by her full name. She now lives in Nashville, Tennessee, where she goes to school. Her daddy is a record producer, and her mommy is a country and western singing star.

The Cunninghams

ABBY   Olivia, call me when you're ready to come home.

OLIVIA   Where?

ABBY   At home, where do you think?

OLIVIA   No, I mean, where should I call you from? Not that many people in the cul-de-sac are still talking to us.

       —Abby and Olivia Cunningham, 1982

Abby Fairgate Cunningham-Ewing

"Well, let me put it this way. If you're stranded in the desert, with no food or water for three days, and you come upon Abby Cunningham with a picnic basket—keep going."
—Karen Fairgate MacKenzie, 1983

She is the most controversial figure in Knots Landing.

Her devotees eagerly cite what qualities they adore most about her: She's staggeringly beautiful, brilliant, dynamic, affectionate, passionate, sophisticated, captivating, and downright thrilling. Her critics, however, vehemently disagree. They say she's scheming, willful, arrogant, vain, manipulative, underhanded, power-crazy, and insatiable. Her devotees playfully compare her to Cleopatra; her critics mutter references to Marie Antoinette and Mata Hari.

Odd thing is, Abby's critics are usually the people who love her.

But then, who can figure a woman who's got millions of dollars of other people's money in her pockets, and yet is striding around with only one kidney because she *gave* the other one away? Only Abby knows; only Abby knows herself completely. And you can bet your bottom dollar that it is a secret she's determined to keep.

Abby Fairgate made her struggling debut into the world in 1950 in New York City. Her mother, Olivia, in her late forties, had ignored her doctor's warnings and had insisted on carrying this most unexpected child. She had a stroke during the difficult delivery and Abby, too, almost died, but both managed to pull through, Abby to complete good health.

Abby's father, Bill, was in his fifties, and her brothers, Paul and Sid, were eighteen and fourteen years old. Since Olivia would never fully recover and the Fairgates couldn't afford outside help, most of Abby's care fell to young Sid. When Abby was almost two, her mother died. Her father's grief hung like a black drape over the apartment. He could barely stand to look at his daughter. Sid took complete care of Abby and loved her more than life itself. In later years, dismissing the huge responsibility he handled, Sid would say that Abby was simply the only thing that had kept him going in those bleak years.

She was an astonishingly gorgeous child. In a family of hulking brunette six-footers, this tiny princess had inherited all the Nordic genes of the sole Swedish ancestor on her mother's side; she had startlingly blue eyes (almost bigger than her face) and platinum blond hair, and Abby bestowed a radiance upon everything she gazed at fondly—particularly Sid. She was starved for attention and incessantly demanded it from him, mainly because he was the only one around to give it to her once Paul moved out to marry. But she demanded it in such winning ways! By telling Sid stories, singing her heart out, or dancing on her tiptoes like a fairy. She couldn't bear it when Sid was sad, and she would do her best to coax smiles and laughs from

Abby Fairgate, the reigning beauty of Stanford University.

him. And in secret, in a hushed voice that couldn't be overheard, Abby would cry to Sid about Daddy—that he never smiled, never talked to her. When she was five, Bill Fairgate died, and Abby didn't understand where he had gone. She knew only to cling to Sid more tightly.

The Fairgates moved into a small two-bedroom apartment in Manhattan, which was what they could afford on Sid's filling station salary. He dropped Abby off at school every morning, where she did fabulously. Well, at least academically. She was crazy about reading, was uncannily good with numbers, but in terms of adjusting to her classmates, did not do nearly as well.

To begin with, until Abby had gone to school, she had no idea that there was anything unusual about her family life with Sid. But in school she found out differently—*everyone* had parents. Their brother didn't come to open house or the school play; their parents came. Parents lived in townhouses, took kids shopping after school, took them on vacations. They did all kinds of things! It wasn't that Abby was in any way unhappy with Sid—she *wasn't*—it was just that she was learning from outsiders that she was deprived. They felt *sorry* for her. And she hated hated *hated* that.

Then she made another disturbing realization; she was going to have to compete for Sid's attention. She had a nightmare one night and went into the living room to find him, and there he was—necking with a girl! Caught, Sid leapt up and steered Abby into the kitchen, making her a hot fudge sundae to bribe her back into bed. Abby made the connection; Sid was buying her off. And so, every time Sid had a date, Abby would have a nightmare and a hot fudge sundae. And every time she did it, she pushed a little more, gaining promises of movies or dresses or books.

By nine, Abby was reading ladies' magazines to see what it was she should be wearing. Acutely aware of her lack of a mother, she became obsessed with not

looking different from other girls; in fact, it was not long before she had Sid outfitting her *better* than the others. That, in combination an inherent acting ability, started building her life-long stance of glamour-as-the-best-defense—one that effectively hid her real circumstances. She became evasive about her parents, not wanting people to know she was an orphan; she didn't bring kids home, and implied she lived in another neighborhood. She didn't want to lie, she just didn't want anyone to *know*.

When Abby was ten, her world as she knew it fell apart. Sid brought home a witch named Susan Philby as his wife. Abby was insanely jealous of her, and Susan felt the same way about her—and won. Abby was shipped off to boarding school just outside the city.

She was miserable, and though she maintained straight A's, she became what school officials described to Sid as "a problem child." She broke every rule she could think of, was contemptuous of her classmates (actually, feeling insecure—they were all from wealthy families), and was forever planning her escape. When the witch left Sid in 1961, Abby's hopes soared—but no, Sid wouldn't let her come home. He kept trying to explain to her how she needed to be with people who could teach her things he couldn't. Abby pleaded, cried, wrote suicide letters (with no intention of carrying out her plans), ran away from school . . . all to no avail.

In 1962 Sid got married again, to Karen Cooper. Abby hated her too, but quickly realized that if she acted otherwise, she might have a chance of moving home. That didn't happen, but Karen did let Abby come home on weekends. Abby eventually got over her hatred for Karen, but never her jealousy. Sid was all she had and, well, it just wasn't fair to have to share him.

When Karen went into labor and Sid called her, Abby bolted from school, took a cab all the way to the hospital, and tried, unsuccessfully, to be admitted to the delivery room. Finally she dressed up with pillows and told them *she* was in emergency labor, got past the front desk, ditched the nurse, and in a gown and mask, snuck into the delivery room. Sid allowed her to stay. And so Abby stood quietly (horrified!) in the corner through sixteen hours of Karen's agonizing labor, and refused to leave Sid when the doctors were forced to perform a cesarean to deliver the baby. Abby was third in line to hold newborn Diana and something stirred in Abby; her love and affinity with this child would last a lifetime.

When Sid, Karen, Diana, Eric, and unborn Michael moved to Knots Landing in 1967, Abby entered Stanford University as an English major. After years alone with Sid and then in an all-girls school, Abby made an astonishing discovery in coed life —constant attention from boys! She was incredibly beautiful by now, her body having grown into womanhood with grace and loveliness, her face being the biggest news around Palo Alto since the opening of the Golden Gate Bridge.

Abby was careful in her selection of boyfriends. She wanted to be adored, loved, and revered, but not *pawed*. She was teasing, alluring, exciting, and still a bit of a brat (purposely), but she always planned to save her sexual life for marriage. In fact, her relationships with all the young men were more like her sister-brother relationship with Sid than romance, but that suited her just fine. In return for making Abby feel wanted, cherished, the focus of attention, "my boyfriends were always very proud to show me off to their mothers. They wore me like a varsity letter they had won . . . a big A for Abby."

Toward the end of her sophomore year, Abby started dating a law student, Jeffrey Cunningham. He was—like the others—madly in love with her, and Abby found his quiet nature, handsome looks, manner, impeccable background, and piles of family money to her liking. As she did with anyone she dated, she brought him down to

Knots Landing to meet Sid, but unlike everyone else, Sid gave his wholehearted approval of Jeff. That was enough for Abby. When he graduated from law school in 1969, she happily dropped out to marry him and settle down in San Luis Obispo.

Abby was severely disappointed by her choice. She had placed so much hope and expectation on the prospect of Jeff making her happy, his drawbacks seemed disastrous. The first was in the area of sex. After being such a "good girl," suppressing herself so effectively no matter how tempted, Abby was anxious to enjoy this marital reward. Her honeymoon baffled her completely. This was *it?* This is what people married for? Fought wars over? What men and women had been writing about for centuries? Scarlet and Rhett? Romeo and Juliet? Lady Chatterly? This is what changed their lives? Five minutes of Jeff's awkward pawing and then rolling off her? All it served to do was make Abby feel terribly lonely.

Another major drawback—Jeff was a workaholic. He never wanted to go out, never felt like playing around, going on a picnic, nothing. Abby felt the way she did when she was five and had to read all afternoon at Sid's filling station, waiting for him to get off work. Only Jeff never got off work!

And the third drawback—now that Jeffrey had Abby, he didn't appreciate her. He expected her, however, to be beautiful at all times (which wasn't so hard), dress like his mother (!), keep an orderly house, and lavishly entertain his clients on a moment's notice. In public, he was proud of her—sort of the way he was about the house—but in private, he seemed unaware of Abby unless she did something that was "unseemly."

And then something wonderful happened. Abby got pregnant. She was filled with a kind of wonderment and gratitude that was foreign to her. Every day was filled with new purpose—to exercise, eat well, listen to beautiful music, read wonderful literature—all in preparation for this little unborn child inside. She positively glowed through her term, filled with an incredible sense of well-being. That day in 1971 when Abby first held Olivia in her arms was the day Abby knew that everything that had ever happened to her had been worth it if it had gotten her to here. To this moment. This tiny bundle, her very own precious child, belonged to her; no one could ever take her away from her.

Olivia so brightened Abby's life that within the year Abby was anxious to conceive again. Her wish came true, and in 1973, she gave birth to a hearty little boy, Brian.

Abby's life with her children grew closer and more intense as her relationship with Jeff further deteriorated. She was impatient with Jeff's ways; what she used to think was "thoughtful contemplation" on his part was, she realized, an inability to make decisions, born out of insecurity. She handled all the money in the family, and whether she liked it or not, had to make every decision—down to what Jeff would wear to work—or nothing would ever get decided. She started to get to know other mothers; behind her ever-ready smile, she felt agony as she realized that other marriages were not like hers. And being around Sid and Karen was painful too, as it only further stressed how mismatched she and Jeff were. Her loneliness and frustration grew.

By 1976 Abby was entertaining notions of divorce. The only problem was the money to do it. She had no intention of depriving Olivia or Brian of *anything,* and reluctantly reminded herself that that meant *two* parents as well, so she continued to stick it out, getting more depressed, feeling more locked in, by the day. She did, however, finish up her degree at the community college in preparation for . . . what? She didn't know yet. How to break away without breaking the children's hearts?

Arriving at the Fairgates after her divorce in 1980. Abby's brother, Sid, is on the left, Karen is on the right, Olivia has a hat on, Michael Fairgate's in the T-shirt, that's the top of Brian's head, and Eric is on the right.

Her nerves frayed, Abby prays for patience as Brian and Olivia fight. The children were so traumatized by the final stages of her marriage to Jeffrey Cunningham, that it would be almost a year before both settled down.

Sid and Gary try to make some sense out of Abby's bookkeeping system at Knots Landing Motors. Abby saw nothing wrong with it; in fact, it was exactly the way she wanted it—detailed to the penny, in a code that only she could read.

When J.R. agreed to finance Gary's cheap parts deal, Abby hosted a dinner party in his honor. J.R. said to her, "We understand each other, you and me. I sure would like it if we had more women like you in Texas." From Abby, going clockwise: Karen, Gary, Valene, Brian, Olivia, Sid, and J. R. Ewing.

Abby is undone by seeing Sid paralyzed in the hospital after his accident, and it was all she could do to get out of his room before bursting into tears. The night Sid crashed, she sat up bolt awake from a sound sleep, knowing something terrible had happened.

Of the many agreements Abby has had with J. R. Ewing over the years, the most important one to him was seeing that Gary stayed away from Dallas. In exchange, he'd happily endorse her marriage to Gary.

ABBY   What makes you think we want to live in Dallas?

J.R.   You're not Valene. As long as he was with her, I knew Gary wouldn't come within spitting distance. But you're different. You want to be Queen of the Ewings.

ABBY   I'll settle for princess.

J.R.   Fine. Take the ermine and the jewels, but the crown stays in Dallas 'cause the crown is mine.

In 1977 Abby got a part-time job as a bookkeeper and Jeff threw a fit. He yelled and screamed and Abby yelled and screamed back, frightening the children. She was adamant; he went on strike. No sex, no kind word, nothing until she quit; Abby said that was the way it always was anyway, so who cared?

It was the beginning of the end. Abby continued in her job, doing very well at it, and her praise from outside of the house started to make her hate Jeff. He wouldn't help with anything, so Abby was frantic trying to look after the children, drive them around, run the household, play maid to Jeff's clients, and still do her job. But she refused to let go of her job—she knew that to do so would mean some kind of personal death for her. Their fights got worse and Abby tried to make it up to the children, but it didn't work. Poor Olivia was a godsend, but Brian started misbehaving in ways that Abby remembered herself doing at boarding school; and she remembered well how unhappy she had been.

In desperation, Abby finally called Sid one night and, crying, told him everything —about the fights, about Jeff's inability to make decisions, about his refusal to let her work, about his unwillingness to help with the family, about their sex problems, about Abby's fear that the children were suffering. He was shocked (Abby's facade had been too good with him too), but supported her in divorce proceedings, which Jeff fought. Finally, in 1980, the divorce went through, and Abby, anxious to start life anew, left San Luis Obispo with the children in their Volvo stationwagon, heading south for San Diego. They stopped to spend a week with Sid and his family.

Although Abby wasn't crazy about the Los Angeles area, before the week was out she decided to buy the last house on the cul-de-sac. She couldn't pass up the opportunity of being so near Sid—besides, the children needed a father figure—and it was a nice house, with a lovely pool and backyard, the schools were excellent, and . . . well, there seemed to be an awful lot of nice men around.

After years of being cooped up with Jeff, Abby was frankly out for a little action— at long last! By November she was having an affair with Richard Avery, since they both had their days free. She quickly got bored, however, and eagerly accepted Sid's job offer as the KLM bookkeeper. She loved the job and was extremely good at it. Ever perceptive, Abby quickly caught on to the cheap parts deal that Gary Ewing was involved in (over his head). She went to J.R. on Gary's behalf and set the stage for Gary to borrow the money he needed. Besides, Sid was in urgent need of some profits at the shop.

Her meeting with J. R. Ewing was really quite something. Abby didn't trust him for a moment, but she saw something in him she admired: He got what he was after, and heaven knew, that was exactly what Abby was after to learn. J.R. liked her a lot, and not just sexually (though they had a marvelous time that way as well). "You're a tough little fighter. I like that. It's a shame my brother's not married to somebody like you instead of that wimp he's been calling a wife." Abby agreed with him; Gary clearly needed someone like her in his life, which planted a seed. Gary Ewing, hmmm.

Gary wasn't without fault. At the moment, if Abby wanted him, she would not only have to go up against his wife Valene, but his current mistress, Judy Trent, as well. So he wasn't exactly the angel he professed to be. Meanwhile, back at the cul-de-sac, Richard was throwing tantrums over Abby's increasing uninterest in him, but since she had been interested in him only to satisfy her sexual curiosity, to find out what other men were like in bed, Abby didn't much care.

In January, Jeff started making trouble for her. He lashed out with a million accusations about how she was an unfit mother, citing that the kids ate only junk food,

Meeting Assemblyman Gregory Sumner for the first time at his campaign headquarters. Little did she know that he would be the source of endless corruption, violence, and extortion as a business partner.

that Richard was hanging around too much, that she had a part-time job when she didn't need to work. Abby's response was, "I'm happy and content for the first time in years. What really bugs you is that I'm doing it without you." Jeff promised to take her to court to win custody of the children, but dropped his suit when he confessed he was doing it only to try and get Abby back. She then set him straight: "The perfect Mrs. Cunningham? I never was. The only place she existed was in your head, Jeffrey, and that's exactly what you can't stand . . . the fact that I'm something other than your fantasy. Take it or leave it—like it or not—I'm *me!*" She was not about to lose her hard-won independence and go back to *that* life.

In February of 1981, Jeff got his revenge. He kidnapped Olivia and Brian, sending Abby reeling into the greatest panic and despair of her life. For weeks and then months Abby followed every lead and employed every means of help available— the police, a private detective, the neighbors, anyone! And in the middle of this, an utterly devastating blow—Sid's accident and subsequent paralysis. When Abby saw him lying there, so defenseless, she felt a kind of terror she could never have imagined, not in her worst nightmares. This couldn't be happening—her children, her brother, dear God! Sid died in October, and her children were still missing. Karen fired her from KLM. Her job had been the sole thing that had kept Abby together. Grieving widow or not, Abby would never forgive Karen for that. Not ever.

Something snapped in Abby then, throwing her defenses up in steel. Without Sid, there was no one to take care of her. No one could take his place. Without his protection, Abby vowed to be on her own—no one would *ever* hurt her again. If it came down to it, she'd simply hurt them first.

At the end of the month, the private investigator finally tracked down Jeff and the children, and Abby lured them back from Jeff by promising to remarry him. Once they were safely in her possession, Abby had the Knots Landing deputy sheriff slap Jeff with a restraining order. If he so much as tried to see the children, she would have him arrested for child stealing.

Feeling terribly alone, Abby's love for her children, particularly Olivia, became tinged with desperate need. Their trusting, loving little faces made her strong; *she* would look after them, *she* would support them, *she* would ensure their future, *she* would give them the life-style they deserved, without interference from *anyone*.

In November, Karen pleaded with her to come back to KLM for the IRS audit, and

after Abby made her point about what a cruel, rotten thing it had been for Karen to fire her, she agreed. Abby wore her sexiest blouse and the auditor was impressed, and not only by her appearance. "If you don't mind my saying so, Mrs. Cunningham, your accounting methods are a bit unorthodox." Abby replied, smiling, "I know. I do everything that way." The audit was a success; Abby had saved KLM thousands of dollars. When Karen offered her old job back, she accepted.

Working with Gary drew them closer. When their methanol motor company got off the ground in January, Abby felt Gary being pulled toward her. Gary Ewing had a lot of potential. Abby felt that his marriage to Val suppressed his natural drive to succeed, which was a part of the Ewing heritage. She wasn't surprised when Gary told her he was a recovering alcoholic—she could see how the suppression of his destiny had led into that. But to make a man like this practically lame—it was a crime! Abby knew she could make him soar, that together their business instincts were fabulous.

In late February of 1982, after clearing the final hurdle for their business venture, Abby and Gary began an affair. It was beyond what Abby had hoped for—not only did they share the same adventurous, daring spirit, but the sex—good heavens! That alone made Gary the catch of the century. And so it began. When Valene started to catch on and confronted Abby, she didn't confirm or deny the affair, but she did make her point:

ABBY   You see only his weaknesses. I see him for what he is
   and what he can be.

VAL   I've seen him the same way I've seen him since I was
   fifteen years old.

ABBY   He's a big boy now, Valene. He doesn't need a crutch
   anymore. He needs someone who believes in him.

By the fall of 1982, when Gary moved out of the cul-de-sac, Abby was including him in many aspects of her family life. The children adored him, which was vital to Abby. Her mind was on Gary for keeps, and a permanent relationship wouldn't be possible if the children did not share her enthusiasm.

After Gary's father died, Abby swapped pages from Valene's novel (about the Ewing family) with J.R. in exchange for an advance tipoff about Jock's will as it pertained to Gary. J.R. told her Gary would be inheriting millions. She refused to sleep with J.R. again, telling him the truth—that she loved Gary and wanted to be faithful to him.

Abby flew to Dallas to support Gary through the ordeal of the will, for which he was deeply grateful. When they returned to Knots Landing, they rented a beautiful house on the beach, and opened a new chapter as partners in business and as partners in life.

Gary's ideas about how he wanted to spend his money appalled Abby. Before the ink was even dry on the first check, he was dragging her up to a godforsaken ranch outside Santa Barbara, where, he said, he wanted to move to and live quietly. Abby pointed out, "You thrive on excitement, living on the edge, risk, the action. So do I." And so what did he want to drop out of the world for? He agreed with her, only to start handing out money all over town; Abby scrambled to make good out of his foolhardy commitments. He'd spend it *all* if she didn't watch it!

She was responsible for Richard's signing an agreement that made Gary and Abby partners in his restaurant, Daniel, instead of charity contributors. She also closely monitored G & K Records and turned it around into a money-making proposition by initiating Ciji Dunne's exposure at Daniel (thus bringing up the revenues of the restaurant), and bringing in a *real* record producer, Jeff Munson, to buy out G & K Records at an enormous profit.

Drying her hair in the executive suite of Gary Ewing Enterprises. Overlooking the harbor and channel of Marina del Rey, the office and attaching apartment were leased by Abby for $72,000 a year. If she came up short on the rent, Laura Avery said she "could rent out the reception area as a trailer park."

On the family front, Abby's niece Diana was having a rough time with her mother (who wouldn't with Karen as a mother, Abby sympathized). Abby invited Diana to go up to Santa Barbara with her and Gary for a weekend. Diana was suddenly taken ill, and Karen, of course, tried to blame it on Abby—when it was kidney failure and had been coming for a long time! And then came a tough decision. Diana needed a kidney transplant or would have to spend the rest of her life around a dialysis machine; and Abby was the only possible living donor. Abby was terrified, of course —what if she were in a car accident or something and lost that one remaining kidney? What about her children's future? God gave people two kidneys because they needed them, right?—but when she went to see Diana, she felt her heart breaking over the life Diana would face without her kidney. Diana said to her, "You're so beautiful—it doesn't seem right. And when I think of what you've been to me. . . . And you've given me so much—I don't want to take any more from you."

Abby agreed to the operation. Karen tried to thank her, but Abby was through with Karen and all her accusations and hostility in recent years, and said, "I'm doing it because I have to—for Diana, for my brother's child. And for myself, so I won't have to live with the guilt of having refused. I'm *not* doing it for you. . . . I don't want us to be civil to each other; I'm not interested in peace offerings. You want to express your gratitude? Save a whale in my name." The operation was a complete success and Diana was given her life back in the fullest sense. As for Abby, except for an occasional frown at her scar, she easily swung back into full action.

Her life with Gary was thrown into a messy cauldron of pain and betrayal in January. Gary started drinking and couldn't stop. On top of that, Diana intimated to Abby that he had been having an affair with Ciji Dunne. Abby was angry, but helpless; no matter what she did to try and get Gary to stop drinking—love, kindness, gentleness, understanding, screaming, refusing to do anything—he started again, disappearing, getting arrested. And then he was arrested for the murder of Ciji. Something happened to Gary after he sobered up in his cell—he just gave up. He seemed to *want* to be convicted. And worse yet, Valene came screeching onto the scene and Abby was fearful of her effect on him. In the end, Gary was cleared, and by that time, Abby had gotten power of attorney over his estate. *He* might blow his whole life, but she was not about to let him blow the life of her family.

Abby supported his decision to buy a beautiful ranch just outside of town. Gary would raise quarter horses and Abby was to run Gary Ewing Enterprises and make them a pile of money. Gary hired Laura Avery to work with her, which annoyed Abby, but the latter proved to be pretty adept at wheeling and dealing herself.

Abby hired attorney Jim Westmont to work for her, the first business at hand being to divert monies from Gary Ewing Enterprises into a secret company, Apolune, from which Abby could operate without Gary's interference. Gary had such nitpicky ways about business—things had to be environmentally sound or for the good of humanity or some such nonsense. When she was to lose her power of attorney, Abby pressed for marriage as insurance for her part of Gary's inheritance. After some question (surrounding Valene, of course), Gary proposed and they were married at the ranch in November of 1983. They had a quick honeymoon in the Colonnade Park Hotel, where Abby introduced more insurance for her future in the form of Ciji Dunne look-alike, Cathy Geary. She knew Gary's obsession with the dead singer would transfer to Cathy, and so keep him occupied while she was left unencumbered to make them all richer.

Things at the office were looking bright and promising. Abby had inherited from her uncle half ownership in an oceanfront apartment building and tract of land just outside Knots Landing. When Laura shopped around, looking for buyers, instead of getting offers of $175,000—what it was worth—she was getting offers like $3,350,400! Something was clearly up with this property; Abby assumed someone had an idea of developing the land and so she changed her plans about what to do with it. She tried to buy out Karen, which Karen refused, so she set up a front, H & O Management, to issue checks to Karen as if the apartment building still existed, leaving Abby free to develop the property into something else.

In November, she really rolled into action, visualizing and drawing up plans for a huge resort complex—Lotus Point. Abby planned to buy out the existing houses

JEFF MUNSON   Astonishing. The way you can shift gears so fast without batting an eye. "Throw Kenny Ward to the wolves! No? You're right: Make Kenny Ward president of the company!"
ABBY   I'm a pragmatist.

adjacent to her property and build on the site, the only opposition coming from strict environmental state laws. Here she enlisted the aid of Assemblyman Gregory Sumner, in exchange for some hefty donations. When Abby threw in a roll in the hay as a part of the negotiations, he agreed. Sumner introduced her to some people who got her a variance from the Coastal Commission so she could get a green light on the construction of Lotus Point.

In January of 1984, Marc St. Clair had the audacity to introduce himself to Abby as her new partner in Lotus Point. When Abby said he was out of his mind, St. Clair explained that his organization, the Wolfbridge Group, had obtained her variance, and if she did not take them in as partners, they would have it rescinded. Abby, mad as all get out, was forced into an agreement. Leave it to Sumner to be mixed up with gangsters!

Gary Ewing Enterprises, which Abby worked on in her spare time, was doing fabulously, branching out in diverse, highly profitable subsidiaries of which Gary approved, such as Ellingson Textile Mills in Massachusetts, a bottling plant in South Carolina, and a video game manufacturer in Hong Kong. Gary was very pleased until he caught the wind of suspicion from Mack MacKenzie that Abby was up to something he should know about, and he ordered an audit of Gary Ewing Enterprises. He didn't find anything (prompting a collective "phew!" from Abby, Laura, Westmont, and Sumner). But Cathy Geary was causing problems. Gary was suddenly suspicious about her background, from where she had come, and Abby moved quickly to fire her. Cathy refused to leave.

Meanwhile, Mack MacKenzie was investigating Wolfbridge and one of many smelly trails was leading aback to Apolune and Abby. Dodging from minute to minute worked for a while—Abby was stuck between Mack, who'd probably try to arrest her, and Wolfbridge, who'd probably break her back—but then everything started to cave in around her. Cathy told Gary about Abby's having hired her; Gary threw Abby off the ranch and froze the assets of Gary Ewing Enterprises, and by virtue of that, unknowingly froze Apolune and Lotus Point. But that was nothing compared to the pain Abby felt when Olivia refused to leave the ranch and live with her. Desperately trying to explain to Olivia why people talked about her the way they did, she said, "When a man conducts business the same way I have, he's admired for his aggressiveness. But I'm a woman. They think of me as a shrew." Eventually Olivia came around and at least lived with Abby.

Gary was completely unforgiving to Abby. She knew it must be because Gary was sleeping with—and leaning on—Cathy Geary. He could never stand alone; always, there had to be a woman somewhere holding him up. In any event, Abby was being threatened by St. Clair to get Lotus Point unfrozen, and she was unsuccessful on all fronts. Finally she resorted to pushing Sumner into doing something. Well, something sure did happen. Gary was murdered. Abby, crazed with grief and anger, immediately went after Sumner, who pleaded innocence and redirected her to St. Clair himself. Killer or no killer, Abby didn't care, she stormed, "I loved my husband, Mr. St. Clair. That may surprise you. I've had my affairs, true. I skimmed the profits. But I did those things for me. I never did them to hurt him . . . *because I loved him.* Because he *counted* in my life. And I won't rest until I settle the score." She was prepared to go to Mack and tell him the whole story, but St. Clair's threatening presence around her children frightened her and she wavered. At night she was sobbing over the loss of Gary, not having realized how very deeply, truly she had loved him. At the office, even her secretary, Elizabeth, quit, saying, "I'm sorry, I—I'm scared here."

And then Abby found out Gary was alive and she screamed and ranted at Mack

Frantic, Abby demands that Sumner do something about madman St. Clair and his killers.

Abby leaves the marina with Gary after the shooting of Marc St. Clair. She nearly died in the course of trying to save his life, but she was still surprised when he insisted she come home to Westfork with him. When she asked why, after all the weeks of hating her, he said, "All I know is, I need to know that the two of us weren't a mistake."

With Karen MacKenzie outside Gary's office at Lotus Point. With Gary and Karen coming in to run Lotus Point, Abby's vote was knocked down more often than not, but occasionally the two women would agree. Here they share apprehension about Gary's dealings with Paul Galveston.

for his deception. She would have done anything to help, she declared, if she had known Gary was still alive. Mack said there was still something she could do, because Gary's life was still on the line. Abby agreed to risk her life by setting St. Clair up. She got him to admit he *was* Wolfbridge, but that wasn't enough evidence and Mack asked her to push harder. When Mack started to close in on St. Clair, St. Clair took Abby along with him, using her as a hostage to make his escape with. She was kept prisoner on St. Clair's yacht, and Abby was stunned when Sumner shot St. Clair in cold blood. But she backed up Sumner's self-defense story. She wanted him to owe her a favor.

Gary, surprised that Abby had willingly risked her life in order to save his, realized the depth of his own love for her, and the couple reconciled. Abby's family was once again back together; and she was relieved, grateful for the respite.

On the business front, Gary and Karen took over Lotus Point, reducing Abby to an impotent third party. She was furious, since it was her project to begin with, but Gary explained, "I love you, Abby. You're exciting, unpredictable, and the perfect lover. But I want to be honest with you: As a businesswoman, you represent everything I loathe. . . . Trust? Are you nuts? I *love* you; I don't trust you. Why should I?" But as compensation, Gary bought Pacific World Cable for her to run. Gary and Karen still needed her help at Lotus Point, however. Abby had to help them out, for example, by employing lawyer Scott Easton to obtain an ample water supply for Lotus Point, an endeavor the two "chiefs" had failed in thus far.

At Pacific World Cable, Abby was responsible for turning it into the second largest news-gathering organization in the country. She promoted Ben Gibson, gave the on-air talent new pizzazz, and fostered new talent like Joshua Rush. While in the newsroom one day, Abby accidentally came across a draft of a letter on Ben's word processor, a letter to Valene that explained he could not deal with the fact that the babies she was carrying were *Gary's.*

Abby was completely undone by this. *Gary had slept with Val? When? How involved were they? Gary didn't know about the babies now, but for how long? Would he leave Abby for them? Would he disinherit her children?* She consulted with Scott Easton on the question of what a paternity suit could do to Gary's estate. The news was not good, and Abby wondered how to keep Val from telling Gary about his paternity.

Easton, in the meantime, explained his plan of action for obtaining water from the neighboring lands of Paul Galveston. He had uncovered a veritable vipers' nest of corruption with Galveston Industries, and was going to use his knowledge to force the water rights from Galveston. Abby said fine, don't tell me any more; she would reward him generously, but leave Gary, Karen, and her out of it. Easton promised to do so and also promised to give Abby a bonus for being such a terrific employer. Bonus?

In November, Val "lost" her babies in childbirth. Abby felt very bad for her, only to receive a mysterious phone call that informed her that the babies were alive and were being put into an illegal adoption ring. Horrified, Abby tried to get hold of Easton, knowing he was behind this—some favor, stealing a woman's children! Easton, in the meantime, had incurred the wrath of Paul Galveston and was murdered on a Galveston Industries jet. In his briefcase had been the adoption papers for the Ewing babies, which made Abby look like the person who had arranged it. The papers found their way to Galveston.

Galveston, who was dealing with Gary in Empire Valley by this time, was quick to use the papers against Abby, telling her that unless she could stop Mack's investigation of Galveston Industries, then he would expose her to Gary. Abby was wild; all

RUTH GALVESTON She seems . . . quite attractive. Was
  she ever an actress?
LAURA I don't think so. Why do you ask?
RUTH She has an air—I'm not sure how to say it—an
  air of . . . professionalism about her.
LAURA I think you said it very well.

Abby with Ruth Galveston.

GREG SUMNER Seeing the two of you there so innocently is
  enough to send a chill down the spine of Ivan the Terrible.

Enjoying the fruits of her labors at Lotus Point, 1986.

she wanted to know was where the babies were so she could get them back to Val! Galveston died in March of 1985, and Sumner announced that he was his real son. Abby immediately went to him, confided in him about the whole awful mess, and pleaded for the adoption papers. Sumner of course toyed mercilessly with her, and it was only in a deal with his mother, Ruth—to get rid of Laura as Greg's girlfriend—that she got the papers back and could destroy them.

The second she destroyed them in May, Abby raced to find Valene and drive her to the address where the babies were. Breathing a sigh of relief, she stepped back from the situation, not knowing if Val would tell Gary or not. But at this point, all that really mattered was getting rid of the guilt she had been carrying over the whole rotten course of this thing.

Back at Empire Valley, Abby was given the assignment to build and run a television station there, but Greg blackmailed her about the babies, forcing her into helping him build his spy complex underneath her station (which he also made her sign over to him). She was also in charge of deceiving Gary. She, in turn, blackmailed the head engineer, Frank Elliot, into falsifying reports to Gary, so he would okay construction of the television site where Sumner needed it. Everything was going ahead as planned when Elliot started to back out. Abby warned Sumner, and the next thing she knew, Elliot was electrocuted at the site. Thinking Sumner had done it, she stormed into his office, sick with fury at what she thought he had done. Sumner thought *Abby* had done it, which made her feel worse. What were they involved in? Together they figured out it had to have been Sumner's colleague, John Coblenz. (Abby, incidentally, gave Elliot's widow $750,000, pretending it was from his insurance coverage. She also got his son a job at the finest law firm in Los Angeles.)

Abby was frightened now—Coblenz was clearly a madman—and she begged Gary to sell his interest in Empire Valley to Sumner. When Gary refused and it became clear that Coblenz was trying to kill both Gary and Abby, Abby warned Gary and sent Olivia and Brian in the care of her maid, Maria, to hide out in Mexico. And then Gary resolved the crisis by blowing Empire Valley up. There. Nothing left to fight over. Abby was relieved (and a little amused too—Gary sure had a way of resolving things).

But it meant endings too. Gary refused to speak to Abby, saying he was through with her deceit and corruption. They stayed together at Westfork for the sake of the children, but for all intents and purposes, their marriage was finished.

With her responsibilities at Lotus Point further demoted, leaving her little to do, and her husband out every night with heaven only knew who, Abby jumped at the governor's appointment to the Land Commission in January of 1986, which Sumner arranged for her out of his own interest.

And then one of the worst experiences of Abby's life began. Somehow Olivia had gotten wind of Abby's knowing that Val's babies were alive when they were allegedly dead, and that Abby hadn't told Valene. Olivia screamed at her mother how much she hated her, and moved in with the MacKenzies', for weeks refusing even to see Abby. Abby tried to explain, plead, but Olivia hated her, that was that. Abby sobbed over the estrangement of her daughter, and worried that Olivia was being eaten alive by the secret she carried. She looked terrible, poor baby.

When Abby persisted in trying to get Olivia to come home, Olivia uncharacteristically turned on her, bitterly blackmailing her mother about the twins. And Olivia wasn't the only one: Sumner, of course, was still trying to use it to force Abby into getting Empire Valley back for him, and eventually that young viper Peter Hollister (with whom, out of loneliness, she slept with one night) tried to use it on her too. The final straw was Gary moving off the ranch and filing for divorce so he could be with that tramp Jill Bennett.

Okay, if everyone wanted to hurt her, threaten all that she held dear, Abby wouldn't argue any longer. *She'd deal with them all.*

At the environmental benefit in March, she publicly explained that, yes, she had known about Valene's babies being alive. She said that she had received a phone call about it—that the caller had thought she was *that* Mrs. Ewing—and she hadn't told Valene because, given her precarious mental condition, she didn't want to get her hopes up. Instead, *she found the babies and brought Valene to them.* At that point, Sumner tried to bring up the paternity question. Abby pretended that, of course, the children were Ben's—right, Gary? He nodded and thereby publicly disclaimed them.

And then Abby swung into action. The first thing she did was march over to the MacKenzies' and drag Olivia home whether she liked it or not. And then when Gary brutally rejected her attempts to reconcile, she informed him that he had to sign over to her *all* of Empire Valley, or she would drag Valene into court to testify about the paternity of the twins. On top of that, she'd drag in Cathy, Jill Bennett, any and all the women he had committed adultery with. Gary, furious, agreed. She also wanted half of all their assets. Gary had to agree.

As for Peter, she let him know that she had proof he wasn't Galveston's son, and promised to ruin his case against Galveston Industries. Or, he could continue to let her pay his legal expenses and, in return, give her 51 percent of everything he won. Oh, and one more thing—he had to lure Jill Bennett away from Gary. He had no choice but to agree.

As for Sumner, she thought having Empire Valley and a chunk of Galveston Industries was enough revenge, but when in April she learned that Empire Valley had formerly been a toxic dump, she quickly moved to sell it to Sumner for millions, plus a seat on the Galveston Board of Directors.

There. All in place. She had her daughter back, she'd get half of everything from her marriage, she'd have a toxic Empire Valley to sell to Sumner for millions, she had 51 percent of Peter's take from his suit, and since she couldn't have Gary back, she could have the next best thing—his relationship with Jill Bennett destroyed. (Just see how long he lasts without a woman, she thought.)

And then the fateful day arrived when her nephew Eric almost died from arsenic poisoning from working in the Lotus Point expansion into Empire Valley. Should she throw Empire Valley and its millions away by telling the world that it was there that Eric was poisoned? Should she risk the success of Lotus Point, located next to the toxic waste dump?

Of course. Eric was her nephew. *Sid's son.* As for Empire Valley, Lotus Point, and all the people causing Abby trouble—well, they could wait for another day, another way, one she would surely find.

When you see Abby, it is next to impossible to feel sorry for her. She's simply too smart, too beautiful, too wealthy, and too powerful to win much sympathy. But if in a generous mood, when next you see her, try to visualize the little girl who lost her mother, lost her father, and lost her chance at a normal life. Try to imagine a vulnerable, divorced young mother of two who lost the brother that meant everything to her. And, finally, try to imagine a smart, beautiful, wealthy, powerful woman who is desperately searching for something that money can't buy, but is condemned to believing she can.

Olivia Cunningham

"Honestly, sometimes Olivia frightens me, she's so smart."
—Valene Ewing, 1981

Olivia was born in San Luis Obispo to Abby and Jeffrey Cunningham in 1971. She was (and is) an exceedingly beautiful child, and as smart and, gentle, and affectionate as her parents were combative. By the time her parents were divorced in 1980, Olivia was a weary child; she was taking care of her brother and, to a certain emotional extent, her mother as well.

She loved living in the cul-de-sac, where her best friend in the whole world was Valene Ewing, and so she was confused about her feelings when Valene's husband, Gary, left Valene to be with her mother. Her mother's marriage to Gary often set off Olivia's old feelings of despair and desperation that she felt in her mother's first marriage. Her greatest agony was trying to figure out why her mother always messed things up! And her obsessive attachment with her mother often conflicted with her love for Gary, who was always clearly in the right. Loyalty to her mother came first, however, and it wouldn't be until January of 1986 that Olivia would finally be unable to forgive her.

She found out that her mom had known that Val's babies were alive and had not told Val, leaving her poor friend wracked in grief, thinking them dead. Olivia moved in with her Aunt Karen, but she refused to tell her why she wasn't speaking to Abby. Missing her mother terribly, yet hating her mother with all her heart for what she had done, Olivia found herself getting high on marijuana as often as she could, in an attempt to make the pain go away.

It wasn't long before the marijuana was more important to Olivia than her anger at her mother. She was smoking first thing in the morning on her balcony, in the bathroom at school, at night when she was supposedly taking a shower. No one but Michael caught wind of her being stoned all the time, and when he was busted for some joints in his car Olivia felt awful about it but nonetheless refused to confess they had belonged to her. She was scared of what her mother would do, but, worse yet, she was scared she wouldn't be able to smoke anymore. But her mother caught on anyway, made her confess, and agreed with the courts that she regularly attend a drug therapy group. Olivia, however, blackmailed her mother about the twins and stayed on at the MacKenzies' *and* continued to get stoned.

In March, her mother told everyone about the babies herself and dragged Olivia home to Westfork. Olivia was very upset that Gary had moved out, felt a bit responsible, and begged her mother to do whatever she could to win him back. Olivia was reassured when her mother said the Ewing marriage wasn't over yet—and said it with *that* special gleam in her eye. This was one of those times Olivia was glad her mother was the way she was. If anyone could fix it, if anyone could make it better, it was Mom.

Brian Cunningham

"Back home we know how to deal with unruly children—we barbecue 'em."

—J. R. Ewing, 1980

He's a *lot* better than he used to be.

Brian Cunningham was born in 1973 to Abby and Jeffrey Cunningham in San Luis Obispo. For many years, people thought he had only inherited his parents' negative traits: Abby's temper, tantrums, and hit-or-miss eating habits; Jeff's indecisiveness, and whining to be cared for. While his older sister, Olivia, was a "good" girl, Brian's response to his familial situation was to act out. His favorite activities were throwing food, pushing people in the pool, hitting his sister, and running away. By the time his parents divorced in 1980, he had stopped talking completely, choosing to communicate by blowing a trumpet.

That, thank heavens, has all changed. With the influence of Valene Ewing, who often babysat for him, and his mother's remarriage to Gary Ewing, Brian has evolved into his true self—a charming, hard-playing, smart boy who is capable of making friends and playing fairly. He loves swimming, eating, and riding, and is devoted to his sister.

While Brian adores his mother and his stepfather, he prefers to spend as much time as possible over at friends' houses. There are too many fights at home.

THE OUTSIDER

"Los Angeles wants no dudes, loafers and paupers, people who have no means and trust to luck, cheap politicians, failures, bummers, scrubs. . . . We need workers! Hustlers! Men of brains, braun and guts!"
—Harrison Gray Otis
   Publisher, The Los Angeles *Times,* 1886

Gregory Galveston Sumner

"You've always understood power, Gregory . . . and craved it. You'll come for it; it's inevitable. You love power more than you value pride."

—Paul Galveston, 1985

Perhaps it's simply that, after watching someone walk the high beam of morality for many years, witnessing their fall makes them appear much worse than those who never had any morals to begin with. Ah, yes, Gregory Sumner. His strong, charismatic aura, once attracting the trust of millions of people, now fosters only rampant suspicion. The confidant smile and adept words, once taken to heart, now only raise one's guard.

It's sad in a way. For Sumner is, despite what his critics charge, still capable of fortitude and courage. Until recent years he was not wont to do anything that wasn't in the public good. But something happened to him, something was crushed and bent. His spirit perhaps. Or his vision. Or maybe, as some have said, Gregory Sumner just got tired. Too tired to fight the hands that were trying to pull him from the beam. Hands that had been there since the day he was born. Hands that found their way to Knots Landing.

The unusual story of Gregory Sumner began sometime before his birth. Formerly roommates at Harvard, best friends Stephen Sumner and Paul Galveston were partners in an airplane company. Sumner, a pilot and aeronautical engineer, was the design and test man; Galveston, a financial genius, was the nuts and bolts production man. Their small plant was outside New York City, where both men lived and pursued the absolutely gorgeous high-fashion model, Ruth Gregory. They were both madly in love with her; and she was madly in love with both of them. As Ruth explained years later, "We were all in love. The three of us. I married the romantic, Sumner. Sumner flew planes, Galveston made them. . . . While one was heroic, the other made a mint." Galveston, a poor sport indeed about not winning Ruth, broke off his partnership with Sumner when they married in 1940. Sumner joined the Air Force and flew mission after mission in Europe, earning the status of Ace and the reputation of a hero back home. Speaking of back home, Ruth and Galveston were having a ball. Galveston, making a fortune on war contracts, showered Ruth with money, furs, and trips. In return, Ruth acted as his wife in every sense; she never tipped off Sumner, although he wrote her every day.

In 1942 Ruth found out she was pregnant, and immediately set about either to get Sumner home on leave or to go over there so as to cover her tracks. Whether she loved Galveston and his money or not, breaking Sumner's heart was not what she wanted. She didn't have long to worry, however; Sumner was shot down and killed. Galveston, now that Ruth was a free woman, promptly dumped her.

Greg's biological father, Paul Galveston.

Greg's mother, former high fashion model, Ruth Gregory Sumner Galveston. Greg often calls her Eleanor, as in Eleanor of Aquitaine.

Gregory Galveston Sumner was born in 1943 in New York City. He was brought up largely in the care of nannies, as his mother traveled extensively on the Continent to pursue a new career behind the camera. His room in their Fifth Avenue apartment was practically a shrine to his "father." Pictures of Sumner adorned the walls, and expensive showcases displayed his military decorations and citations. Greg's most reliable comfort came from hours spent rearranging scrapbooks of articles about his father. He was Greg's hero, and his memory was Greg's best friend. Ruth supported the young boy's worship with stories about him. How he helped people, how he was a self-made man, and how handsome, brave, and smart he was. How people loved him.

Greg thought his mother a mysterious beauty—a suitable match for his deserving father—but learned early on that maternal love and affection were not qualities she possessed. Once though, she suffered a spurt of domesticity and learned to crochet. She made him a sampler of her motto in life: NEVER ASSUME. He still has it.

When Greg was eight, he was sent to a boarding school. With lots of other boys around to play with, Greg was happy. Perhaps because he had been left on his own so much, Greg had an overdeveloped sense of responsibility. He just seemed to know what needed to be done and did it long before it would occur to anyone else, his teachers included. His studies were superb, and his papers—particularly in history and social studies—were remarkable for his age. He was also an excellent athlete and that, in combination with extraordinary leadership skills, made him the team captain, *always*.

As he grew through his teenage years, students and teachers alike were mesmerized by him. He had become a fabulous orator (what with all the speeches he had to make as president of everything), and with four years on the debating club, it became increasingly difficult to ever find fault with his reasoning. In short, Gregory Sumner, the handsome, dynamic athlete and brilliant scholar, was king of the school. He enjoyed the attention and admiration; it did much to fill a lonely place he had in his heart.

He was all set to attend Harvard University when everything in his life came to a grinding halt. Just before leaving for school, his mother and Uncle Paul (Galveston) had dinner with him to announce what his mother thought was wonderful news. Uncle Paul, who had paid all of Gregory's expenses at boarding school (this was news to Greg), was now prepared to pay for all his college expenses, including a generous allowance. Wasn't Gregory grateful? Greg was confused. *Why* was Uncle Paul doing this? Ruth explained that she had no money of her own. *Why not?* Because Stephen Sumner had left her nothing. Well, a few thousand from a GI policy, but Gregory could hardly expect that that had bought them anything. Stunned at the realization that was beginning to dawn, Greg demanded to know how they had lived the way they had all these years. His mother looked to Uncle Paul. Greg then said he appreciated his offer of assistance, but he couldn't accept it; his father wouldn't have liked it. Galveston blew his stack and told Greg that he *was* his father, and that past that point, Sumner had been an idealistic patsy who couldn't have made a buck if his life depended on it.

Greg was reeling. But not idle, for he packed his bags and moved out that night, not to speak to his mother for almost four years. As for Galveston, he swore never to have anything to do with him. Forget Harvard, he'd find his own way. And he did. He got a full-time job with the city and worked his way to a Fordham University degree in three years, served in the Air Force for three years, and then in 1966, came back to New York to attend Fordham's law school on the GI Bill.

There he met Mack MacKenzie, who became his best friend and roommate. Mack was bent on making piles of money, and as Sumner listened to him on the subject, he thought about his own future. It wouldn't hurt to make a little money first, before deciding what he actually wanted to do in law.

Greg had many girlfriends over the years, but none of them had ever been serious. In 1967 he met Jane Stillman. It was funny how he fell for her; she reminded him a lot of his mother, but the way he wished his mother would be. Nice. Beautiful, fiercely bright, competitive in her own right, Jane was from a wealthy old family and was the model Bergdorf's kind of girl.

They married in 1967, and Jane gave birth to an enchanting baby girl, Mary Frances, the day after Greg passed the bar in 1969. He landed a lucrative job on Wall Street (at the same firm as Mack) and the Sumners moved into an apartment in the East Seventies in Manhattan. Everything was wonderful, except that Greg was bored to tears. He had always volunteered his time and energy to political cam-

Standing in front of his official campaign poster for the U.S. Senate race, 1983. Mack kidded him on the night of his fundraiser by pointing out, "You knew in third grade that you wanted to be President!" Greg just laughed, replying, "Everybody in third grade wants to be President. I just never grew up."

As Greg's wife, Jane, explained to their daughter, Mary Frances, "Politics is more than a job to your father. It's the way he is able to give and receive love."

paigns, so after deciding that money was definitely not everything, Greg quit Wall Street and followed his heart into politics.

Greg ran for the Manhattan City Council and narrowly lost, but then went to work for Governor Chester Kesey, who, in appreciation for his fine work, paved the way for Greg to a West Coast constituency where he was bound to do well. Jane was not adverse to the Los Angeles area, and so the Sumners moved there and Greg got politically active. He was elected to the Los Angeles City Council in 1972 on a platform that would never change over the years: environmental causes, social reform programs, consumer protection, judicial reform, civil liberties, and corporate abuses. He did a fabulous job in that capacity, and people loved him. So much so they elected him assemblyman in 1974. He was even better in that capacity and he began to fantasize about the Presidency. But . . . nothing.

Greg was stuck in the Assembly for eight years, and he couldn't understand why. Every time he tried to get backing for a congressional or senate seat bid, his party support would falter at the last minute. In addition, his constituency was made up largely of the downtrodden, the poor, the victimized, hardly the kind of voters, his advisors pointed out, that could fill the campaign coffers. And he surely wasn't about to be backed by corporate money! His career had been largely devoted to stopping corporations such as Galveston Industries from riding roughshod over California and its land. In fact, every major industrial concern in California had Sumner on their political hit list. He was too idealistic, too squeaky clean, too uncompromising. He was a pain in the neck and, worse yet, a constant pain in the corporate pocketbook with his environmental protection bills. It wasn't as if Gregory felt he was getting anything done in the Assembly, however. Getting anything passed felt like trying to turn the *Queen Mary* on a dime. As he later described, "I was dying in Sacramento. . . . My lofty ideas and my celebrated principles and my lousy integrity were starting to atrophy. There's only so much great work you can do in the State Assembly, you know? I tried the high road. It got me no place."

In early 1982, Marc St. Clair approached Sumner with a tempting offer. It was simple. The businessmen St. Clair represented would help Greg get elected senator, in return for Greg's just keeping them apprised of pending legislation that might affect them. Greg didn't have to *do* anything, only let them know in advance what might become approved. By himself, Greg agonized over the offer. If he took it, it would mean that Greg could *really* have the power to get things done.

He accepted St. Clair's offer and even Greg was shocked at how quickly and easily his name came up for nomination. He had people—important people—making devout endorsements for him, people he had never met. And worse yet, half of them were people he had gone after as corporate abusers! When Greg found out that St. Clair represented the Wolfbridge Group, his heart sank. What had he done? But as St. Clair happily reminded him, there was no turning back now. . . .

Greg's election bid was off to a great start in October of 1983, and one of his first visitors to his campaign headquarters was Abby Cunningham-Ewing, who had come to make a hefty donation on behalf of J. R. Ewing. Sumner refused the check, and though beautiful Mrs. Ewing was not pleased, they parted amicably. Days later she turned up at a fundraiser with her husband, Gary Ewing, who was there to make a donation on behalf of an environmentalist group. Ah ha, Greg was quick to see, Mrs. Ewing had an interesting life . . . In with the dirty boys, married to Mr. Clean, eh?

In November, Greg hired Mack MacKenzie to head his Crime Commission, planning on his work to help him win the election next fall. He gave Mack carte blanche to investigate whatever he wanted, only for Mack to choose the Wolfbridge Group. Greg started getting tension headaches.

Mrs. Ewing became a flirtatious Abby, and Greg was slow to understand what she was after. Finally, he got it; she needed a Coastal Commission variance to proceed with a beachfront resort project. In exchange, she'd make heavy campaign contributions from a "political action committee" she'd whip up. Greg—whose marriage, at this point, was next to nonexistent—slept with her first and then gave her the bad news—no deal. He changed his mind, however, when he realized all he had to do was introduce her to Wolfbridge and let them work it out. He didn't anticipate, however, that St. Clair would not only get the variance for her, but force the Group on her as partners in the project. She was not pleased; Greg was nervous.

Meanwhile, St. Clair came to Greg with a demand for him. Get Mack off their backs. Greg threw a couple of wrenches into Mack's investigation, but when he announced he had enough on Wolfbridge to go to the DA, St. Clair made him fire Mack, and discredit him by raising a question of conflict of interest. Mack went wild, of course, and Greg was genuinely sorry to do it, but what else could he do? Let St. Clair kill him or something?

Greg blows his top when Laura doesn't believe him when he says he is clean of Wolfbridge. Deceiving Laura was never just to protect his own skin and hers; he desperately wanted not to lose her.

Greg and his wife, Jane. Just before the election, she informed him that she would be divorcing him and warned, "You're not going to make it, Greg. You may win the election, you may even get to Washington. But sooner or later you'll lose; you'll bring yourself down."

Greg won the primary and now was really in the home stretch toward winning that Senate race. A nice aside, at this point, was Greg's meeting of Abby's number one person on Lotus Point, Laura Avery. She was rather cold to him, but Greg saw something underneath her attitude that he liked. At the very least, he loved what he saw on the outside. In February, the two began an affair. Despite declarations to the contrary from both, it rapidly became an intense involvement.

Mack, though not employed, was nonetheless still snooping around, demanding answers from Greg. He denied knowing that Abby was Apolune, the company in with Wolfbridge on building Lotus Point; but when St. Clair started threatening Laura's children, then Greg had to start worrying about what *she* might tell Mack. To ease the tension on everyone, Greg found Mack "vindicated of all charges" and asked him to come back as commissioner. To his surprise, Mack did, with the condition that he could drop his Wolfbridge investigation, because it was threatening the well-being of his family. Relieved, Greg reported back to St. Clair and Abby that the heat was off. For the moment.

After Gary unknowingly froze the assets of Lotus Point, Abby came begging to Greg for him to get Gary to unfreeze Lotus Point before St. Clair did something rash. Greg tried, but Gary wouldn't listen to him. When Gary was then (allegedly) killed, Sumner was stunned. He told St. Clair he was through with him. St. Clair said he doubted it.

In October of 1984, when Mack came closing in on St. Clair (having been secretly working on the case for the governor), St. Clair kidnapped Abby and, with the entire city alerted in an APB, demanded that Greg come to his boat and lead him out of the harbor to open waters. If Greg didn't, then he could kiss his career good-bye; oh, yes, and Abby Ewing too. Greg threw Mack's tail off and arrived at the boat. Alone in the main cabin with St. Clair and Abby, Abby managed to grab a gun and toss it to Greg. St. Clair sat there, smiling, saying that Greg didn't have the guts to shoot him, which was too bad since he would be revealing to the world how crooked aspiring Senator Sumner was. Greg pulled the trigger. St. Clair was dead, damaging documents were destroyed, and Abby backed up his story of shooting in self-defense.

Greg was sick with self-loathing afterward. Now free of Wolfbridge, he vowed to clean up his act and resume the work he had always wanted to do. However, it didn't quite work out that way. After telling his staff that he would not be dealing with Mrs. Ewing any longer on *any* level, she informed him that that would not be possible, not if he didn't want to go to prison for murdering St. Clair.

With a heavy heart, Greg won the election in November of 1984 and became a United States senator. Jane announced that following his inauguration, she would be divorcing him. Pledging honesty to Laura, he brightened at the prospect of getting out of Knots Landing and going to work in Washington, with Laura at his side. But just before leaving, Abby came flying in on her broomstick to demand that he get something on Paul Galveston for her. *Galveston.* The very name made Greg's blood run cold. He bitterly refused to have anything to do with it. And then Galveston himself contacted him. Galveston was dying, he told Greg, and he wanted Greg to take over his empire in Galveston Industries after he died. Greg thought, *Is this guy for real?*, and said no way. Greg then started to help Mack in his investigation of Galveston Industries, and warned him—and Abby—that Galveston made St. Clair look like Goldie Locks by comparison.

Greg started receiving phone calls from Washington, telling him that he was already being bounced from committees—and he hadn't even gotten there yet! Within days, Greg's political career was being unraveled—by guess whom. Come work for me, Galveston urged him again. Prepared to fight him to the end, Greg confided to Laura about his biological relation to Galveston. She vowed to stay at his side; Galveston was quick to start threatening the well-being of her children.

When Galveston died in March, Greg still had no intentions of taking his offer. His mother then appeared on the scene, announcing that she had married Galveston and was holding everything in her legal custody until Greg took over. His mother and Galveston's right-hand man, John Coblenz, had a heart-to-heart with Greg, explaining exactly what he was giving up: billions, and more power in the Empire Valley project than he had ever dreamed of. What was Empire Valley?

Paul Galveston had masterminded this project years ago. A communications center capable of intercepting any electronic signal anywhere in the world. With it, the controller could monitor any electronic transaction, or maybe even tamper with it, if so he wanted. Gary Ewing was the front for Empire Valley, the guy not even knowing what he was building.

Greg deals with reporters as he leaves Pier 7 following the shooting of St. Clair. He claimed St. Clair had been holding a gun, and shot him in self-defense.

Ruth watching the press conference, with top Galveston aides at her sides. Their biggest area of disagreement was over Laura Avery. After Ruth repeatedly insulted her at the dinner table one night, Greg warned her, "If you so much as speak to her again, I will rip your lungs out," to which she coolly replied, "Don't threaten your mother, Gregory; it's unseemly."

What could someone do with this complex? Something as simple as destroying someone's credit rating, or something as big as starting a world war. Greg stopped to think of the implications. The project would go ahead with or without him; with him, it meant he controlled it. Coblenz also hastened to remind Greg that they could easily destroy his career, if he was still thinking he could go to Washington. After all, it was Paul Galveston who had gotten him elected. Greg was not surprised.

At a press conference held at the ranch, Greg announced the death of Paul Galveston, that he was his son, and that he was stepping down from the Senate to become chairman of the board of Galveston Industries. He moved to the ranch with his mother that afternoon.

First on the agenda for Greg, he wanted the Ewings out of Empire Valley. If it was to be his, then it had to be *all* his. Unfortunately that SOB who had been his father had second-guessed his probable course and had bequeathed all the land that Empire Valley was on to Gary Ewing. Ha, ha, nice trick. And so Greg was forced to reveal a little of the truth about Empire Valley to Gary to gain his cooperation. He got it, to an extent.

In the meantime, his mother made noises to him about how unsuitable Laura was as his significant other—she wanted a daughter-in-law like Abby Ewing! Greg told her to lay off Laura (which she didn't), and as far as Abby went—well, there was an interesting development. . . . In Galveston's files he discovered paperwork that said Abby had arranged for Valene Ewing's babies to be stolen and sold into an adoption ring. Abby wanted those papers *badly,* and Greg took his time in thinking how best to use this information to his advantage. He hit on it; he put Abby to work to make Gary let Greg build buildings where he needed them.

Then, with no explanation, Laura suddenly walked out of his life. It wouldn't be

until September that Greg found out that his mother had been responsible, and for that, he threw her out on her ear.

Alone, undeterred by Laura's influence, Greg pushed full ahead on Empire Valley. Reading Paul Galveston's files, listening to Coblenz, he gained the history of what had gone on before him to make it a reality. First, it was the site itself. Out of everywhere in the world, this was the spot best suited for the center. The only problem had been that a town, Wesphall, was on part of it. So Galveston Industries purposely poisoned the water, claimed it was an accident, and paid the residents off to keep silent. With a little money in their pockets, the residents couldn't get out of there fast enough. *Paul Galveston had murdered for this project.* And when the head engineer was murdered on the site in November of 1985, Greg realized that Coblenz would murder too. He had some unruly rough boys on ship with him and he frantically tried to figure out how to get them off.

And then Gary blew up the entire complex in December. Sure, it got Coblenz and his thugs to drop out of sight, but what was Greg left with? In the space of three years he had managed to lose everything important to him: his wife, Laura, the affection of his daughter, the friendship of everyone, his career, his self-respect, and even his play for power.

Laura came back to him in January. Tipped off by his assistant, Peter Hollister, Laura stood by him as he teetered back from the edge of complete failure. Her strength, her belief in him, and their love started building him back up. He talked about getting married, but she was noncommittal; he knew she'd come around.

Once he felt like himself, Greg reassessed the damage of the past few months. He had given up his career for Empire Valley, and all he had done was lose billions of dollars because of that nutbag Ewing, who was sitting there with all the Empire Valley land in his lap! For what?

At the end of January, Peter Hollister hit Greg with a surprise—that he was Greg's half-brother. His mother, too, had been a "friend" of Paul Galveston's. Greg shrugged—it certainly was plausible—and put Peter to work on earning his inheritance. Get Empire Valley back to the rightful owners—Galveston Industries.

But something wasn't right. Greg wanted more than anything—at least he thought he did—to get back all 50,000 acres of Empire Valley. He had Peter working on it, he had Abby working on it, he himself was working on it, but his attempts felt and looked lackluster. He found himself more often sitting and ranting and drinking in his office than he did in accomplishing anything. Laura nagged him about dealing with Peter's suit against the Galveston estate, but he didn't particularly worry about it. He did, however, get mighty upset when that crazy Ewing first tried to *give* half of Empire Valley to his illegitimate children and, when that didn't work, started *giving* acres away to Lotus Point.

In April, Laura put it on the table in a way he couldn't ignore. She said he wasn't the dynamic mover and shaker she had fallen in love with. She asked him why he didn't try to be President or, if not, find a candidate he'd like to make President. She had hit upon it. Greg was sorely missing his public life, his life as an honest mover and shaker, and here Laura, the woman he loved, was begging him to be that kind of man again. Hmmm . . .

In May, Greg swung into action. First, he married Laura. Second, when a toxic waste dump was discovered (leaking) under Empire Valley, he held a press conference and announced that since Galveston Industries had (legally) buried the chemicals there, he was willing to buy the land back and clean it up. And third, he made a

A rare moment of relaxation at the ranch.

generous out-of-court settlement with Peter Hollister; it included Greg's promise to make him a California State Senator.

On the surface, these were very admirable deeds. On the more practical level, however, it simply meant that Greg had Laura's support, the means to bankrupt Lotus Point (by delaying the cleanup), and a puppet in the State Senate to protect his business interests and undermine those of his enemies.

Gregory Sumner was on the move.

Given some of the less-attractive traits of city living, like crime, one can understand why some families seek safety by living in the suburbs. But what happens when the very things they moved to get away from follow them out there?

Greg, even three years ago, would be sick at the thought that he is the kind of thing people are trying to get away from. He understands that today, though, and the realization makes him uncomfortable. (There is nothing worse than realizing you've become exactly like the hated person you grew up vowing you'd never be like.)

Despite what people think, Greg doesn't want to be like Galveston. On the other hand, his sole tie to Sumner, the idealist, is his love for Laura Avery. And he cannot continue the way he is without hurting the people and place that make up Laura's home. Will he change, will he try to change at all? Will he ever abandon the drive to be king, and settle for being one of the kingdom?

All of Knots Landing would like to know.